BEFORE CHAPPAQUIDDICK

BEFORE

CHAPPAQUIDDICK

The Untold Story of Mary Jo Kopechne and the Kennedy Brothers

WILLIAM C. KASHATUS

Potomac Books
An imprint of the University of Nebraska Press

Potomac Books is an imprint of the University of Nebraska Press. Manufactured in the United States of America.

Library of Congress Cataloging-in-Publication Data
Names: Kashatus, William C., 1959– author.
Title: Before Chappaquiddick: the untold story of Mary Jo Kopechne and the Kennedy brothers / William C. Kashatus.
Other titles: Untold story of Mary Jo Kopechne
Description: Lincoln, NE: Potomac Books, an imprint of the University of Nebraska Press, [2020] | Includes bibliographical references and index.
Identifiers: LCCN 2019036771
ISBN 9781640122697 (hardback)
ISBN 9781640123465 (epub)
ISBN 9781640123472 (mobi)
ISBN 9781640123489 (pdf)
Subjects: LCSH: Kopechne, Mary Jo, 1941–1969. | Kennedy, Edward M. (Edward Moore), 1932–2009. | Congressional secretaries—United States—Biography. | Kennedy, Robert F., 1925–1968—Friends and associates. | Single women—Washington (D.C.)—Biography. | United States—Politics and government—1961–1963. | United States—Politics and government—1963–1969.
Classification: LCC E840.8.K35 K38 2020 | DDC 973.92092 [B]—dc23
LC record available at
https://lccn.loc.gov/2019036771

Set in Minion Pro by Mikala R. Kolander.

A portion of the proceeds from this book will be contributed to the Mary Jo Kopechne Scholarship in political science at Misericordia University, Dallas, Pennsylvania. Contributions can be made through the university's Office of Institutional Advancement at 866-262-6363.

To the memories of
Mary Jo Kopechne
and her parents,
Gwen and Joseph

The truth will set you free.

—JOHN 8:32

CONTENTS

ILLUSTRATIONS

ACKNOWLEDGMENTS

This book is dedicated to Mary Jo Kopechne and her parents, Gwen and Joseph. Although I did not know them, I came to admire and sympathize with this small family over the last decade. Their devotion to each other as well as the integrity of their examples provided the inspiration and drive to continue my research and writing when I despaired that this book would amount to little more than a good intention. I can only hope that my efforts will set them free from the bold-faced lies, rumors, and innuendo that have been written during the last half century. Deep down I know that Mary Jo, Gwen, and Joe are together again and have found eternal happiness. Nor would the book have come to fruition without the blessing, support, and assistance of Georgetta Nelson Potoski, the executor of the Kopechne estate, and her son, William Nelson. Not only did they grant access to Kopechne family documents, but they also granted permission to reprint family photographs and reviewed earlier drafts of the manuscript. For those gifts I am especially grateful.

Unfortunately, the Kennedy family; Margaret Carroll, Mary Jo's roommate at the time of her death; and the five Boiler Room Girls who attended the Chappaquiddick Party, Maryellen and Nance Lyons, Esther Newberg, Susan Tannenbaum Osterhout, and Rosemary Keough Redmond, declined to be interviewed for this book. But there were others who were generous with their time and recollections. Among them are Mary Jo's childhood and college friends: Sister Rita Margaret Chambers, Carol Caprik Dougherty, Elly Gardner Kluge, Judith Hadden Lutoff, Patricia Ann Murphy McGarrity, Nancy Smack McMurtrie, Alan Stenfors, and Emalene Fargnoli Renna. Others knew Mary Jo from volunteering on John F. Kennedy's 1960 presidential campaign in New Jersey: Carol Teague Condon, John Mohrhauser, and Dick Toole.

Some were Mary Jo's students at the Montgomery Catholic High School: Lynn Jehle Downs and Maureen Clark Trussell. Still others were colleagues who worked on Robert F. Kennedy's Senate staff and his 1968 presidential campaign: Judith Cromwell, K. Dun Gifford, Jeannie Main, Melody Miller, and Adam Walinsky. Owen M. Lopez dated Mary Jo during her years in Washington DC. Michael Bonafede worked with her as a political consultant for Matt Reese Associates. Finally, there were those who were involved in the Chappaquiddick investigation—Joseph Flanagan, Leslie H. Leland, and Donald McFadden—or covered it in the media, like Liz Trotta. I am extremely grateful to all of these individuals for their willingness to participate and to provide unique insight into Mary Jo's life and political career.

Special thanks are due to Barbara Ann Perry of the Edward M. Kennedy Institute for the United States Senate and the Miller Center Foundation at the University of Virginia, who granted permission to print excerpts of interviews from the EMK Oral History Project; Stacey Chandler, archivist at the John F. Kennedy Presidential Library, who granted permission to print excerpts of interviews from the Robert F. Kennedy Oral History Project; and to Les Leland, Don McFadden, Walter Mears, and Georgetta Nelson Potoski, who reviewed earlier drafts of the manuscript and wrote endorsements. I am also grateful to Tom Swanson and his editorial staff at Potomac Books and the University of Nebraska Press for their support in the publishing process; Patricia Tracz of the Photography Center in Malvern, Pennsylvania, for resizing the images used in the book; attorney Janet Fries of the Washington DC law firm of Drinker Biddle, who vetted the manuscript for any potential legal issues; and Michelle Zabriski of Misericordia University's Office of Institutional Advancement, who served as the liaison for the Mary Jo Kopechne Scholarship.

Finally, I am grateful to my parents, William and Balbina, and to my wife, Jackie, and our three sons, Tim, Peter, and Ben. Few men admit to having heroes, but I am grateful that they are mine.

INTRODUCTION

On Saturday, August 29, 2009, Senator Edward M. Kennedy of Massachusetts was laid to rest at Arlington National Cemetery.[1] He was buried next to his older brothers, President John F. Kennedy and Senator Robert F. Kennedy of New York. Ted, who had died four days earlier of brain cancer at age seventy-seven, had been the youngest son of the most glamourous political dynasty in United States history.

Propelled into the public spotlight after the assassinations of his brothers, Ted Kennedy was expected to carry on the liberal agenda by the Democratic Party and was recruited every four years to run for the presidency. Lacking the keen intellect and eloquence of John and the uncompromising moral stand and compassion of Bobby, Ted doubted his abilities for executive office. He felt more comfortable on Capitol Hill, where he exercised a powerful influence for nearly a half century. There, Kennedy used his good looks, wit, charm, wealth, and power to seduce voters, interest groups, and congressional colleagues. That exceptional ability enabled him to win reelection to the Senate seven times and to champion legislation addressing economic and social justice, including measures on civil rights, education, cancer research, health insurance, apartheid, and disability discrimination.[2] But Kennedy's personal behavior was not always as virtuous as his political image.

Several Kennedy biographers have pointed out that the senator had a voracious appetite for alcohol and attractive young women as well as an arrogant belief that he could do exactly what he pleased and evade any charge leveled against him.[3] That volatile combination resulted in a divorce from his first wife, two highly publicized legal cases, and the death of Mary Jo Kopechne, a twenty-eight-year-old woman who was killed when a car Kennedy was driving plunged off a bridge on Chappaquiddick Island, Massachusetts.[4] Thus while the rest of the nation was glued to CNN, FOX, and MSNBC for regular updates on Kennedy's funeral, I found it difficult to mourn the death of a man who had been widely hailed as the "Lion of the Senate."[5]

Instead, I visited Kopechne's grave at Saint Vincent's Catholic Cemetery on Larksville Mountain in Luzerne County, Pennsylvania, just a few miles from her hometown of Forty Fort. I wanted to honor her memory and the potential that was lost at Chappaquiddick on that summer evening forty years earlier. It is a modest grave, with just a simple gray marble stone bearing her name and those of her parents. There is nothing to distinguish it as the final resting place of a woman who became the focus of a national scandal—no suggestion that her memory is forever tied to Ted Kennedy and his failed bid for the presidency.

Mary Jo Kopechne was a bright, attractive young woman who appeared to have a promising future in politics. Born on July 26, 1940, she was the only child of insurance salesman Joseph Kopechne and his wife, Gwen. When she was still a child, the family moved to East Orange, New Jersey, where Mary Jo attended parochial schools. She had seriously thought about becoming a nun, but after graduating from Caldwell College she turned to public service. Inspired by President John F. Kennedy's challenge to "ask what you can do for your country," Kopechne became part of the civil rights movement, taking a job as a schoolteacher at the Mission of Saint Jude in Montgomery, Alabama.[6] Three years later, the slender, five-foot-four blonde joined the Capitol Hill staff of New York senator Robert F. Kennedy.

A devout Catholic, Kopechne lived in Georgetown with three other women. She rarely drank, didn't smoke, and was offended by profanity, yet she was irresistibly drawn to the fast-paced, glitzy world of Washington. She served as a secretary to RFK's speechwriters and distinguished herself during his 1968 presidential campaign by working long hours at his Washington headquarters. Along with five other young women collectively known as the "Boiler Room Girls"—after the windowless room where they worked—Kopechne tracked and compiled data on how Democratic delegates from different states might vote at the convention. The job involved keeping in contact with field managers and the press. Like the other women on RFK's staff, Kopechne was fully devoted to the New York senator and was devastated by his assassination on June 5, 1968. Feeling as if she could no longer work on Capitol Hill, Mary Jo took a job with a political consulting firm in Washington.[7]

On the evening of July 18, 1969, Kopechne attended a party on Chappaquiddick, near Martha's Vineyard, in honor of her and the other Boiler Room Girls. Ted Kennedy hosted the party as a gesture of personal gratitude for all the hard work they had invested in his late brother's campaign. Later that night, Mary Jo accepted Kennedy's offer to drive her back to her hotel. His car swerved off a narrow, unlit bridge and overturned in the water. The senator escaped from the submerged car, but Mary Jo died after what Kennedy claimed were "seven or eight" unsuccessful attempts to rescue her.[8] By the time he reported the accident to police the following morning, Kopechne's body had been recovered. The diver who found her stated that she had positioned herself near a backseat wheel well, where an air pocket had formed, and had apparently suffocated rather than drowned. The diver added that he "could have saved her life if the accident had been reported earlier."[9]

Afterward, some journalists unjustly suggested that Kopechne was an opportunist who sought to attach herself to the Kennedy family or that she was having an affair with the senator.[10] As the years unfolded, many writers blamed her for Kennedy's failure to be elected to the presidency.[11] The tabloid writers had made Mary Jo the offender when she was in reality an innocent victim of the senator's poor judgment.

Although I was a great admirer of President Kennedy and his brother Robert, it was difficult to respect Ted Kennedy, who easily could have been charged with involuntary homicide and sentenced to significant jail time for Kopechne's death. Judge James A. Boyle instead sentenced him to two months' incarceration, the statutory minimum for leaving the scene of an accident with bodily injury, and immediately suspended the sentence. In announcing his decision, Boyle said Kennedy had "already been, and will continue to be, punished far beyond anything this court can impose."[12]

The senator was unable to apologize to Gwen and Joseph Kopechne, who remained heartbroken over the death of their only child for the rest of their lives. But he went on national television to ask the people of Massachusetts for their forgiveness, and they forgave him each time he was reelected to the U.S. Senate during the next four decades. For Ted Kennedy, Mary Jo's life—and death—weren't as important as his political career. But on that summer evening when I visited her grave, Mary Jo Kopechne became important to me.

I began researching her past only to discover that precious little information existed about her personal life. Her parents had already died, and she had no siblings. The Boiler Room Girls, the five women who worked with Mary Jo on RFK's 1968 presidential campaign and attended the Chappaquiddick party, chose to remain silent. As a result, I was limited to three feature stories that appeared in women's magazines, two shortly after Mary Jo's death in 1969 and a third on the twentieth anniversary of the incident in 1989.[13] Using leads from the three articles, I contacted those who knew Mary Jo. Some were classmates from elementary, high school, or college. Others worked with her on Capitol Hill, and still others knew Mary Jo at the time of her death. I spent the next decade interviewing those individuals who agreed to share their memories as well as their feelings about Mary Jo, her career potential, and her untimely death.

Before Chappaquiddick is a biography based on those interviews as well as recently declassified FBI documents, a privately published Kopechne family memoir, and newspaper and magazine accounts that focus on Mary Jo's personal life. Chappaquiddick is addressed at length because it brought her into the national spotlight, but the book adheres to Senator Edward Kennedy's account of the accident, highlighting its inconsistencies as well as the questions that remain unanswered half a century later. I do *not* offer a new interpretation of the accident.[14]

Instead, *Before Chappaquiddick* explores the life and death of a devoted Kennedy staffer in the broader context of the period she lived in. Caught between the silent generation of the 1950s and the politically active generation of the 1960s, Mary Jo belonged to an exclusive group of females who worked on Capitol Hill and committed themselves unconditionally to the Kennedy brothers and their noble vision for a better, more humane nation. She was both a participant in and product of that vision. Inspired to pursue a career in public service by President John F. Kennedy, Kopechne worked on the congressional staff and 1968 presidential campaign of his brother, Senator Robert F. Kennedy, and was killed in an automobile recklessly driven by their youngest brother, Senator Edward M. Kennedy. In the process, Mary Jo came to embody the best ideals of the sixties: compassion for the underprivileged, social idealism tempered by political realism, and a fierce devotion to just causes. At the same time, Kopechne's attraction to the Kennedy brothers proved to be a fatal one, as she paid for it with her life.

I wrote this book because the only information the American public learned about Mary Jo Kopechne after her death was filtered through a sensationalist press motivated by political agendas. Hiding behind the First Amendment, those writers sullied her reputation in a web of salacious rumors, scandalous innuendo, and bold-faced lies. I wrote this book because Kopechne could not defend herself against those damaging allegations. When I visited her grave on that summer day in 2009, I promised Mary Jo that I would tell the truth in order to restore her integrity. Ultimately, I wrote this book to set her free.

BEFORE CHAPPAQUIDDICK

1 Humble Origins

Tucked away between the mountain ranges of northeast Pennsylvania was once a small, tranquil haven of rolling hills, fertile meadowlands, and thick forests abundant with wildlife. Delaware Indians who inhabited the land referred to the scenic vale as Wyoming, or "land of the plains." Seeking to build a new life on the frontier, Connecticut Yankees migrated west in the late 1760s and discovered the picturesque valley while traversing the Susquehanna River. They hoped to build a community there that resembled the New England towns whence they came. But within months of settling, the Yankees learned they would have to fight for the land against the Indians who had preceded them and the Pennsylvanians who also claimed title to it. The dispute erupted into a prolonged civil conflict known as the Pennamite Wars and, later, during the American Revolution, into a bloody Indian massacre of white settlers.[1] It was another revolution that occurred at the turn of the nineteenth century, however, that altered the Wyoming Valley's geographical and demographic landscape forever.

The Industrial Revolution was fueled by northeastern Pennsylvania, which once contained three-quarters of the earth's anthracite coal deposits. Bounded on the west by the Susquehanna River, on the east by the Lehigh River, and to the south by the Blue Mountains, the anthracite region was divided into four large coalfields that covered eight counties and provided the entire nation with the fuel required for consumer heating and industrial production.[2] A monopoly of seven large railroad companies joined by interlocking boards of directors and connected by joint stock ownership to New York and Philadelphia Banking interests controlled the region. Their subsidiary mining companies accounted for more than 70 percent of anthracite production and all the employment in northeastern Pennsylvania.[3]

Of the four coalfields in the anthracite region, the northernmost bed, which dominated Luzerne County, was the most productive and served as the lifeblood of the Wyoming Valley.[4] Virtually all the valley's adult males worked in the northern coalfield for one of four companies: the Alden Coal Company; the Delaware, Lehigh, and Western Railroad; Lehigh and Wilkes-Barre Coal Company; and the Susquehanna Coal Company.[5] The power of the coal companies was absolute. Miners and their families lived in poorly constructed company-owned houses. They bought groceries at company-owned stores, which charged prices higher than those outside the coal region and did not honor credit. Rent and grocery purchases were deducted from a laborer's meager pay each week. Miners were reduced to wage slaves, earning anywhere between $0.75 to $1.25 per day, depending upon the number of coal cars they filled. The poor pay was only surpassed by the industry's hazardous working conditions.

Coal miners faced the daily threat of death. Cave-ins were common, especially if wooden supports were improperly installed when a coal vein was mined out. Flooding was also common because the mining was done hundreds of feet below the Susquehanna River bed. Runaway mine cars and unpredictable explosions were daily concerns. Even if a miner was fortunate to escape these immediate dangers, he would eventually be forced to contend with black lung, a respiratory disease caused by years of inhaling coal dust. The majority would end up coughing themselves to death for less than subsistence wage. No wonder the taprooms were the most popular places in the Wyoming Valley. Liquor was the miner's tonic, providing him with the only release he had from a miserable existence.[6]

While high prices, low wages, and poor working conditions were common to every miner, those who had recently immigrated to the anthracite region fared even worse. Between 1875 and 1915, about one hundred thousand of the fifteen million immigrants who came to the United States settled in northeastern Pennsylvania's anthracite region.[7] Lured by the American Dream and the prospect of employment in a prosperous hard coal industry, the new arrivals came primarily from eastern and southern Europe. But they were not welcomed by the more established groups who immigrated to the area from northern and western Europe before the American Civil War. Primarily English and Welsh Protestants, the "old immigrants" were skilled laborers, foremen, and colliery operators who established the coal industry. The "new immigrants," on the other hand, were Catholic and largely unskilled workers who arrived from Hungary, Ireland, Italy, Lithuania, Poland, and Ukraine. Settling in the company towns of Edwardsville, Kingston, Pittston, Plymouth, Swoyersville, and Wilkes-Barre, they created their own ethnic ghettos and became the backbone of labor in the Wyoming Valley. The differences between the two immigrant groups were cultural but often manifested themselves in the living conditions, working relationships, and patterns of mobility and physical violence that characterized the life of the valley's anthracite culture.

Regardless of ethnicity, the residents of the Wyoming Valley encouraged ambition and personal enterprise, but never at the expense of community solidarity. They trusted others, but only others of their own culture. Their social and religious lives did not extend beyond the ethnic enclaves in which they lived. Children were taught to play with their own kind. Church attendance and marriage were observed exclusively in the parish of one's ethnic origin. Marrying out of the faith was strictly forbidden and cause for family disownment. Individual achievement was respected as long as the individual remembered "where he came from" and acknowledged the support he received from others. The people of the Wyoming Valley were also very passionate. If they "liked" somebody, they "liked 'em hard." But God help the person they didn't like. They were stubborn, resistant to change, sometimes at the expense of their own and their family's welfare. Yet for all their ambivalence and passion, the people of the Wyoming Valley were essentially genuine human beings who believed that self-respect, a good education, and plain, honest hard work would enable the individual to rise above his humble circumstances and become a "somebody."[8]

Mary Jo Kopechne's humble origins can be traced to the Wyoming Valley's anthracite culture and the immigration of her ancestors Joseph Kopechne from Hungary and William R. Jennings from Wales at the turn of the nineteenth century. Both family patriarchs settled in the valley hoping to realize the American Dream of upward social and economic mobility. What they found instead was a hard and unforgiving life. Kopechne, his wife, Johanna, and their ten children arrived in 1891 from Pécs, a large mining town in southwest Hungary.[9] Kopechne, who struggled to support his family by working in the mines, wanted a new start in America.[10] Sailing on the ss *Moravia* of the Hamburg-American Line, the Kopechnes arrived in New York on October 29, 1891, and settled in Maltby, Pennsylvania (present-day Swoyersville).[11] Joseph died a year later at the age of fifty-two, leaving Johanna to raise their seven children. Frank, the eldest of the four sons, went to work at the Maltby coal colliery to help support the family until he married Mary Leitinger on October 3, 1898. The couple eventually purchased a home at 1214 Murray Street in neighboring Forty Fort, where they raised eight children, five boys and three girls.[12]

Large families were the norm among Catholic immigrants, not only because of religious beliefs on the duty of procreation, but as a matter of economic necessity. Sons were sent out to work as breaker boys as young as age eight. For twenty-five cents per day, these youngsters sat on a wooden plank on the ground floor of the breaker, separating the coal by hand from slate, rock, and wood refuse as it chortled down metal chutes from the top of the breaker, where it had been sorted by size. Despite an 1885 law stipulating that boys had to be at least twelve years of age to work in the breaker, parents often lied about their sons' age to gain the additional income. Since Pennsylvania had no compulsory registration of births, the law meant little in actual practice, as a youngster could be passed off as "small for twelve."[13]

Neither Frank nor Mary were schooled beyond the sixth grade, but they did value education and wanted their children to have as much as possible.[14] Unfortunately, those hopes were dashed when Frank was severely injured in a mining accident. Unable to continue his mining work now that he used a wheelchair, Frank was forced to send his sons off to the mines before they could complete their high school educations. Joseph, the third-eldest son, claimed that his father became a "frustrated and bitter man" who "cursed his fate and made life miserable" for the family until he died in 1950. Mary, on the other hand, was a kind and gentle soul. She encouraged her children, cultivating their self-esteem and a strong worth ethic. Joe adored his mother, who somehow managed to hold the family together until her death in 1947.[15] He would later name his only child Mary Jo in memory of her.

As the Kopechnes were establishing roots in Forty Fort, Jonah and Lydia Jennings were raising two sons in Plymouth, just six miles away. Shortly after the family immigrated from Wales in 1881, Jonah became one of the founders of the Ebenezer Baptist Church and, like Lydia, a respected member of the Welsh community. Their sons, William and Thomas, grew to adulthood working in the coal mines, first as breaker boys and later as laborers. Bill lived with his parents until 1902 when he married Mary Jane Jones, a "proper Welsh girl." Within the next year, Mary gave birth to a son, Willie, who quickly became his father's pride and joy. But two years later, Mary died in childbirth, and Bill and his young son went to live with Jonah and Lydia.[16]

To help with Willie and his ailing parents, Bill hired a caretaker named Marie "Mame" Evans, who was thirteen years younger than him. The two fell in love almost immediately, but the social mores of the time prohibited marriage between different religions. Since Bill was a staunch Baptist, Mame, a less devout Irish Catholic, converted to Protestantism, against the wishes of her family. When the couple wed in 1905, Mame's father promptly disowned her for marrying out of the Catholic faith.[17] After the birth of their first child, Byron, Mame lost four babies in infancy. As she struggled with bouts of depression after each death, Bill began spending more time at the local saloons, drowning his sorrow in alcohol. Making matters worse was Richard Evans, Mame's father, who insisted that the deaths were divine retribution for her unforgivable sin of marrying a Baptist. In fact, infant mortality was common at the time due to the primitive state of prenatal care. Curiously, Evans remained silent when his daughter gave birth to three healthy babies between 1915 and 1920. The eldest, Sarah, was born in 1915, followed by Gwen in 1918 and Thomas in 1920.[18]

By 1920 Bill had been promoted to mine foreman by the Lehigh Coal Company. Willie, his son, was married with an infant daughter and also worked in the mines. To save money, both families lived together in the same house in Edwardsville. Pooling their salaries each week, Bill and Willie apportioned money for rent, groceries, household expenses, and a small allowance for each of them to spend at the local tavern. Often a few pennies remained for Sarah, Gwen, and Thomas to buy some candy. The two families created their own entertainment. Bill, who played the piano and harp, gave each of the children lessons on both instruments, and the evenings were filled with music and song. It was a simple but happy life until about 1924, when Bill suffered a severe mining accident that left him hospitalized for months.[19]

No longer able to rely financially on Willie, whose own growing family required that he move into his own home, Mame sent her eldest son, Byron, to work in the mines and took in boarders to support the family. The responsibility of caring for three young children and the stressful demands of operating a boardinghouse led her to a premature death in 1925 at age forty-three. In Mame's last days, her aunt, Emma Dempsey, came from Ireland to care for the children. Emma also insured that her niece received the last rites of the Catholic Church before she died and that she was buried at Saint Vincent's Catholic cemetery in nearby Larksville.[20]

When Emma, a practical and resourceful woman, discovered that Sarah, Gwen, and Thomas were eligible for financial assistance from the Catholic church, she promptly had them baptized. The additional income allowed her and Byron to eke out a meager existence for themselves and Mame's young children. Of course, Bill, still hospitalized, was not informed of these arrangements. It was painful enough to deal with his wife's death, but when Bill finally returned home and learned that Emma had converted his late wife and youngest children to the Catholic faith, he turned to the bottle to soften the devastating blow. After being committed to Retreat State Hospital in West Nanticoke, Bill Jennings died of alcoholism in 1931. His youngest daughter, Gwen, chose to remember him as a loving father who toted her around Edwardsville in a large red wagon visiting friends and relatives.[21] The importance he attached to family would remain with her, and she would cultivate those same feelings in her only child, Mary Jo.

By the mid-1930s, the Great Depression was in full swing, and the Wyoming Valley, like the anthracite region itself, fell on hard times. A growing United Mine Workers union demanded better wages, shorter hours, and collective bargaining from the railroad cartel that monopolized the anthracite industry. Tired of doing battle with labor, the railroads resorted to leasing their subsidiary mining operations to smaller and often non-union operators. At the same time, the urban northeast, once the primary market for hard coal, turned to cheaper fuel alternatives such as electricity, oil, and natural gas. As a result, anthracite production fell to 46 million tons in 1938, less than half the tonnage of twenty years before. The coal operators and the United Mine Workers agreed to a policy of job equalization that limited the weekly work schedules of miners throughout the anthracite region. Although the policy saved many jobs, it also resulted in a drastic reduction of salaries. Job equalization and rising unemployment had a profound emotional as well as economic impact on families.[22]

Men, once the breadwinners of the family, began to rely increasingly on their wives to find work for meager wages in the cigar and garment industries, which had relocated from New York City to the valley. Struggling with feelings of uselessness and embarrassment, miners turned to the bottle to ease their pain, often returning home drunk to disrupt the lives of their family members. Women felt the stress of working outside the home in addition to their household and caregiving responsibilities. Although children were now protected by child labor laws and remained in school longer, they bootlegged coal to heat the family home and usually left high school to find whatever employment was available. President Franklin D. Roosevelt's New Deal alleviated some of the economic distress by providing residents with work relief programs. The Works Progress Administration, for example, hired and paid workers to construct public buildings, build bridges, pave roads, and install street lighting.[23] While such projects restored a semblance of normalcy, they did not end the Great Depression or the personal hardship that accompanied it.

Nevertheless, the valley's residents never lost hope. A growing sense of compassion emerged, especially for the sick, indigent, and dispossessed. Food and clothing were frequently distributed to those down on their luck. Somehow the valley's residents even scraped together enough money to pay for the medical care of those suffering from serious health problems. Inspired by the generosity of donors, "Little Bill" Phillips, a broadcaster for WBRE Radio in Wilkes-Barre, referred to the Wyoming Valley as the "Valley with a Heart."[24] Indeed, the valley was changing for the better in spite—or perhaps because—of the economic hardship. Poverty is a great equalizer, and if nothing else the Depression created humility by making most people poor. Ethnic and religious animosities that once defined the social conventions of the valley slowly melted away as residents began to view each other primarily as human beings who were simply trying to get by. The young in particular did not define themselves by their ethnic background, though many spoke their immigrant grandparents' native languages at home. Nor did differences in religion seem important, especially between Catholics and Protestants, who both embraced the Christian tradition. Instead, the valley's young people defined themselves by their Americanness and a willingness to judge others by their character. It was in this more compassionate, more tolerant society that Joseph Kopechne and Gwen Jennings met and fell in love.

The two teenagers first noticed each other while crossing the Market Street Bridge in Wilkes-Barre. They were on their way to Kirby Park to meet with their respective groups of friends. Gwen was a petite, attractive girl with curly dark hair and sparkling blue eyes. Joe was smitten. Using all the charm he could muster, the tall, handsome teen attempted to strike up a conversation, but he was promptly rebuffed. Joe was not a quitter, though. For weeks he pursued Gwen, until she finally agreed to let him walk her home. Like Joe, Gwen was independent and did as she pleased. But she was also committed to her family, and she worked in a tobacco factory to support her Aunt Emma and her young brother, Thomas. Joe respected those qualities.[25] They talked of marriage, but they were concerned about their families' approval because of the money each was contributing to the household. They decided to marry secretly in January 1939 but to continue to live at home to support their respective families. The arrangement lasted for four months.[26] During that period, Joe found work with the Civilian Conservation Corps, a New Deal program for young men. Attached to a CCC unit in Fredericksburg, Maryland, Joe earned $30 per month building bridges and roadways in the surrounding forests. "It was structured like an army camp," he recalled years later. "We wore uniforms, marched and trained. But instead of military training, we took classes in forestry, carpentry, welding and, for those who needed it, reading and writing."[27]

Gwen visited Joe on weekends, when wives could join their husbands who were attached to the unit. The couples camped, swam, and fished, enjoying each other's company. But Gwen soon tired of being away from Joe and in May informed his parents that they were married. To her surprise, the Kopechnes forgave them and accepted the marriage. When Joe returned home in June, the couple took a room in a boardinghouse, and he found employment with a tree-trimming service.[28] A little more than a year later, Joe, age twenty-six, and Gwen, age twenty-two, were blessed with the birth of their first and only child. Mary Jo Kopechne was born on July 26, 1940, at Nesbitt Memorial Hospital in Kingston, not far from Forty Fort, where her parents lived at the time.[29] "If we were to have only one child, God surely chose the very best one for us," Joe said. He was a doting father from the beginning. "He cared for Mary Jo as lovingly as Gwen and participated fully in her care," said Georgetta Potoski, his niece.[30] But Joe also wanted to give his daughter many of the opportunities he did not enjoy growing up and realized he could not afford to stay in the Wyoming Valley if he wanted a better future for her.

By World War II the anthracite industry had violated the Wyoming Valley, leaving mountainous black banks of coal refuse, waste piles of slate and rock, and only scrawny little birch trees to dominate a region once rich in woodland evergreens, oaks, and pines. The industry polluted the sparkling streams and creeks, turning many of them black with coal dust and redolent with the stench of sulfur. Even the Susquehanna River, which once wove through the valley like a silver thread, bore a permanent dark tinge. Electricity, oil, and natural gas had replaced hard coal as the primary means of heating in most American homes, leaving employment opportunities in the anthracite industry as bleak as the valley's terrain. With fewer and fewer jobs in the anthracite industry and the closing of many related businesses, Joe and many other young men from the Wyoming Valley relocated to New Jersey, where there were greater employment opportunities.[31] He took a job as a stevedore at the Port of Newark and secured an apartment for his small family in nearby military housing.[32]

Newark was a melting pot of religious and ethnic groups. Mary Jo grew up playing with black and Hispanic American children as well as whites, developing an early respect for social diversity. Her father's love for the Brooklyn Dodgers, baseball's first integrated team, reinforced that quality. Joe and his young daughter spent many summer afternoons in the bleachers at Ebbets Field cheering on the Dodgers and their favorite player, first baseman Gil Hodges. For her seventh birthday, Mary Jo received a small glove, bat, and baseball so Joe could play catch with her on the small playground beside their apartment building.[33] "No question, Mary Jo was a tomboy," said Alan Stenfors, a childhood playmate. "I remember that she loved baseball, and when her father wasn't around, we played catch together. She was good, too."[34]

After the war, Joe took a job with Washington National Insurance Company in East Orange, and the family moved to the Newark suburb.[35] They lived at Bradley Court, a collection of small, brown-brick condominiums at the corner of Shepard and Rhode Island Avenues. Mary Jo would spend her high school and college years in this cozy, family oriented, blue-collar neighborhood of mostly Irish and Italian residents. The Kopechnes joined Our Lady of the Most Blessed Sacrament, an Irish parish, where Mary Jo received confirmation and completed her grade school education.[36]

"She was a very reserved girl," recalled Emalene Fargnoli Renna, Mary Jo's closest friend in the neighborhood. "She really didn't volunteer much about herself, but we enjoyed each other's company. We spent a lot of time in the park playing games like hopscotch and jump-rope or at one of our homes playing board games like monopoly or just talking." According to Renna, Mary Jo remained the "same person in high school as she was in the sixth grade." When asked to describe herself for the high school yearbook, she used one word: "introvert."[37]

Indeed, Mary Jo was careful in her dealings with those outside of her family, a trait she inherited from Gwen and Joe. "The Kopechnes were insular, quiet people," recalled Renna. "They kept to themselves. I knew the mother, Gwen, better than the father. She worked as a cosmetics saleswoman at a lovely little department store, but it was only part-time when Mary Jo was at school. Gwen was always home whenever I visited. Mary Jo was her life."[38]

Family was of utmost importance to the Kopechnes. In fact, they never intended to settle permanently in New Jersey. It's probably the reason Joe and Gwen preferred to rent instead of purchasing a home there. Instead, the family returned regularly to the Wyoming Valley on holidays and summer vacations to visit with relatives. It was always assumed they would return to the valley for good when Joe could find gainful employment there. During these visits, Mary Jo bonded with relatives from both sides of the family. Her younger cousin, Georgetta, the daughter of Gwen's older sister, Sarah Mathews, became her closest companion and the peer she confided in most. Whenever Joe and Gwen visited the valley, they would stay with the Mathews family in Plymouth, and the two girls spent all their time together. "Mary Jo was two years older than me, but she was more of a sister than a cousin," said Georgetta. "We enjoyed sharing each other's lives, loves and joys because we trusted each other unconditionally. I looked to her to show me the way, never doubting that in any situation Mary Jo could be counted on for the proper behavior, protocol or response. Like a younger sister, I might've argued with her because doing it her way was harder, but I never doubted that she was right."[39]

Mary Jo endeared herself to other members of the family as well. Georgetta's mother, Sarah Mathews, doted on her niece as if she was "one of her daughters." Byron Jennings, Gwen's older brother, was Mary Jo's favorite uncle. Although he was a taxi dispatcher, Byron was at heart a poet who regularly quoted Tennyson and Keats. He appealed to Mary Jo's childhood imagination as well as her love of books. Bouncing his little niece on his knee, Byron taught her the ABC's as she laughed and sang along. She nicknamed him "Uncle Putchy Pie" and was devastated at age nine when he died of tuberculosis.[40]

In the fall of 1954, Joe and Gwen enrolled their daughter at Our Lady of the Valley Catholic High School in East Orange. OLV was a small traditional co-educational Catholic high school with an enrollment of fewer than five hundred students, mostly from blue-collar families. It was also less expensive than the elite, single-sex high schools in the Archdiocese of Newark. Since an entrance exam was required and admission was limited to those scoring highest, there were few if any problem students at the school. Academic standards were high but reasonable. Matriculation to college was about 50 percent, though the rate for females was lower. Mary Jo made a decision to be successful academically and worked hard to earn good grades. "The group of girls she hung out with were all honor roll students," said Renna. "She wasn't a popular girl, but she was involved in many activities, including the glee club, the drama club, the school newspaper, and the yearbook."[41]

Carol Caprik Dougherty, another close friend, remembers that Kopechne was "not an extraordinary student, but a solid B student," and she was "more active than others in Sodality, a school organization that promoted Christian charity." "I'm sure that's why the nuns liked her so much," she noted. But what endeared Dougherty to Mary Jo were her easygoing personality and loyalty. "She was easy to talk to and have good, clean fun with, but what I remember most is that Mary Jo was always there for me."[42] That didn't mean she was a milquetoast, though. Kopechne had a sense of humor that bordered on the irreverent. During her junior year, for example, she was enrolled in the same history class as Renna, who was infamous for baiting the nuns who taught there. On one occasion, the rebellious student took exception to the instructor's praise of Spain's dictator General Francisco Franco.

"Sister, can you explain something to me?" Renna asked as she raised her hand.

Mary Jo, seated nearby, rolled her eyes, knowing that her friend intended to get a rise out of the nun.

"I don't understand why it's okay for Franco to be imposing the Catholic religion on Spain when you criticized Queen Victoria for imposing

Anglicanism in England," said Renna. No sooner had Renna completed the sentence than the sister banished her from the classroom for contrariness. As Emalene was leaving, she caught a glimpse of Kopechne, who was desperately trying to hide a wicked smile.

"Mary Jo was a good kid," admitted Renna, "one who would *never* contradict a nun. The nuns liked her. But she was the first to laugh about an incident like that because in her own quiet way she appreciated the humor." Above all, Mary Jo wanted to please her parents. She strived to meet their high expectations and was delighted when she excelled. The bond between them ran deep. Gwen and Joe were protective of their daughter but also trusted her judgment. Rarely did she waiver when confronted with a difficult decision. If she was unsure, Mary Jo assessed the situation carefully, gathering as much information as possible, and used her strong moral code as a filter before making her decision. Nor did she test her parents as most adolescents do. In all these ways, Mary Jo was very mature for a teenager.[43]

Renna can only recall one occasion during their high school years when Kopechne was unsure of herself. It was over a boyfriend who, by appearance, was the kind of "preppy, clean-cut guy" Mary Jo liked to date. In fact, he was "a fast-talker" and "not the kind of boy you could trust," according to Renna. "All of our friends knew the guy was bad for her, but Mary Jo was too naïve to believe it," she explained. "When I tried to warn her, we got into an argument and she didn't speak to me for weeks. But Mary Jo eventually broke up with him, and we never discussed the matter again. To be honest, I think she was more upset that her private life was being discussed in the neighborhood than she was about her poor decision to date the guy. But Mary Jo could be stubborn, too."[44]

Like many of the girls who attended OLV, Kopechne thought about becoming a nun. She was active in the League of the Sacred Heart, whose members assisted with weekly mass, and in Sodality, a religious fellowship of students. But Mary Jo was also active in several other organizations. She wrote for the school newspaper, sang in the glee club, participated in the drama club, and in her senior year served as secretary of the student council and an editor of the yearbook.[45]

When she graduated from OLV in June 1958, Mary Jo Kopechne was, by all accounts, an all-American girl: an attractive and obedient daughter who was devoted to her religious faith, a good, hardworking student who participated in many extracurricular activities and got along with everyone, though she had only two close friends. She also had ambitions to attend college, but after that the future was uncertain, or as she wrote: "It's not for me to say."[46]

The Call to Serve 2

Mary Jo was undecided about where to go to college after her graduation from Our Lady of the Valley, and she didn't have much help in making the decision. Neither of her parents nor anyone in her extended family had a college degree. Initially, she planned to enroll at a Katharine Gibbs secretarial school in Montclair, New Jersey, but discovered a similar program at Caldwell College for Women closer to home. She enrolled at Caldwell in the autumn of 1958 with the intention of completing a two-year degree in business administration with an emphasis on secretarial skills.[1]

Caldwell was a small Catholic liberal arts institution in suburban New Jersey, about twenty miles from New York City. Founded in 1939 by the Sisters of Saint Dominic, the college was affiliated with the Archdiocese of Newark and the Catholic University of America in Washington DC. It placed a strong emphasis on theology and philosophy with the objective of producing "Catholic cultured leaders."[2] Caldwell was a natural place for Mary Jo to matriculate considering her Catholic school background and her strong commitment to the faith. It was also a small college with only 298 full-time students.[3] Mary Jo was one of just 114 freshmen, some of whom were classmates at Our Lady of the Valley. Although she was a "day dodger" who commuted from East Orange, Kopechne quickly felt at home on the close-knit campus.[4]

In addition, the choice of a business major not only complemented Mary Jo's organizational skills and diligence but offered one of the few avenues for employment that existed for young women in the late 1950s and early 1960s. "Mary Jo was very talented at taking correspondence, filing and other secretarial work," said Sister Rita Margaret Chambers, chair of the English department. "Like many of the students at the college, she held a work study position and was assigned to me in her sophomore year. She was indispensable because she was extremely meticulous and took great pride in her work."[5]

But Mary Jo was also intelligent and ambitious. Increasingly drawn to history and politics, she began taking courses in those subjects and decided to remain at Caldwell to pursue a four-year bachelor's degree.[6] "It wasn't unusual," said Chambers. "Many of our students were like Mary Jo, the first to attend college in their family. She was especially eager to receive a good education. I also believe that Mary Jo took very seriously the college's mission to develop a sense of moral and civic awareness in the students. She had a close friendship with Sister Regina, who taught history and political science. I believe that Sister Regina, more than anyone else, inspired Mary Jo's interest in politics."[7]

It was the late 1950s, a time of innocence on college campuses. The war in Vietnam and the demand for civil rights at home had not yet stirred widespread protest.[8] Caldwell was a staid place, where conformity to traditional values and behaviors prevailed. Students held fast to a conviction against premarital sex and expected to assume roles as wives and mothers upon graduation. "We did not think of ourselves as 'rebels,'" insisted Nancy Smack McMurtrie, who graduated in 1962. "Most of us were convinced that we'd go straight to hell if we violated the Ten Commandments, especially when it came to adultery. Many classmates were engaged to be married right after graduation, and a few were secretly married during senior year. In fact, one classmate got married in January of our senior year, and when the administration found out she was expelled because it was against college policy to graduate a married woman."

"Mary Jo was much more religious, much more conformist than I was," added McMurtrie. "She was also very close to the Dominican priest who taught a required course on marriage. He was adept at instilling the fear that sex before marriage was the ticket to hell. So I cannot imagine Mary Jo ever being promiscuous. She simply wasn't that kind of girl."[9]

Even political awareness, while encouraged by the college, was integrated with a heavy dose of Catholicism. "All students were required to take theology all four years," recalled Patricia Ann Murphy, who graduated in 1960. "Most of the events on campus involved a mass, and the nuns were a constant presence. But within that religious framework there were opportunities to become politically aware. For example, Mary Jo and I belonged to the National Federation of Catholic College Students, an organization composed of local Catholic colleges. It provided a forum for students to meet and discuss the social and political issues of the day, especially those relevant to our campus."[10] Peter McKeown, a student at Seton Hall in the early sixties, shared Mary Jo's interest in current events and dated her for two years. Initially, they were attracted to each other by a shared love of dancing, but as their relationship grew the couple often found themselves immersed in political discussions. "We spent many an evening in very serious conversation about the state of the world," recalled McKeown, shortly after Kopechne's death in 1969. "Mary Jo was a person of genuine substance—not a phony. She was a rare girl, who was truly concerned about the future of the country."[11]

Kopechne possessed other intangible qualities, too. Classmates were impressed by her "quiet congeniality," "dauntless charm," and "unusual perceptiveness." They predicted she would go on to "enrich the world by adding her perfectionist touch to even the simplest undertakings."[12] Such a constellation of traits suggested that Mary Jo would have a bright future in politics if she chose to pursue that arena. Indeed, Kopechne's interest in public service grew stronger during her sophomore year, when Pope John XXIII encouraged Catholics to work together with Protestants and Jews in the common cause of human rights and social justice.

Anticipating a Second Vatican Council, the Pope promoted interdenominational cooperation as a means of modernizing the church and bringing Catholics into the American mainstream.[13] Catholic colleges like Caldwell answered the call by offering students opportunities for "practical expressions of charity." "I can't ever say that the college was insular because our students were always involved in service projects," said Sister Rita Margaret Chambers. "But in the late 1950s after Pope John's encyclical, our students became more active in social outreach than ever before."[14]

Among the most popular involvements were fundraising for the poor in Appalachia, protesting local establishments that barred blacks, and tutoring minority students in Montclair, Newark, and Jersey City.[15] Upon graduation, some of the most dedicated students became lay apostles, "giving a year of their life to God" as volunteers on Native American Indian reservations or teaching children in the Deep South.[16] Inspired by these opportunities, Mary Jo invested more time in her political science courses than in her business major and told friends that she was planning to use her degree to get a job in politics after graduation.[17] But the experience that had the greatest impact on her future came in 1960, when she volunteered for John F. Kennedy's presidential campaign.

Kennedy, a young, Irish Catholic senator from Massachusetts, was the son of Joseph P. Kennedy, former U.S. ambassador to the Court of St. James's and a multimillionaire who made his initial fortune on Wall Street.[18] The ambassador's own political ambitions were dashed during World War II after he remarked that "democracy is finished" in Europe. Viewed as a Nazi sympathizer, Joe Kennedy was recalled by President Franklin D. Roosevelt. He remained an intensely controversial figure in America because of his suspect business credentials, his Roman Catholicism, and his opposition to Roosevelt's foreign policy.[19] Unable to secure elective office, Joe Kennedy, fueled by a personal resentment against the white Anglo-Saxon Protestant establishment, viewed his four sons as the means to achieve his own political ambitions. Accordingly, the Kennedy patriarch used his wealth and connections in the Irish American community to build a national network of supporters that became the base for the senatorial and presidential campaigns of his son John.[20] He also enlisted the services of *New York Times* political columnist Arthur Krock as a paid speechwriter and political adviser to JFK.[21]

Popular mythology surrounding the Kennedy family maintains that Joe Kennedy wanted his eldest son, Joe Jr., to become president, but after Joe Jr. lost his life in World War II, he became determined to secure the White House for his second son, John.[22] There is some truth to the myth, too. JFK had demonstrated little interest in politics before the 1940s and had planned to pursue a career in journalism or college teaching. But after he was discharged from the navy in 1945, he decided to run for Congress. "It was like being drafted," he admitted years later. "My father wanted his eldest son in politics. 'Wanted' isn't the right word. He demanded it."[23] However, Thomas Oliphant and Curtis Wilkie, in their recent work *The Road to Camelot*, show that John Kennedy wanted the highest office for himself and took steps as early as 1956 to gain the national exposure to launch a presidential campaign. According to Oliphant and Wilkie, the junior senator from Massachusetts had been in Congress for nearly a decade, and he had the reputation of a socialite and war hero; not a serious contender for higher office. Indeed, JFK in 1956 had no identifiable philosophy, nor was he attached to any significant national cause. His congressional colleagues considered him an "indifferent Democrat with occasionally independent tendencies." To gain greater visibility, Kennedy wrested control of the Massachusetts Democratic Party apparatus from John McCormick, speaker of the U.S. House of Representatives, to be elected chairman of the state's delegation to the 1956 national convention in Chicago. The tactic placed Kennedy in a commanding position. Not only did he insure that the Massachusetts delegation would support former Illinois governor Adlai Stevenson for the nomination, but JFK also gained for himself serious consideration as Stevenson's running mate.[24]

Joe Kennedy opposed his son's idea of courting the vice presidential nomination as "seeking fool's gold on a ticket that was doomed to defeat" by President Dwight D. Eisenhower, the popular incumbent. But Kennedy's top aide, Theodore Sorensen, encouraged him to pursue the nomination as a "first step to overcoming the religious obstacle to his becoming president in the future."[25] Sorensen reinforced his argument by preparing a sixteen-page report with statistics on Catholic voting patterns in postwar presidential elections. The report challenged the popular notion that Al Smith, the Catholic governor of New York, was trounced by Herbert Hoover in the 1928 presidential election because of his religion. Ever since, Smith's defeat had been interpreted to mean that Catholicism was an ironclad disqualification from the presidency. Instead, Sorensen argued that "the Catholic vote is far more important than its numbers—about one out of every four voters who turn out—because of its concentration in the key states and cities of the North" and that millions of Catholic Democrats who had voted for Eisenhower in 1952 would "return home to the Democratic Party if a Catholic were chosen as Stevenson's running mate."[26] Thus Kennedy's Catholicism could actually benefit him in a later bid for the White House. Although Kennedy lost the vice presidential nomination to Senator Estes Kefauver of Tennessee at the 1956 Democratic National Convention , he emerged as a potential future candidate for the presidency.

Between 1957 and 1959, Kennedy increased his national exposure by traveling across the country and speaking at annual Democratic Party fundraising dinners in many states. He hired Lou Harris, a thirty-six-year-old pollster, to gain leverage in the sixteen primaries scheduled for the 1960 presidential campaign and create grassroots campaign organizations to court Democratic leaders in key primary states. In all these ways Kennedy created a clear advantage for himself over other Democratic presidential hopefuls like Senator Lyndon B. Johnson of Texas, Senator Hubert Humphrey of Minnesota, and Senator Stuart Symington of Missouri, all of whom did not begin to lay the groundwork for their campaigns until the autumn of 1959 or later.[27]

In 1960 JFK took advantage of the economic prosperity and optimistic mood of the country to launch his bid for the presidency. In the previous decade, personal incomes had ballooned by more than 80 percent across all classes, and disposable income had increased by 50 percent. Americans enjoyed more leisure time and an improved quality of life. Middle-class demand for cars, better roadways, and air travel resulted in the growth of suburbs and shopping malls. Family vacations became more common. Television overtook radio as the popular means of daily entertainment and news. Material prosperity also resulted in social change. Women were entering the work force in greater numbers than ever before. A post–World War II baby boom created the need for more schools and a greater demand for college education. Bound together by growing highways systems, television, and suburbia, Americans were beginning to abandon local and regional identities and embrace a truly *national* identity.[28] Kennedy exploited these developments by introducing a new style of political campaigning that appealed to young voters, women, and other groups that were becoming politically active.

At age forty-three, JFK projected the image of a youthful, dynamic, self-confident politician who represented a decisive shift away from the business-as-usual politics of an older generation. He exploited the growing medium of television by introducing thirty-second commercials that began with popular catchphrases like "Senator Kennedy goes to the people," and showed footage of Kennedy speaking about an issue like education, unemployment, or the Cold War. Unlike earlier paid political advertising, which consisted of infrequent, five-minute segments, Kennedy's spots were quick, dynamic, and carried by the three major networks on a regular basis.[29] He was photogenic and worked hard to keep his tan dark to enhance his television appearance.[30] He courted the press, saddling up to such prominent journalists as Arthur Krock of the *New York Times*, Ben Bradlee, the Washington Bureau chief for *Newsweek*, and Theodore White of *Time*. In fact, White unabashedly wore a "Kennedy for President" button while writing his Pulitzer Prize–winning account of the election, *The Making of the President, 1960*.[31]

Kennedy's youth, natural wit, movie-star good looks, and media-oriented campaign captured the attention of first-time voters on college campuses across the nation. The more serious-minded students, however, were just as impressed by his platform. JFK was a Cold War liberal. He identified himself with the Democratic Party's liberal reform tradition established by Franklin Roosevelt and Harry Truman and promised a new surge of legislative innovation in the 1960s. Specifically, Kennedy advocated an activist government to protect the interests of the poor, working, and middle classes against corporate capitalism at home while embracing a fierce anti-Communism abroad. But what most attracted young voters was his call to public service.

Mary Jo Kopechne, like thousands of college-aged youth, was smitten with JFK because of the dynamic image he projected and his more substantive positions on the issues that confronted the nation. But Kennedy's Catholicism endeared him to her in a more personal way.

Predictably, when the local Catholic Youth Organization created a "Flying Squad for Kennedy," she was among the first to volunteer. "We were from the 'silent fifties' generation, and the 1960 election was our 'coming out,' so to speak," recalled John Mohrhauser, a high school teacher who directed the Kennedy campaign in Essex County, New Jersey. "We grew up during World War II and didn't have a lot of material comforts. Our parents raised us to be responsible, to work hard, and to sacrifice. We weren't like the rebellious Sixties generation. They were given everything and, as a result they were irresponsible. Many of them dropped out of college or remained in school to stay out of Vietnam or simply for the sake of protesting."

Those who joined the Flying Squad, on the other hand, were attracted by Kennedy's "message to make a difference in our country and around the world through public service," according to Mohrhauser. "We really believed in Kennedy and that he could shape this country for the better." At the same time, Mohrhauser admitted, the thirty members of the Flying Squad were "very naïve" in terms of fundraising. "We used to have cocktail parties to raise money for plastic straw hats with 'Kennedy' written across them. We'd sell the hats for $2 each and the profits would go toward more cocktail parties. We had no sense whatsoever of politics or money, but people loved us."[32]

The Flying Squad campaigned in blue-collar towns like Bloomfield, Newark, and East Orange, which tended to vote Democrat, especially the Italian and Irish Catholic wards. Since most of the college students came from working-class families, they understood the needs of the community and were welcomed by residents. Although Kopechne joined in the fundraisers and marched in a few parades waving a "JFK" banner, she was more comfortable fielding questions at the Essex County campaign headquarters. She was well-prepared with an impressive command of Kennedy's position on various issues. "Mary Jo was one of our most committed volunteers," said Mohrhauser. "If you spoke with her, you knew you were dealing with someone who was extremely bright and extremely dedicated."

Once, while Mary Jo was taking a phone call, she overheard another volunteer give misinformation about JFK's position on education. He was speaking with an attractive blonde and doing his best to impress her. Afterward, Mary Jo corrected him in private. Embarrassed, he berated her, walked out of the office, and never returned. "If you were a bullshit artist—and we had some of those—Mary Jo would tolerate you just so long," Mohrhauser admitted. "She would let you know that you were insufferable. She had no pretense. She was a *very* direct individual, but she was also very professional. I never heard a word of animosity towards her, probably because she exercised discretion."[33]

Dick Toole, another campaign worker, confirmed the observation. "Mary Jo was very direct," he recalled. "You didn't have to sniff around to know what she was thinking. Sometimes she expressed her opinion in a sharp-witted, cute way. But she was careful not to insult others." Toole dated Kopechne for a year, but their relationship was not as much a "romance" as a "close friendship." They met through the local Catholic Youth Organization, which had an acting group for young adults. Toole, recently graduated from Notre Dame University, had returned home to Bloomfield, New Jersey, to look for teaching jobs. To relieve the boredom, he joined the Catholic Youth Organization and thought it would be interesting to try acting. "No one had ambitions for Broadway," said Toole. "It was just good clean fun and a way to meet other young single Catholics." The group performed plays like *Carousel* and *Brigadoon*. It also formed an orchestra and built the set designs. "We would perform mostly at prisons and mental institutions," chuckled Toole. "I guess you could say that we had a *captive* audience. But it was also a form of outreach because the guys at the prison were especially delighted to watch pretty young women up on the stage! Mary Jo and I joined the drama group independently and acted in a few productions together. Neither of us were very talented actors. We'd just take bit parts. What we really enjoyed was going out together after the play practices. Initially we went out with the group, about ten guys and fifteen girls. After a while we started to date."[34]

Toole described Mary Jo as "very thin and almost tomboyish, not glamorous at all." Instead, he was attracted by her natural appearance, especially by her smile, which he described as "simply beautiful, even radiant." Toole also admired Mary Jo's character. "She was a lady in every sense of the word," he explained. "She wasn't amused by dirty jokes or profanity. Nor was she a party girl. When we were together she hardly ever drank."

Toole and Kopechne joined the Flying Squad in the spring of 1960. Both were idealists who believed Kennedy would make a difference in the lives of the poor and working class. "Mary Jo was especially concerned about civil rights," said Toole. "She came from East Orange, which had a growing black population, and saw firsthand some of the police discrimination they faced. I also think she felt guilty because she enjoyed the advantages of a safe home and an education, things that most blacks didn't have. I noticed that Mary Jo would gravitate to black youngsters whenever they were at a parade or a rally. She was especially sympathetic with them."[35]

Toole was surprised years later when he learned that Kopechne went into politics. He thought that she would be a much better history teacher or college professor. But Mohrhauser knew better. "Mary Jo made it very clear that she intended to go to Washington to work for the Kennedys," he said. "That was her ambition. She was even more dedicated to Robert Kennedy because he took such a strong stand on civil rights. She spoke of him as being 'the answer' to civil rights and later 'the answer' to Vietnam."[36]

Throughout the spring and summer of 1960, in his speeches and meetings with Democratic leaders, JFK emphasized that excluding Catholics from the White House was unacceptable bigotry. The West Virginia primary in May represented a turning point in his campaign. Until then, Senator Hubert Humphrey of Minnesota appeared to hold an edge among the liberal and moderate wings of the Democratic Party because of his strong support of civil rights, labor, public education, and health care. Kennedy's legitimacy as a candidate would be tested in West Virginia because the state had such a small Catholic population. To his credit, JFK focused on those voters who were genuinely fearful of a Catholic president rather than appeal to those who were outright bigots. He insisted that he "would not accept the right of any ecclesiastical official to tell me what I should do in the sphere of my public responsibility." "And if my church attempted to influence me in a way that affected adversely my Constitutional responsibilities as a public servant," he added, "I would tell them that it is an improper action on their part."[37]

Humphrey dropped out of the race after the West Virginia primary as the religious issue began to recede.[38] Kennedy won ten of the sixteen primaries he entered and prevailed over three other rivals who hoped to be drafted as the party's nominee at the Democratic convention: Senate Majority Leader Lyndon B. Johnson of Texas, Senator Stuart Symington of Missouri, and Adlai Stevenson, who had won the nomination in 1952 and 1956 and lost in the general election to Dwight D. Eisenhower. On July 15, at the Democratic National Convention in Los Angeles, JFK won the party's nomination on the first ballot.[39]

If voters had any reservations about Kennedy's Catholicism, the Democratic nominee put them to rest on September 12, 1960, in an address to three hundred Protestant clergymen at the Greater Houston Ministerial Association. "I am not the Catholic candidate for President," Kennedy said. "I am the Democratic Party's candidate for President, who happens also to be a Catholic. I do not speak for my church on public matters—and the church does not speak for me." Although Kennedy insisted that he would "not disavow my Church," he "pledged to resign" if ever he had to choose between his personal conscience and his presidential duty.[40] Instead, the general election raised questions among voters about JFK's youth and whether he had the experience to be president.

While Kennedy promised to "get the nation moving again" and to "resist communism around the world," his Republican opponent, forty-seven-year-old vice president Richard M. Nixon, exploited his background in the Eisenhower administration to assure voters that he would maintain American prestige, leadership, and military strength.[41] Nixon, who impressed many voters as more mature and experienced than Kennedy, initially led in the polls. But after a series of televised debates, Kennedy held the advantage. His photogenic appeal and his ability to speak directly to the cameras and the national audience gave him more credibility with viewers who watched the debates. Nixon, on the other hand, relied on a traditional debating style in responding directly to Kennedy and appeared uncomfortable and tense in the first debate. Although the vice president was more poised and relaxed in the last two contests, the first encounter left a stronger impression with the viewers. Studies would later show that of the four million voters who made up their minds based on the debates, three million voted for Kennedy.[42]

JFK appealed to urban minorities, ethnic voting blocs, and organized labor and appeared to win back conservative Catholics who had deserted the Democrats to vote for Eisenhower in 1952 and 1956. By naming Senator Lyndon B. Johnson of Texas as his running mate, Kennedy was also able to hold his own in the South. In November he defeated Nixon in one of the closest presidential elections in American history. When the votes were tallied, the Massachusetts senator earned 49.7 percent of the popular vote to Nixon's 49.5 percent. Kennedy polled only about one hundred thousand more votes than Nixon out of more than sixty-eight million votes cast. Despite Nixon winning more states than his Catholic opponent, the electoral college awarded the election to Kennedy by a 303–219 margin.[43]

In an inaugural address that has become a poignant reminder of the idealism of the 1960s, JFK challenged the American people to "ask not what your country can do for you—ask what you can do for your country."[44] By issuing such a challenge, the new president inspired a strong sense of national purpose and pride, especially among young Americans. His New Frontier programs ushered in a refreshing spirit of voluntarism by urging citizens to commit themselves to solving the problems of poverty and social injustice, both at home and abroad. Kennedy's agenda proved both ambitious and energizing. He advocated such programs as a higher minimum wage, the creation of new jobs, greater federal aid to education, and increased Social Security benefits. In foreign policy he sought to counter the communist threat by supporting democratic movements in Third World nations, especially Vietnam, and to land an American on the moon before the end of the 1960s. But few of these efforts, especially civil rights, were achieved without failure or suffering.[45]

Kennedy came late to the civil rights struggle. Fearing that the fight for racial equality would divide the Democratic Party, he stalled for two years on his campaign pledge to ban discrimination by executive order in federally financed housing. Instead of attacking segregation head-on by supporting congressional liberals who pushed civil rights legislation, Kennedy quietly pursued desegregation through litigation. His reluctance earned him harsh criticism from black activists, whose nonviolent resistance to segregation often resulted in injury and imprisonment.[46] But Kennedy also learned from his mistakes and grew as a leader because of it.

The sobering drama of police dogs and high-powered fire hoses unleashed on school children who voluntarily joined the Southern Christian Leadership Conference to protest segregated public facilities in Birmingham forced Kennedy to reconsider the morality of his civil rights position. "If an American, because his skin is dark, cannot eat lunch at a restaurant open to the public," he said in a June 11, 1963, television address, "if he cannot send his children to the best public school available, if he cannot vote for the public officials who represent him, if, in short, he cannot enjoy the full and free life which all of us want, then who among us would be content to have the color of his skin changed and stand in his place?" Eight days later, Kennedy introduced the strongest civil rights measure proposed up to that time. Not only did the bill guarantee the rights of blacks to vote and to use public accommodations, but it charged the Justice Department with enforcement and cut off federal funding to those states that refused to uphold the new measure.[47]

Kennedy demonstrated similar growth in his foreign policy. After he led the world to the brink of a nuclear war during the Cuban Missile Crisis in October 1962, he pursued a more open dialogue with the Soviet Union, which resulted in the Nuclear Test Ban Treaty of 1963.[48] There are also indications that the assassination of South Vietnamese president Ngô Đình Diệm in early November 1963 made JFK realize that the United States could not control events in Southeast Asia and that a gradual withdrawal of American special forces would be necessary.[49]

Inspired by Kennedy's challenge to "ask what you can do for your country" and a personal commitment to her religious faith, Kopechne, after her graduation from Caldwell in 1962, decided to join a Lay Apostolate organization, a Catholic version of the Kennedy-inspired Volunteers in Service to America. "Mary Jo really wanted to teach on an Indian reservation in Oklahoma," recalled her mother, Gwen, in a September 1970 interview with *McCall's Magazine*. "But when she realized that that would prevent her from coming home for an entire year, she decided to teach at the Mission of Saint Jude in Alabama. This kind of work was called 'giving a year to God.' At that time, all Catholic girls were encouraged to spend such a year."[50] In fact, Mary Jo's work was missionary, a call to serve her Catholic faith and her country.

The Mission of Saint Jude was founded by the Archdiocese of Mobile in 1938 and located in the City of Saint Jude in West Montgomery, Alabama. Among the various forms of outreach was Montgomery Catholic High School, an integrated school with an enrollment of four hundred students. Most of the students came from middle-class families, but there were also some from affluent and working-class backgrounds. The high school was supported financially by tuition and donations from Saint Jude's Parish, alumni and "individuals and groups who believe in the importance of a Catholic education." The school's mission was to "serve the educational and spiritual needs of single young men and women in grades 9–12, integrating faith into daily life, making moral choices and acting in a manner that respects the rights and dignity of each person." In addition, the high school aimed to "educate students for Christian living in a global society" so that they become "mindful of the importance of loving service, concern for the poor and a deep faith in God."[51]

Kopechne was one of three lay female teachers during the 1962–63 school year. She was paid $50 per month to teach typing, shorthand, and office practice and to supervise the school newspaper, *Dixie Echoes*.[52] Her classes were small, between eight and fifteen students, and all female, which allowed for greater intimacy than those taught by the nuns. "Mary Jo was awesome," recalled Lynn Jehle, one of her students. "Since she was just 22 years old and closer in age to the juniors and seniors, we were able to have a friendship. She was a blessing not only to me but to the other students she taught as well."[53]

Kopechne lived in a home owned by Saint Jude's Mission in the Normandale section of Montgomery, a middle-class neighborhood just a few miles from the high school. She shared the house with two other lay apostles, Janet Casha and Jean O'Leary. Sometimes students would visit them "just to say hello" and to "share the latest news about school and their classmates." "Miss Kopechne was a wonderful person," said Maureen Clark, another student. "She talked about wanting to be involved in the civil rights movement as much as possible. I have a sneaking suspicion that she was planning to make that her focus after the school year ended. We were just fortunate to have her at the school for the brief time she was with us because she was well read, very intelligent, and she cared very deeply about the students."[54]

Others spoke of Kopechne as someone who "enjoyed good, clean fun." Judith Hadden, a former lay apostle, had been hired as a full-time teacher at Montgomery Catholic High School the year Kopechne arrived. They had known each other from high school at Our Lady of the Valley and quickly connected. "My memories of Mary Joe from OLV were of a cute blonde with a very boyish figure," said Hadden. "She was friendly with everyone and seemed unimpressed by anyone's status or position within the hierarchy of the school. In the five years since, Mary Jo had developed into an attractive young woman. Her hair was shorter and much blonder, and she wore much trendier clothing."[55]

Hadden and Kopechne spent a lot of time together. They chaperoned dances, went on double dates, and frequented piano bars. Hadden, who was dating an Air Force lieutenant from nearby Maxwell Air Force Base, introduced Mary Jo to another lieutenant, Paul Sanchez. "Mary Jo and Paul became an item that spring," recalled Hadden. "The four of us often went out together. We'd go to a piano bar, have a drink, and sing along with whoever was there. Other times we went dancing. But Mary Jo and I always insisted on going home early either because we had school the next day or we had had enough. Mary Jo usually led the way. She liked a good time, but she was no party girl. She would've had just as much fun at the ice cream parlor, which we also frequented."[56]

Kopechne loved to dance. She was a naturally introverted individual who used dancing to "let loose." She once confided to her cousin Georgetta that the "swinging and swaying and turning and dipping was like setting your soul free to fly."[57] Hadden believed her friend's dancing skills were "remarkable," but "not necessarily in a good way." "Mary Jo had an intensity about her that affected everything she did," explained Hadden. "Hence, there was nothing relaxed about her dancing, and it was rather awkward to watch."[58] Essentially, dancing was Mary Jo's primary outlet, a way to release some of the anxiety she felt about an uncertain future as well as the restless energy pent-up inside an otherwise disciplined person. And there were those occasions when Mary Jo was compelled to keep her opinions to herself.

One Saturday afternoon Kopechne and Hadden were invited to the home of an affluent white student whose family had deep roots in the history of Montgomery. When the mother began to express her opinions on President Kennedy's efforts at integrating public transportation, it was clear that she was not a supporter. "Mary Jo somehow managed to bite her tongue," said Hadden. "I know it took a lot of discipline. She loved the president and admired his brother Robert's defense of civil rights. So I just thanked God she kept quiet because she could be very candid in her opinions when it involved the Kennedys."[59]

Most of the families who sent their children to Montgomery Catholic High School were "progressive" in their attitude toward civil rights. Saint Jude's Mission employed blacks at Saint Peter's Church and its rectory as well as in the grade school and high school. Students were taught to treat blacks with respect.[60] But the City of Saint Jude was not like the rest of Montgomery, which had a national reputation for racial intolerance.

The modern civil rights movement began in Montgomery on December 1, 1955, when Rosa Parks, a black seamstress, refused to give up her seat to a white man on a public bus. The driver summoned the police, who promptly arrested Parks for violating the city's segregation ordinance. This single act of defiance triggered a mass boycott of the buses by the city's African American residents and thrust the movement's leader, the Reverend Martin Luther King Jr., into the national spotlight. The boycott lasted for 381 days and ended, on December 21, 1956, with the desegregation of the Montgomery bus system. The following year, King became the president of the Southern Christian Leadership Conference and began to coordinate protest activities across the South. Montgomery was at the forefront again in 1960, when three dozen students from Alabama State University attempted to eat at a segregated lunch counter in Woolworth's department store and were expelled from the university at the insistence of Governor John Patterson. The following year a racially integrated group of Freedom Riders arrived in Montgomery on May 20. They were traveling on Greyhound and Trailways buses across the South to test compliance with the U.S. Supreme Court's 1960 ruling in *Boynton v. Virginia*, which forbade racial discrimination in interstate travel. Instead of protecting the Freedom Riders, the city police allowed a group of whites to attack them as they disembarked, sending several to the hospital. The violence embarrassed and infuriated U.S. Attorney General Robert F. Kennedy, who pressured Governor Patterson to provide them with safe passage into Mississippi. Once there, the Freedom Riders were arrested and jailed. But their demonstration was a turning point in the civil rights movement because it refocused attention on segregation and racial violence in the Deep South and forced President Kennedy to take decisive action to protect the civil rights activists. Unfortunately, the president did not make protecting civil rights workers a permanent priority, which left them exposed to white violence.[61]

In 1962 the battlefront of civil rights movement shifted to Birmingham, the most segregated city in the nation. Baptist minister Fred Shuttlesworth, the president of the Alabama Christian Movement for Human Rights, secured a promise from white civic leaders to desegregate downtown water fountains and restrooms. But when the white leaders reneged on the agreement a year later, King's Southern Christian Leadership Conference organized an elaborate campaign to desegregate the city with a series of sit-ins, marches, and a boycott of downtown stores. Joining in these efforts was the Student Nonviolent Coordinating Committee, founded in April 1960 by young people dedicated to nonviolent, direct action tactics. Like the Southern Christian Leadership Conference, the Student Nonviolent Coordinating Committee was an integrated organization and included the college-aged children of northern white liberals. They had grown up with a naïve faith that civil rights could be achieved through principled action and were shocked when their protests resulted in some of the most unspeakable violence of the era.[62]

"For a northerner to go down South to teach in the 1960s was gutsy enough, but Mary Jo was risking her life because she was a double minority down there being both female and Catholic," said her cousin Georgetta Potoski. "But Mary Jo believed strongly in the civil rights movement. Our family rolled our eyes and shook our heads. We thought she was crazy. Whenever her parents visited her down there they tried to persuade her to leave. They feared for her."[63]

To be sure, Kopechne was feeling the same pressures of many white, middle-class young women from the North who had joined the civil rights movement. Sarah Evans, author of *Personal Politics*, argues that parental concern for their daughters' safety was just one of those pressures. Hundreds of young white women who went south to become involved in the civil rights movement between 1962 and 1965 were forced to confront fears of their own safety, the culture shock of living in the South, and the pressure of young African American men who challenged them to prove their sincerity by engaging in sex.[64] In addition to these pressures, Mary Jo was wrestling with her future. She understood how emotionally attached she had become to her students and wondered whether she possessed the discipline to create the distance she needed to have a life of her own.

Near the end of the school year, Kopechne decided that "teaching wasn't for her because she was so emotionally involved with the students." She confided to her mother that she "wasn't quite mature enough to know how to reserve a part of herself for her own life." Gwen Kopechne later admitted that she was "proud that her daughter was mature enough to recognize the problem" and "relieved about her decision to return home" because of the mounting tensions in the civil rights movement. But Mary Jo did not plan to return home. Instead, she told friends, she planned to "go to Washington and work for John Kennedy." It was, as Mary Jo put it, her "career ambition."[65]

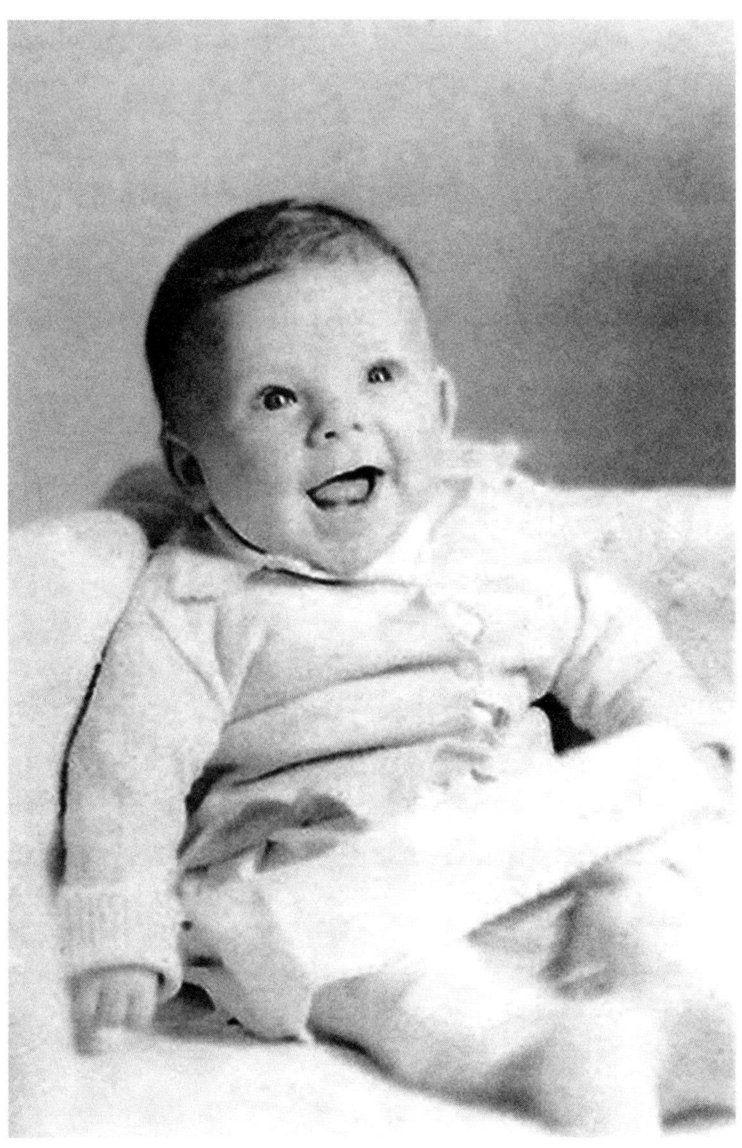

1. Mary Jo as a baby, 1941. Kopechne Estate.

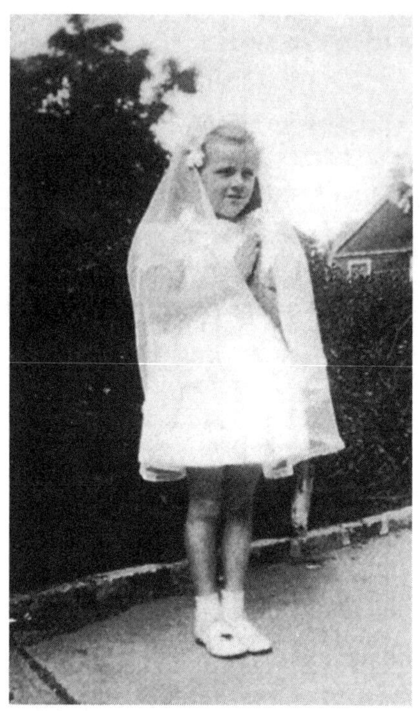

2. (*left*) Raised to be a devout Catholic, Mary Jo posed for her first Holy Communion at age seven in 1946. Kopechne Estate.

3. (*below*) Gwen, Mary Jo, and Joseph Kopechne, Christmas 1946. Kopechne Estate.

4. Mary Jo was a serious and involved student at Our Lady of the Valley Catholic High School, where she was an active member of the glee club, student council, Latin club, and a host of religious societies. She graduated in June 1958 undecided about her future. Kopechne Estate.

5. Portrait of Kennedy family at Hyannis, Massachusetts, 1930s. *Seated from left*: Robert Kennedy (1925–68), Edward Kennedy (1932–2009), Joseph P. Kennedy Sr. (1888–1969), Eunice Kennedy (1921–2009), Rosemary Kennedy (1918–2005), and Kathleen Kennedy (1920–48). *Standing from left*: Joseph P. Kennedy Jr. (1915–44), John F. Kennedy (1917–63), Rose Kennedy (1890–1995), Jean Kennedy (1928–), and Patricia Kennedy (1926–2006). Bachrach/Getty Images.

6. The Kennedy brothers, in August 1963, pose in Washington: Attorney General Robert, Senator Edward, and President John. Cecil Stoughton/ National Archives.

7. Mary Jo Anne Kopechne, Caldwell College, class of 1962. Kopechne Estate.

8. In 1966 Mary Jo realized a longtime ambition by going to work for her political hero, Senator Robert F. Kennedy of New York. Kopechne Estate.

9. (*above*) RFK meets with members of his secretarial staff in summer 1967. Mary Jo is seated at far left. Kopechne Estate.

10. (*opposite top*) After RFK's death, Joe Gargan, Teddy's cousin, hosted several gatherings for the Boiler Room Girls to stay connected in the event that the youngest Kennedy brother would launch his own presidential campaign. *Top row, left to right*: Betty Gargan, Joe Gargan, Maryellen Lyons, Mary Jo Kopechne. *Bottom, left to right*: Terri Gargan, Rosemary Keough, Susan Tannenbaum, Esther Newberg, and Nance Lyons. Kopechne Estate.

11. (*opposite bottom*) Lawrence Cottage on Chappaquiddick Island, the scene of the July 18, 1969, party attended by Senator Edward Kennedy and friends, including Mary Jo Kopechne and five of the late Bobby Kennedy's Boiler Room Girls. Boston Globe/Getty Images.

12. Ted Kennedy's Oldsmobile plunged off Dike Bridge on Chappaquiddick Island in the early morning hours of July 19, 1969. The Massachusetts senator escaped, but his passenger, Mary Jo Kopechne, was killed in the accident. Bettmann/Getty Images.

13. Mary Jo Kopechne's body is removed from a charter plane at Avoca Airport in Wilkes-Barre, Pennsylvania, on July 20, 1969. The body was transported to the Kielty Funeral Home in nearby Plymouth, where it was prepared for burial. Bettmann/Getty Images.

14. (*left*) Mary Jo's casket leaves Saint Vincent's Catholic Church. Reverend William Burchill (*foreground*) conducted the Catholic funeral mass. Kopechne Estate.

15. (*below*) Joseph and Gwen Kopechne leave Saint Vincent's Church. Gwen was so distraught she had trouble remembering any details of the funeral years later. Kopechne Estate.

16. Senator Edward Kennedy and wife, Joan, leave Saint Vincent's Church after attending Mary Jo's funeral mass. Bettmann/Getty Images.

17. The five Boiler Room Girls who attended the Chappaquiddick party arrive at Edgartown, Massachusetts, on January 8, 1970, to testify in the inquest into Mary Jo Kopechne's death. *Left to right*: Rosemary Keough, Maryellen Lyons, Nance Lyons, Susan Tannenbaum, and Esther Newberg, with one of the lawyers, Daniel Day (*back right*). Bettmann/Getty Images.

18. Joseph and Gwen Kopechne leave the Luzerne County, Pennsylvania, courthouse on October 21, 1969, after Judge Bernard C. Brominski ruled against the exhumation of their daughter's body. Bettmann/Getty Images.

19. (*top*) Senator Ted Kennedy shakes hands with President Jimmy Carter before the 1980 presidential campaign. Carter would go on to defeat Kennedy for the Democratic nomination, ending the Massachusetts senator's one and only bid for the White House. National Archives.

20. (*bottom*) Kopechne gravesite at Saint Vincent's Catholic Cemetery, Larksville Mountain, Pennsylvania. Courtesy of the author.

True Believer 3

When Kopechne arrived in Washington DC in the late summer of 1963, she quickly discovered that there were no secretarial positions available in the Kennedy administration. Determined to work for the president, she assumed a more passive-aggressive strategy to achieve her goal. Mary Jo interviewed with several congressional offices, including those of Harrison A. Williams of New Jersey and George Smathers of Florida.[1] John O'Keefe, Smathers's administrative assistant, was impressed by her quiet demeanor, wholesome appearance, and educational background and offered her a job.[2] "Smathers is a close friend of the President's," Mary Jo told her mother excitedly when she phoned to tell her parents the news. "Well, then," replied Gwen Kopechne, "there's no question about who you're going to work for, is there?"[3]

George Smathers had been John Kennedy's closest friend in the Senate. Both men began their congressional careers in 1947 and forged a strong bond as young senators in the early 1950s. In fact, Smathers was the only member of Kennedy's wedding party who was not a relative of his or the Bouvier family, and during the 1960 presidential election he managed Kennedy's campaign in the southeastern region of the country.[4] Both men also had notorious reputations for "womanizing." According to journalist Roger Mudd, Smathers and Kennedy were "wolves on the prowl, always able to find or attract gorgeous prey." Once, Mudd, a CBS network representative assigned to the press boat following the presidential yacht, saw Smathers aboard sharing the company of several beautiful young women with Kennedy. "It was a joke," explained Mudd, "our pretending to be covering the president as we squinted through binoculars to find out who was coming and going, but always having our view blocked by a Secret Service boat just as another long-legged beauty climbed aboard."[5]

That JFK enjoyed an active extramarital sex life is common knowledge today, as is the fact that his indiscretions were hidden from the public by the Secret Service, journalists who covered the White House, and those who worked in the West Wing.[6] Although rumors of Kennedy's infidelities circulated on Capitol Hill, Mary Jo, if she heard the gossip, refused to believe it. "Mary Jo believed that President Kennedy could do no wrong," recalled Gwen Kopechne. "If anyone criticized him, she would defend him. She just refused to believe anything bad about him."[7]

"Mary Jo came from a different background than the rest of us," recalled a friend who worked on Capitol Hill and shared a townhouse with her at 2921 Olive Street in Georgetown. "Most of us came from wealthier backgrounds and attended Ivy League schools or small exclusive liberal arts colleges. Mary Jo came from a working-class background and had graduated from a Catholic women's college. She impressed me as bright-eyed, enthusiastic, and a bit naïve. I remember another housemate who was promiscuous," said the Olive Street friend. "Mary Jo was taken aback by her behavior, which told me that she was pretty straight."[8]

The "other housemate" was Nancy Carole Tyler, a former beauty queen from Loudon County, Tennessee, who worked for and dated Bobby Baker, secretary to Senate Majority Leader Lyndon B. Johnson.[9] Together with Tyler, Baker, who often mixed politics with personal business, founded the Quorum Club, a private club in the Carroll Arms Hotel adjacent to a Senate office building. Club membership was composed of "senators, congressmen, lobbyists, Capitol Hill staffers, and other well-connecteds who wanted to enjoy their drinks, meals, poker games, and shared secrets in private accommodations."[10] Many of the same activities soon spread to a townhouse at 308 N Street SW, just a short ride from the Capitol, that was owned by Baker and later occupied by Tyler. According to the November 8, 1963, issue of *Time*, the townhouse was "well-furnished with prints on the walls, silk draperies in the bedrooms, and lavender carpeting in the bathrooms. Lively gatherings were hosted by chain-smoking, martini-drinking, party-loving Carole. The twist was danced both inside the house and on the patio outside; the convivial drinking and animated chatter lasted long into the night. Some nearby residents noted that visitors appeared in the daytime as well as the evening. 'A lot of people used to come through the back gate,' recalls one neighbor. 'That struck us as strange. Most of our guests come through the front door.'"[11]

Young women and parties defined the nightlife of Washington DC, where "single girls outnumbered other people by a wide margin," according to George Schreiber, author of *The Bobby Baker Affair*. "A passably attractive girl in a government office can go off to a party given by free-spending lobbyists as often and as far as her schedule and her scruples allow. She can go with a male colleague who prefers not to take his wife, or a business executive from out of town who hates to eat alone."[12] But Washington, with its fast pace and glitzy temptations, was an exception to the U.S. norm.

In the early 1960s, young women were far less sexually sophisticated than females of the same age today. They deferred to men in dating and relationships. To ask a man on a date was considered "brazen" if not "promiscuous." Nor did they date more than one man at a time. They were serial monogamists who tended to give serious consideration to what kind of husband and father their boyfriends would make. Marriage was never far from their minds. This was especially true of young women like Mary Jo, who were raised in strictly Catholic households where the definitions of "marriage" and "motherhood" were deeply entrenched in the canon of religious faith.[13] Popular culture and the media reinforced these traditional roles, as women's magazines and television commercials depicted the stay-at-home wife and mother as "happy" and "personally fulfilled." Although Mary Jo expected to use her college education to pursue a career, she also planned to follow her mother's example and marry and raise a family at some point in the future.[14] If Mary Jo felt any tension between her educational status, career ambitions, and the traditional expectations of becoming a wife and mother, she kept those feelings to herself. Nor did she compromise her rigid morality.

Unlike many of the young female secretaries who worked on Capitol Hill, Kopechne did not drink, smoke, or do much partying. "Most of my friends and I had a lot of fun, staying out way too late and partying, but not Mary Jo," recalled Elly Gardner Kluge, a Caldwell classmate who lived and worked in nearby Arlington, Virginia. "If she joined us, she would have just one drink and then ask for a ginger ale because she preferred the taste of nonalcoholic beverages. If there was too much drinking, profanity, or lewd behavior, Mary Jo was always the first to leave. Unlike the rest of us, who were pretty immature, she was balanced, mature, and well behaved." Kopechne held herself to a high moral standard, so high that she was often kidded about it by friends and family.[15] "Mary Jo was modest in her speech, clothing, and behavior," said her cousin Georgetta Potoski. "I never knew her to flaunt herself in suggestive postures or to participate in questionable conversations or behavior. She was a self-confessed 'cradle Catholic' with a firm belief in her faith."[16] As a result, Mary Jo struggled initially to reconcile her straitlaced view of the world with the looser morality that defined Washington.

Despite her discomfort with the risqué lifestyle of Washington, Kopechne eventually found a way to blend in without compromising her ethics. While working for Smathers, she distinguished herself by completing her duties with diligence and perfection and was willing to go above and beyond those duties by assuming various menial tasks, something her "more sophisticated" coworkers considered beneath them. In fact, there was a standing joke that in a senatorial office full of chic, glamorous secretaries, Mary Jo was the only one who knew how to take dictation. In addition to her impressive work ethic, Kopechne, according to Georgetta Potoski, was "a delightful companion who dedicated herself to co-workers. She was tenderhearted, but never sloppily sentimental. She encouraged, supported and assisted anyone in need." As a result, Mary Jo endeared herself to the other secretaries in Smathers's office. She could be a team player without compromising her moral standards and be respected for it. As one of her coworkers said, "Mary Jo had no enemies." She also continued to be a stalwart defender of the president whose photograph she kept on her office desk. "If anyone criticized JFK or his brother Robert," said a coworker, "Mary Jo always had a quick comeback."[17]

Kopechne was a true believer in the Kennedy brothers' vision for the country. That vision was based on equal rights and opportunities for all Americans, regardless of race; a peaceful revolution grounded in diplomacy that would reduce the threat of nuclear war and improve U.S. relations with Third World countries; the responsibility of all Americans to improve the lives of the less fortunate at home and abroad, especially children; and the pursuit of scientific discovery, especially to land a man on the moon before the end of the decade. "Her ideas were very similar to John and Robert Kennedy's," said her mother, Gwen, "especially their belief in helping the poor, the downtrodden."[18]

Kopechne's loyalty was rewarded on November 16, 1963, when Smathers introduced her to the president. He told Kennedy that Mary Jo was one of his "biggest supporters" and that she hoped to work for him in the future.[19] But the hard reality of power politics hit home for Kopechne four days later, when President Kennedy was assassinated in Dallas, Texas. The loss of her political hero was "traumatic," according to friends. Unlike Smathers's other secretaries, Mary Jo did not burst into tears when she heard the news of the president's death. Instead, she "sat at her desk for hours, speechless and staring straight ahead," recalled a coworker. Staff members became so worried about Mary Jo that two secretaries volunteered to take her home.[20]

JFK's assassination was one of the most tragic events in modern American history, not only because a young leader was violently murdered in the prime of his life but because of the lost potential for meaningful change in the nation. First Lady Jacqueline Kennedy seized the moment to insure a prominent place in history for her late husband by mythologizing his presidency. Beginning with the orchestration of JFK's nationally televised funeral and continuing over the next few years in a series of interviews, the First Lady crafted an enduring myth about the Kennedy administration as Camelot, a reference to the legendary King Arthur, his lofty principles, and the idyllic kingdom he created in medieval England. "President Kennedy was strongly attracted to the Camelot legend because he was an idealist who saw history as something made by heroes like King Arthur," she told Pulitzer Prize–winning journalist Theodore White in an exclusive interview for *Life* magazine one week after her husband's death. Extolling the potential and achievements of the Kennedy presidency as "one brief shining moment" in American history, the First Lady insisted, "There will never be another Camelot."[21]

White's essay appeared on newsstands on December 6, 1963. *Life*, which boasted a readership of thirty million, insured that the article received the widest possible audience in the United States and abroad. It also made White a reluctant accomplice to mythologizing the Kennedy administration. According to the journalist's notes, released by the John F. Kennedy Library and Museum a year after Jacqueline Kennedy's death on May 19, 1994, the former First Lady was "obsessed" with being sure that her husband was remembered as a hero. To do so she exploited the popularity and instant recognition of Camelot due to the success of Alan Jay Lerner and Frederick Loewe's 1960 Broadway musical of the same name starring Julie Andrews and Richard Burton.[22] White later admitted he "regretted the role [he] played in transmitting the Camelot myth" to the public because JFK was "not a liberal idealist, nor did he believe that history was made by heroes."[23]

Jacqueline Kennedy was also concerned that historians—"bitter old men," as she referred to them—would portray JFK unfavorably after the shock of the assassination passed.[24] But Harvard-trained historian Arthur Schlesinger Jr. insured that she did not have to worry for long. Shortly after JFK's death, Schlesinger, who served on Kennedy's cabinet, embarked on writing an ultimately voluminous manuscript titled *A Thousand Days*. Published in 1965 by Houghton Mifflin, the selective history of the three-year presidency portrays Kennedy at his best. Its decidedly one-sided and exceedingly generous interpretation suggests that Kennedy was a martyr for civil rights and a dove who sought to achieve world peace despite hawkish advisers and an antagonistic Soviet Union bent on spreading communism around the world.[25] That the book received the 1966 Pulitzer Prize for Biography served to reinforce these images of Kennedy among the American public, which had become blinded by the painful loss of a dynamic leader violently cut down in the prime of his life. In fact, Schlesinger's book does almost as much disservice to the real understanding and assessment of Kennedy's presidency as has the former First Lady's comparison to Camelot and the mystique that has endured for more than a half century. Both interpretations ignore the fact that the New Frontier was defined more by style and sophistication than by substantive achievements. Few of the nation's later presidents would enjoy the same public affection or trust that Kennedy did. Instead, JFK's assassination led to conspiracy theories involving the Central Intelligence Agency and organized crime, widespread disillusionment with and protest over American involvement in Vietnam, and popular distrust of the presidency itself.[26]

President Kennedy's death also marked a sea change in the life of his younger brother Robert. Until then, Robert Kennedy had devoted himself unconditionally to his brother's political career. Beginning in 1946, when JFK first ran for Congress, and continuing through the 1960 presidential election, Bobby put his own career on hold either to work on or manage his brother's campaigns.[27] RFK could be brusque, if not arrogant, with subordinates and strangers who volunteered for those campaigns. "That young man never says 'please,'" complained Adlai Stevenson, a two-time Democratic presidential nominee. "He never says 'thank you,' he never asks for things, he *demands* them."[28] Bobby's rudeness was due, in part, to his goal-oriented nature. He wanted things done, and he didn't care if he offended others in the process. "He was a very cross, unhappy and angry man during those years," observed historian Arthur Schlesinger.[29] After JFK was elected to the White House, Joe Kennedy insisted that the president-elect appoint his younger brother to the cabinet as attorney general. The ambassador realized that his eldest son needed a confidant as well as someone to cover up his extramarital indiscretions, which could damage or even destroy his presidency.[30] "He's a great kid," Joe Kennedy said of Bobby. "He hates the same way I do, not like Jack, who forgives all his enemies and courts them."[31] While the family patriarch may have intended the remark as a colorful figure of speech, there was some truth to it. RFK was a clone of his father in terms of their ruthlessness, specifically the will to win regardless of the means. But that quality came at a price.

During the Kennedy administration, Bobby solidified his alleged reputation as a callous shadow president who waged moral crusades against communist adversaries like Fidel Castro of Cuba and Nikita Khrushchev of the USSR. He acted more ruthlessly against domestic enemies, prosecuting corrupt unions and the Mafia, specifically Jimmy Hoffa of the Teamsters and mob bosses Sam Giancana and Johnny Rosselli.[32] Bobby even made enemies within the Justice Department as he routinely undercut the authority of FBI director J. Edgar Hoover, who regarded RFK as a "sneaky little son of a bitch."[33] After his brother's assassination, Bobby publicly accepted the Warren Commission's conclusion that a lone gunman killed JFK, but personally he could not escape the feeling that he had caused his brother's death by making such powerful enemies.[34] Nicholas Katzenbach, his deputy at the Justice Department, believed that RFK purposely distanced himself from the investigation because he "worried that there might have been some conspiracy and that it was his fault." Katzenbach explained, "I think that Bob worried that the investigation would somehow point to him and his responsibility for his brother's death."[35]

Many friends felt Bobby's nagging belief that he might have caused JFK's death resulted in a serious depression and possibly a nervous breakdown. Robert Blakey, who worked in the Criminal Division of the Justice Department, noted that his boss looked like a "walking zombie." "Looking at Bob was like looking right through him to the wall," he explained.[36] RFK's compulsive behavior suggests that his brother's death had a devastating impact on him. For nearly a year after the assassination, the attorney general removed portraits of his deceased brother from the wall and turned over magazines with Jack's picture on the cover as if to avoid the painful reality of his death. On other occasions, he clung to his brother's memory by donning JFK's brown leather bomber jacket bearing the presidential seal or by slipping into quiet conversations. Ken O'Donnell, a close friend and the president's former chief of staff, initially thought Bobby was talking to himself until he listened more closely and realized he was talking to his deceased brother.[37] On the other hand, Richard Goodwin, one of JFK's speechwriters, believed that the president's death and the personal anguish it caused forced Bobby to "explore new worlds of thought, poetry and manifold varieties of human intimacy," almost as if he were "deliberately preparing himself for a larger role that would make him worthy of succession to his romanticized vision" of JFK.[38]

One of the most moving examples of Bobby's struggle to come to terms with his brother's death came a month later, at a Christmas party for orphans arranged by Mary McGrory of the *Washington Star*. It was Robert Kennedy's first public appearance after JFK's funeral. When he arrived at the party, the dozens of children who had been screaming and playing suddenly stopped and became quiet. Edwin Guthman, Bob's press secretary at the Justice Department, recalled that a six-year-old black boy sprang forward and said, "Your brother's dead! Your brother's dead!" "The little boy knew he had done something wrong," said Guthman, "but he didn't know *what*; so he started to cry. All the adults pretended as if they didn't hear the remark. But Bobby did. He stepped forward, picked up the child and held him very close for a moment. Then he said, 'That's all right. I have another brother.'"[39]

RFK was also struggling to redefine his political future. According to John R. Bohrer, Bobby was embroiled in a competition with his political nemesis, the new president Lyndon B. Johnson, for the control of the Democratic Party. Initially, he sought to become Johnson's running mate on the 1964 Democratic presidential ticket. But their differences were too great. Bobby realized he would have to forge his own path if he hoped to carry out the vision of America he shared with his late brother. The turning point came on Thursday, August 27, 1964, during the Democratic National Convention in Atlantic City, New Jersey. Dressed in a black suit and the black tie he had worn almost continuously since his brother was assassinated, RFK had come to Convention Hall to introduce a memorial film about President Kennedy. But after he was introduced, some twenty thousand delegates and spectators stood in an outpouring of respect and affection unlike anything ever seen. Unable to speak, Kennedy, who had announced his candidacy for the U.S. Senate seat from New York five days earlier, stood behind the podium, his eyes welling with tears. The applause continued for nearly twenty minutes. When the cheering finally subsided, Bobby thanked the delegates for all they had done for President Kennedy, "for the encouragement and the great strength" they had given to him.

After asking the audience to give "the same dedication" to President Johnson, RFK paid tribute to his brother:

> When I think of President Kennedy, I think of what Shakespeare said in *Romeo and Juliet*:
> "When he shall die,
> Take him and cut him out in little stars,
> And he will make the face of heaven so fine
> That all the world will be in love with night,
> And pay no worship to the garish sun."[40]

With those words, Robert Kennedy said his final farewell to his brother, the president, and left the past behind. No longer was he a moral crusader or a ruthless prosecutor. In the next four years a softer, more compassionate Bobby emerged, one who identified with African, Hispanic, and Native Americans, the poor and working classes. Robert Kennedy would become his own man.

Kennedy's Republican opponent in the 1964 senatorial election was incumbent Kenneth B. Keating, a moderate. Bobby focused his campaign on the substantive issues facing New Yorkers: the need for racial harmony, lowering unemployment, better education, and higher quality of urban and suburban life.[41] But Keating, to overcome Kennedy's fame and name recognition, emphasized his Democratic opponent's reputation for ruthlessness and the fact that he was a native of Massachusetts who had spent only part of his childhood in New York and only recently established residency in the state.[42] Bobby managed to overcome the "carpetbagging" accusation by pointing out that his parents had owned a house in New York since 1926, that he attended New York schools for six years, and that he was legally qualified to run for political office as a New Yorker.[43] On November 3 Kennedy defeated Keating by a margin of 719,693 votes. The Democratic landslide after JFK's assassination helped carry the younger Kennedy into office, reflected by the fact that Bobby polled about 1.1 million votes fewer in New York than Johnson did.[44]

On January 4, 1965, RFK was sworn in as the junior senator from New York. Many members of his staff from the Justice Department followed him. Joseph Dolan, an assistant deputy attorney general, served as chief of staff. He knew Bobby so well that the two men communicated in a monosyllabic style understood only by each other. Adam Walinsky and Peter Edelman were the legislative assistants. Both men were in their late twenties and had been junior attorneys at Justice. Their personalities and skills complemented each other well. Walinsky was brash, if not arrogant, but possessed the eloquence of a seasoned speechwriter. Edelman, on the other hand, was gentler and a meticulous researcher who drafted legislation. Together they were a formidable team, providing Kennedy with fresh ideas, brilliant insight, and effective strategies. Both men were passionate about their work and idolized the junior senator. While their constant needling might have worn down a lesser politician, Bobby valued their counsel and listened to them patiently, argued with them, and, when necessary, overruled them.[45]

Frank Mankiewicz was the press secretary. A hefty, chain-smoking World War II veteran, Mankiewicz had served as Peace Corps director in Peru during JFK's administration. His smart-aleck remarks and acerbic wit endeared him to the press core.[46] Wendell Pigman, a Korean War veteran who worked at the National Aeronautics and Space Administration, initially assisted Mankiewicz but had a wide range of legislative duties as well. The secretarial staff was headed by Angela Novello, RFK's indispensable administrative assistant at Justice. Novello, who never married, knew Kennedy better than anyone else on staff. She was unconditionally devoted to him. "Angie was not officious, as some secretaries in her position can be," recalled Judith Cromwell, who worked as her assistant. "She was a very warm person, and that came through in her voice and interactions with others. Angie was also very well organized and extremely good at what she did. She was also on call all the time, but that was true of all of us."[47]

Esther Newberg, who joined RFK's staff in 1967, observed that those who worked for the junior senator had a reputation for being "young and brash": "We didn't fit into the conventional mold of people who had been on [Capitol] Hill for thirty years. Those people switched loyalties and could work for a variety of senators. That wasn't true with Senator

Kennedy's staff. You were working for him only."[48] Their schedule, like Kennedy's, was exhausting, too.

RFK's staff worked Monday through Saturday and often on Sundays. "If you worked for Senator Kennedy you basically gave up any life outside the office," said Cromwell. "But we did so happily because we believed in him and what he stood for." Indeed, RFK's New York constituents and other Americans placed overwhelming demands on his staff. During his first three months in the Senate, the office phone lines were constantly busy, and Kennedy was receiving more than one thousand letters a day. His staff could hardly keep up, responding to fewer than six hundred of those letters daily.[49] Initially, chief of staff Joe Dolan, who did the hiring, intended to operate within the official allowance to hire and pay staff. But that became impossible, and Kennedy contributed $100,000 of his own for salaries.[50] He also directed Dolan to employ additional staff. Mary Jo Kopechne was one of the first hires.

After JFK's assassination, Kopechne's career seemed to have lost purpose until she shifted her loyalties to the late president's brother. When Bobby was elected senator of New York in November 1964, Mary Jo made no secret of her ambition to work for him. She occasionally trailed the new senator down the corridors in the Senate office building in awe of him. A photo of RFK replaced the one of President Kennedy on her desk. She asked John O'Keefe, Smathers's administrative assistant, to get the photo autographed, and he did. Kopechne's silent adoration of the New York senator became so obvious to Smathers that he finally introduced the two of them. Walking into his office suite with RFK in tow, the Florida legislator pointed to the photo on Mary Jo's desk and said to Kennedy: "Take a look at your admirer." Bobby smiled and Kopechne blushed. "It's *my* office," complained Smathers, tongue in cheek, "and I don't see any picture of *me*!"[51]

In March 1965 Smathers allowed Kopechne to work for RFK on a temporary basis until the junior senator could hire more staff. Dolan quickly noted and admired her thoroughness, hard work, and discretion and hired her full time.[52] Thrust into a high-pressured operation, Mary Jo did more than hold her own. Although she was Dolan's personal secretary, Kopechne often worked for other male staff. Legislative assistant Wendell Pigman considered her a "crackerjack secretary" who could be "delegated responsibility for a complete operation"—taking dictation, typing a speech, reading proof, making corrections, and then arranging for the finished copy to be sent by shuttle plane to Kennedy's New York office. Kopechne also floated between Frank Mankiewicz to work on press releases and Jeff Greenfield to type up RFK's speeches. "Mary Jo was a very valuable, prized member of the staff because she was so willing to go above and beyond the duties that weren't in her job description," said Jeannie Main, a personal secretary to Adam Walinsky.[53] Perhaps the highest compliment came from RFK's personal secretary, Angela Novello. "In times of crisis and urgent need, Mary Jo was the one you could depend on," said Novello. "Many times on a weekend when a crisis inevitably arose, hands and heads were needed, and she always made herself available. She'd give up an evening with friends, sometimes an entire weekend, to do what was needed and never complained. That's why Bob Kennedy liked and respected her so much."[54]

One of those times of "urgent need" came in October 1966, when RFK needed someone to advance a hastily scheduled visit to Wilkes-Barre, Pennsylvania. Since Mary Jo was familiar with the town, having spent her early life in nearby Forty Fort and returned there to visit during the summers, she volunteered to give up her weekend so she could advance the trip. Don McFadden, an aide to Pennsylvania state senator Martin Murray, recalled how impressed he was by Kopechne's attention to detail:

> Bobby Kennedy was scheduled to speak on Public Square in Wilkes-Barre. We had directed the speaker's platform to be built on the center of the Square. But when Mary Jo saw the location she explained that we could get as many as 2,000 spectators on the Square but when the television crew filmed from that angle the crowd would look very small.
>
> She suggested that we relocate the platform to the Market Street side between the First National Bank and the old Miner's Bank

Building. That way even if we drew a crowd half the size, the television camera would make it appear as if 10,000 people were present. Mary Jo realized that that side of Public Square was more narrow and that the crowd would have to overflow onto the Market Street Bridge, making it appear as if thousands had come to the rally. I thought it was extremely clever.[55]

Indeed, RFK's staff was passionately dedicated to him and inspired by his commitment to social justice and the way he treated them. He trusted the people who worked for him and tended to give them broad authority. He rarely read briefs or position papers, reserving his time for the most important legislation and speeches that demanded his input. "Bob Kennedy treated people decently," insisted Nicholas Katzenbach, deputy attorney general under RFK at Justice. "He didn't duck or shift blame and brought out the very best in everyone who worked for him."[56] As a result, staff members felt a personal connection with him. "Those who worked for Robert Kennedy did not think of themselves as mere employees," wrote Ronald Steel in his book *In Love with Night*. "Each felt connected to him personally by iron bonds of belief and commitment. There was no rigid staff hierarchy among those who worked for Kennedy, but only an interlinked nexus of real and assumed personal ties with him."[57]

Mary Jo was drawn to RFK's shy, introspective nature and his quick wit. "The senator was a very shy man," said Judith Cromwell, Angela Novello's personal assistant. "Socially, he didn't do a lot of talking. He was a great listener, though. It took a while for him to warm to others. He needed to know that he could trust you. After Mary Jo broke the ice, it was very easy for the senator to approach her. She could be very bubbly and vivacious, like his wife, Ethel. Once he knew Mary Jo and knew he could trust her, Senator Kennedy became extremely loyal to her."[58] Kopechne also shared RFK's quick-witted, sometimes self-deprecating, sense of humor. In an office full of attractive, party-going secretaries, Mary Jo often joked about "swinging party girls" and then "mocked herself for not being one."[59] Nor did she spare Kennedy from her humor. Once, after staffers gave him a globe as a birthday present, Bobby, in mock appreciation, said, "Gee, it's just what I've always wanted." He hardly completed the sentence before Mary Jo quipped: "Yes! The *whole* world!"[60]

"We all laughed," recalled Melody Miller, a college intern who joined RFK's staff in 1965. "The exchange was so funny not because the senator had a huge ego but because he was a humble man who was considering a run for the presidency and because he was so beloved around the world. The comeback was also characteristic of Mary Jo's quick wit."[61] "Bob enjoyed Mary Jo's delightful sense of humor," added Novello. "In spite of—or maybe because of—the sophisticated voices around her, Mary Jo would come out with a funny phrase that would have him laughing."[62] But Kennedy was also known to tease her.

Once, Kopechne responded to a constituent who asked that the senator intervene with the U.S. military so one of their abandoned bases on a small island off Long Island Sound near New Rochelle could be used as a home for physically disabled children. Appreciating RFK's love for children and his family's commitment to the disabled, Mary Jo wrote that the senator would "certainly approve of such a project." However, she did not realize that Kennedy had already signed off on other plans for the abandoned base. After Bobby learned of the gaffe, he took pleasure in chiding Kopechne about it. "Mary Jo, given away any islands today?" he would inquire.[63] On another occasion, after Kopechne spent several evenings at the office, Kennedy took a photo of her from behind her desk. He had it developed and left it on her desk with the inscription: "You work so hard. This is the only way I ever see you!"[64]

There were also occasions when RFK and Kopechne had a good laugh at the expense of others. According to Kennedy biographer Burton Hersh, Mary Jo and Bobby "knew each other well enough" to share "Kennedy-style humor and 'inside' jokes" that were often based on the "drolleries of personality." Once, when they were in the company of a prominent Louisiana politician, the two could not refrain from giggling over his silk suit, loud tie, and alligator shoes.[65]

Mary Jo also possessed an innocence that endeared her to RFK and his staffers. "We worked together for two years, never more than a few feet away," said Frank Mankiewicz, RFK's press secretary. "It was no secret that Mary Jo was my favorite. She was the antithesis of the sophisticated urban woman; a natural, unassuming and unworldly person. It pleased me to see her and make her smile." Kopechne's former boss, Senator George Smathers, called her "young, sweet and impressionable." He even admitted to assuming the role of "father confessor" feeling as if he had to protect her.[66] Similarly, Mankiewicz noted that Mary Jo was "the kind of girl you wanted to be a father to." "The guys in the office were always looking out for her and protecting her," he explained. "She looked like she was only 5'2" tall and so thin that she was called 'Twiggy.' Mary Jo was in her late twenties, but she looked like she was much younger, like a kid." Angie Novello also took a maternal interest in Kopechne. She saw a younger version of herself in Mary Jo and worried that she would allow her devotion to RFK consume her. "Angie always encouraged Mary Jo to have more of a life outside the office, to date and to have more time with family and friends," recalled Judith Cromwell, who was close to both women.[67]

Aside from her family and a few college friends, however, Kopechne limited her social life to "Honorary Kennedys," those like her who dedicated themselves to Bobby. She was the catcher on the office softball team, which played on the mall near the Washington Monument after work. She improved her tennis game and played touch football at RFK's Hickory Hill estate in McLean, Virginia, where she often joined other staffers at the invitation of Bobby and Ethel.[68] She occasionally invited a boyfriend to come along. "Mary Jo took me to a few of those gatherings," said Owen Lopez, a law school student who dated Kopechne. "It was Robert Kennedy's way of rewarding her hard work. It was fun. We played touch football with his kids, did some charades. But there was also intelligent, articulate conversation going on. It was a good blend, and one that was very appealing to Mary Jo." Even when she took a few weeks' vacation to Ireland in the summer of 1967, Kopechne made sure to visit the Kennedys' Irish relatives at Dunganstown, the family's ancestral home. Mary Jo's personal and professional lives had become so intertwined with the Kennedy family that Ethel asked her to become an au pair for her ten children. Kopechne was particularly fond of the Kennedys' third-eldest child, Bobby Jr., but she declined the offer, wanting to remain on Capitol Hill.[69]

Mary Jo dated but was never serious about a man. Those who dated her in the last few years of her life said that Kopechne had evolved from the naïve tomboy of her earlier years in Washington to an "attractive young woman with a sparkle in her eyes." While she did not adopt the appearance or behavior of the more glamorous secretaries, who favored miniskirts and long, over-the-shoulder hair and spoke with charm-school accents, Mary Jo's beauty came from her natural disposition and wholesomeness. Owen Lopez described her as "a devout Catholic, a straight girl, and very conservative socially." When Kopechne visited him at Notre Dame Law School, she refused to stay in the house he was renting, believing it was "improper." Instead, Mary Jo stayed with his landlady, who lived across the street. Lopez was also attracted to Kopechne's intelligence as well as her strong commitment to "justice and equality." But he realized that marriage was not in her immediate future. "Mary Jo was completely dedicated to the Kennedys," observed Lopez, who once admitted to her father that "she'll never marry me because she's married to the Kennedys."[70] Another suitor was more persistent but finally gave Mary Jo the ultimatum, "It's either the Kennedys or me!" Of course, she took the Kennedys.[71]

At the same time, Kopechne's hero-worship of Robert Kennedy was primarily based on his political beliefs, especially his commitment to the poor, minorities, and children. During his years in the Senate, RFK initiated several projects that benefited those groups, including assistance to underprivileged children and students with disabilities and the establishment of the Bedford Stuyvesant Restoration Corporation to improve living conditions and employment opportunities in depressed areas of Brooklyn.[72] The Bedford Stuyvesant legislation encouraged private industry to create jobs for those who wanted to work and stay off welfare. In this way, RFK diverged from President Lyndon B. Johnson's multibillion-dollar War on Poverty, based on federally funded projects and welfare payments. Instead, Kennedy emphasized individual initiative, self-reliance, and business participation as the formula to address poverty. He also insisted that the poor must be given a share of government power through local institutions like the Bedford Stuyvesant Corporation.[73] Bedford Stuyvesant became a model for Kennedy's larger effort to address the needs of the dispossessed and powerless in America. Traveling into urban ghettos, Appalachia, the Mississippi Delta, and migrant workers' camps, RFK appealed to the conscience of the American people to address the issue of poverty. He was especially moved by the children he saw and angered by their plight. "There are children in the Mississippi Delta whose bellies are swollen with hunger," he said in an April 4, 1968, speech at Notre Dame University. "Many of them cannot go to school because they have no clothes or shoes. These conditions are not confined to rural Mississippi. They exist in dark tenements in Washington DC, within sight of the Capitol, in Harlem, in South Side Chicago, in Watts. There are children in each of these areas who have never been to school, never seen a doctor or a dentist. There are children who have never heard conversation in their homes, never read or even seen a book."[74]

Harvard child psychiatrist Robert Coles, who often testified at congressional hearings on anti-poverty legislation, believed that childhood poverty was "very personal" to Kennedy. Coles, a close friend to Bobby, was fascinated by the New York senator's childlike qualities. "He had a gentleness and playfulness and a trace of innocence," said the psychiatrist. "He was a little boy in his enthusiasms, capable of showing childlike delight over something so simple as liking ice cream."[75] Coles attributed Kennedy's "hypersensitivity to poverty," as well as his decision to devote himself to public service, to his empathy for children. Some who worked for RFK made similar observations. "I think if his father did not expect him to go into politics, Bob would've been a child psychologist because he loved children so much," said Judith Cromwell, a secretary. "He thought that they were the only honest people in the world, the only ones you could fully trust. If Bob walked into a room and there was one child and thirty adults, he would go over to the child, sit down and talk with him, one-to-one. I saw him with his own children. He was completely engrossed by them."[76]

Kopechne was also impressed by RFK's stand against Vietnam. Bobby, as a member of JFK's cabinet, originally supported American involvement in the divided Southeast Asian country.[77] While he continued to support the Johnson administration's involvement there, the New York senator also called for a greater commitment to a negotiated settlement and a renewed emphasis on economic and political reform within South Vietnam.[78] But as America's involvement deepened, Kennedy began to have serious misgivings about President Johnson's escalation of the war. In February 1966 RFK publicly distanced himself from the president, proposing participation in South Vietnam's government by the Communist National Liberation Front, the Viet Cong's political arm. Finally, on March 2, 1967, Kennedy, in a speech typed by Mary Jo Kopechne, rose in the U.S. Senate and urged Johnson to cease the bombing of North Vietnam and reduce the war effort.[79] "The United States has sent more than 400,000 men into the ever-widening war as the most powerful country in the world turns its strength and will upon a small and primitive land," he declared. Then, speaking to the conscience of the American people, he insisted that the war was "not just a nation's responsibility, but yours and mine." "It is we who live in abundance and send our young men out to die," he continued. "It is our chemicals that scorch the children and our bombs that level the villages. We are all participants."[80]

"Mary Jo spoke very highly of Robert Kennedy," said Elly Gardner Kluge, "especially for his views on civil rights and against the war in Vietnam." In February 1967 Kopechne told Kluge that she hoped Senator Kennedy would "eventually throw his hat in the ring for the presidency." "It would," she added, "be very exciting for me."[81] Mary Jo would get her wish one month later.

Boiler Room Girl 4

Serving in the U.S. Senate was a demotion for Robert Kennedy after heading the Justice Department and serving as JFK's closest adviser. In those capacities, Bobby wielded the influence and power of a shadow president, always being at the center of the most critical events. In the Senate, however, he quickly became bored with the legislative minutiae, parliamentary procedure, and horse trading that defined the business of the chamber. Lacking the necessary patience to navigate a bill through the Labor and Public Welfare Committee, RFK tried to persuade other members with his passion. Once, he spoke too long at a hearing, and his brother Ted, who also served on the committee, passed a note: "Stop talking! You just lost [Chairman] Lister [Hill]. Just let us vote or you will lose the others, too."[1] Nor did Bobby's lowly status at the bottom of the senatorial pecking order make his situation any easier.

RFK sat at the back of the Senate chamber in a fifth row that had been added to accommodate the Democratic Party's gains in the 1964 election. He shared the row with three other young, liberal—and irreverent—newly elected members: Walter Mondale of Minnesota, Fred Harris of Oklahoma, and Joseph Tydings of Maryland. The foursome were often seen whispering to each other as they gave running commentary on the proceedings.[2] Committee hearings were just as frustrating since senators asked questions in the order of seniority. Kennedy, who ranked ninety-ninth, was reduced to silence at those hearings. Once he became so frustrated he asked Ted, "Is this the way I become a good senator—sitting here and waiting my turn?"

"Yes," replied his brother.

"Then how many hours do I have to sit here to be a good senator?" Bobby snapped.

"As long as necessary," said Ted, ending the conversation.[3]

Although RFK had other friends who had served in the Senate longer, Ted was his only confidant.[4] Bobby constantly consulted with his brother, who did his homework by learning every detail of each bill as well as parliamentary procedure to be accepted by his Senate colleagues. Ted also realized how frustrated his older brother was with the slow pace of the legislative process and the tedious but necessary bills that consumed a senator's time. Accordingly, the brothers reached a tacit understanding on the issues each would address. While Bobby would concentrate on higher-profile issues like Vietnam, Ted would focus on immigration and health care.[5] But even this agreement did not end RFK's frustration. He desperately wanted to return to the executive branch.

During the winter of 1968, Robert Kennedy struggled over whether to enter the Democratic presidential primaries. Senate colleagues urged him not to run, fearing he would divide the party and pave the road to victory for Republican candidate, Richard Nixon, in the general election. JFK's former advisers and his younger brother, Ted, also discouraged a run. They constantly reminded him that a sitting president had not been denied the nomination of his party in the twentieth century and that Johnson's supporters controlled the delegates in most of the large, delegate-rich states where there were no primaries. Under the circumstances, they argued, Bobby could only be defeated.[6]

At the same time, the polls and RFK's advisers were pressuring him to run. Adam Walinsky, Peter Edelman, and Frank Mankiewicz warned that he had a moral obligation as an antiwar and socially progressive Democrat to enter the race. Other voices he respected, like those of journalists Jack Newfield and Peter Hamill, warned him that staying out of the campaign would cost him a part of his soul. But Kennedy continued to waffle, and his indecision opened the door for another antiwar candidate, Senator Eugene McCarthy of Minnesota, who immediately won the support of college-aged voters.[7]

When Kennedy saw McCarthy's strong showing against Lyndon B. Johnson in the March 12 New Hampshire primary, which LBJ won by just 7.2 percentage points, he believed the incumbent president could be defeated. Four days later, on March 16, 1968, RFK, in a statement typed by Mary Jo Kopechne, announced his candidacy for the Democratic presidential nomination.[8] He insisted that his decision was based on principled disagreement with Johnson over the Vietnam conflict and the deteriorating state of race relations at home. Bobby identified his experience in the Kennedy administration on the National Security Council during the Cuban Missile Crisis, the Berlin Crisis, and later the negotiations on Laos and the Nuclear Test Ban Treaty as teaching him "about the uses and limitations of military power" and about the "opportunities and dangers which await the nation in many corners of the globe." Kennedy also pointed to his experience as a member of the executive cabinet and as a member of the Senate that revealed to him the "inexcusable and ugly deprivation which cause children to starve in Mississippi; black citizens to riot in Watts; young Indians to commit suicide on the reservations because they lack all hope and feel they have no future." All these experiences convinced RFK that the United States was "on a perilous course" and that he not only had "strong feelings about what must be done" to correct them, but that he was "obliged" to do all that he could to address the problems.[9] Indeed, Robert Kennedy had more experience to prepare for the presidency than his brother had in 1960 when he ran for executive office and more than any other candidate in the 1968 election, with the exception of the incumbent president. But he was far from securing the Democratic Party's nomination.

Ronald Steel argues that Kennedy faced several obstacles, some of his own doing. First, young, college-aged voters were suspicious of Kennedy for not committing himself to the race earlier, viewing him as an "opportunist." Many of those who protested the war had hoped to support him but now gave their allegiance to McCarthy. Second, the white South was hostile to Kennedy because of his support for civil rights and because he had used the weight of the Justice Department as U.S. attorney general to integrate the University of Alabama and to protect the Freedom Riders. Third, after Johnson withdrew from the race on March 31, the Democratic chiefs threw the weight of the party machinery behind Vice President Hubert Humphrey. Finally, Kennedy faced tough competition in the most important states. Of the fourteen primaries, the most critical states were New Hampshire, Wisconsin, Indiana, Nebraska, Oregon, South Dakota, and California. Kennedy entered the race late, so he never campaigned in New Hampshire. In subsequent primaries, where he competed directly against McCarthy, the Minnesota senator defeated him in Wisconsin and Oregon. While RFK won the primary elections in Indiana, Nebraska, South Dakota, and California, he did not secure the support of organized labor because of his earlier prosecution of Jimmy Hoffa and the Teamsters Union. Labor would have a strong influence in determining the winner in the remaining primaries, especially in Pennsylvania, Ohio, and New Jersey.[10] Thus Kennedy's campaign staff—and those who monitored delegates in particular—would play a crucial role in his quest for the presidency. Kopechne was one of those individuals.

Mary Jo was not just a secretary to Kennedy's speechwriters, either. "Her value to RFK," according to Burton Hersh, a Kennedy biographer, "was such that she was consulted by him and Ted Sorensen as to the particular phrasings of those speeches." She also distinguished herself during the campaign by working long hours at Kennedy's Washington headquarters, monitoring and communicating with delegates across the country. Kopechne was the sort of staffer who "seemed always to be present, while seldom particularly noticeable," wrote Hersh.[11] At the same time, Mary Jo was part of a dedicated team that included Rosemary Keough, Susan Tannenbaum, Esther Newberg, and sisters Nance and Maryellen Lyons. Collectively, they were known as the Boiler Room Girls, after the windowless room they worked in at 2020 L Street.[12] Dun Gifford, who supervised the team, described their work as an "intelligence operation, but also an amazing constituent service operation." "Our job was to persuade those delegates who were not firmly committed to another candidate to vote for Bobby," he explained. "To do that, we learned as many details about the delegates as possible and how they were elected by the states. We also tried to persuade delegates by doing things like getting them a hotel room for the convention, or having Bobby write a letter to get their kid admitted to a particular college."[13]

The Boiler Room contained desks divided by regions of the country. The northeast region, for example, included Massachusetts, Connecticut, Vermont, New Hampshire, and Maine. Each of the women was assigned a regional desk and was responsible for gaining as much intelligence as possible on the delegates in their region, including age, phone number, occupation, marital status, if the delegates were at large, district, or alternate, if they had a full vote or a fraction of one, if they were running for office, their opinion of RFK, what would most influence their vote, and any advice for the campaign that would help RFK to secure their vote. The desk officers were also responsible for daily communication with each state director in their regions. They discussed issues and compiled a daily decision book for RFK and his campaign manager, brother-in-law Stephen Smith. Kennedy and Smith discussed the issues and the following morning the Boiler Room Girls conveyed their decisions to the state director in their respective regions. Issues could be as complex as RFK's position on abortion rights or as simple as the need to provide a delegate with bumper stickers. Thus the Boiler Room became "an important conduit for policy statements" that were crafted by Kennedy's press secretary Frank Mankiewicz, who would plant those statements in newspapers across the nation. As each state primary was held, the Boiler Room Girls kept track of the delegate count for all three candidates—RFK, McCarthy, and Humphrey—leading up to the convention. Just before the Democratic National Convention, the operation would be relocated to a temporary office off the convention floor, where the Boiler Room Girls would continue to monitor their assigned delegations. "Essentially, the Boiler Room was the heartbeat of Bobby's campaign," said Gifford. What made it work, though, was the intelligence and perseverance of the young women who worked in it. They were hand-picked and turned out to be real jewels."[14]

According to a September 5, 1969, article in *Time* magazine, the Boiler Room Girls were "uniformly bright, efficient, fascinated by politics and cultishly pro-Kennedy." Rosemary "Cricket" Keough, age twenty-two, had volunteered for JFK's 1960 presidential campaign in her hometown of Philadelphia. After graduating from Manhattanville College, she joined Bobby Kennedy's staff in 1967 to answer constituent mail from children and stayed on to work in his presidential campaign. Susan Tannenbaum, twenty-three, attended Centenary College in Hackettstown, New Jersey, and later Miami University of Ohio. She also went to work for Robert Kennedy in 1967. Esther Newberg, twenty-five, was the daughter of a former Democratic national committeewoman from Connecticut. She worked for the Senate subcommittee on government reorganization before she joined RFK's campaign staff in 1968. Maryellen Lyons, age twenty-five, worked as an administrative assistant to Massachusetts state senator Beryl Cohen, a protégé of Senator Ted Kennedy's, after graduating from Regis College in 1963. Ted recruited her in 1968 to help in his brother's presidential campaign. Maryellen's sister, Nance Lyons, twenty-six, shared a Georgetown townhouse with Kopechne and two other girls. A 1964 graduate of the College of the Sacred Heart in Newton, Massachusetts, Nance did public relations for the Norfolk County Tuberculosis and Health Association before Ted Kennedy recruited her to work on Bobby's campaign.[15]

At age twenty-seven, Mary Jo was the oldest of the Boiler Room Girls and the one who had worked for RFK the longest. Kopechne, who was assigned the critical states of Indiana and Pennsylvania, among others, tracked and compiled data on how Democratic delegates might vote and kept in constant contact with field managers and the press.[16] Pennsylvania was a battleground state, the polls predicting that the race between Kennedy and Humphrey would be close. Jimmy Smith, a campaign coordinator in Allegheny County, desperately needed volunteers to help him with field work. Mary Jo located two individuals who lived in the region and recommended them: one was "a Vietnam veteran and freelance writer who knows two delegates who could be picked off," and the second was president of a small company in Erie who had worked for JFK in 1960 and was a "delegate-at-large and Democratic Committee chairman." Kopechne also circulated memos on policy statements as well as her own suggestions on how to promote Kennedy's candidacy while discouraging that of Vice President Hubert Humphrey, who became his chief rival after Johnson withdrew from the race. Among those suggestions were:

1. Humphrey had time after Johnson's withdrawal to enter primaries in California and South Dakota like Kennedy and McCarthy but waited until filing deadlines passed to avoid submitting his candidacy and the Johnson administration's record in Vietnam to the people.
2. Now, a gang-up to stop Kennedy is under way—combining southern governors from Lester Maddox of Georgia to John Connally of Texas with Labor union leader George Meany (whose organizers are totally blanketing the country high-pressuring political and labor leaders to support Humphrey), and enlisting both the special interest lobbies from Wall Street to oil and major Republican newspapers. But the people are with Kennedy and they are fed up with this kind of power politics and propaganda.
3. By supporting Humphrey, the candidate of the status quo, by picking him in the back room instead of the primaries, and by trying to label Kennedy "ruthless" because he is tough-minded and determined, or "too young" because he has energy and drive, this unholy alliance of southern governors, labor, and special interests is playing right into Republican candidate Richard Nixon's hands. The people want leadership, not labels; and they want Kennedy, not Humphrey.

Still, Mary Jo deferred to the judgment of the field managers, directing them to "use whichever [suggestion] they felt was the best for their state, or not use any at all." Smith considered Kopechne and her Boiler Room colleagues to be "politically savvy, not mere secretaries."[17]

Indeed, by 1968 Mary Jo had become more sophisticated, both in her professional and personal lives. She had always been industrious and competent, but her experience in the Boiler Room made her more confident, more politically savvy, and, when necessary, tough. She remained fiercely dedicated to Kennedy, never complaining about her demanding workload or modest salary. Like the other secretaries on RFK's staff, Mary Jo was paid $6,000 a year when she was hired, while the male legislative assistants started at a salary of between $12,000 and $15,000 a year.[18] In the four years she worked for RFK she never earned more than $7,500 a year, just enough to share a Georgetown townhouse with two other secretaries and maintain a light blue Volkswagen Beetle.[19]

By today's standards, Kopechne appears to have been grossly underpaid, extremely overworked, and dismissed as a "secretary" when her responsibilities suggested she deserved the more respectable title of "political consultant" and to be paid accordingly. But she, like the other young women who worked for Robert Kennedy, belonged to a transitional generation of women who paved the way for the feminists of the 1970s and their fight for gender equality.[20] Born in the 1940s, the generation came of age in the 1960s, when the proportion of female college graduates age twenty-five to thirty-four in the workforce increased from 42 to 65 percent.[21] These young, college-educated women accepted the social conventions of the era, which dictated that women were "not meant to compete with men, not to act independently of men, nor earn the same salary as men for doing the same jobs."[22] However, unequal pay did *not* mean they believed themselves to be any less capable than the men for whom they worked.

"I never considered the title 'secretary' to be demeaning," said Jeannie Main, who was secretary to Adam Walinsky, a legislative assistant. "That's one of the things the women's movement did. They made the title 'secretary,' like 'housewife,' a demeaning thing. True, we had good secretarial skills and we were expected to perform competently, but we did more substantive work than most people realize." According to Main, serving as secretary to a legislative assistant required a "familiarity with the major political, economic, and social issues that were important to RFK." Kennedy's secretaries were also "expected to know how the legislative process operated, where to locate earlier bills that he sponsored as well as the laws that informed the legislation Kennedy intended to sponsor." With such demanding responsibilities, Main considered herself to be part of the "inner circle" when legislation was being drafted.[23]

Male staff members who worked on RFK's presidential campaign also recognized the capabilities of their female colleagues. "The Boiler

Room Girls were much more than women who took dictation, typed letters and speeches," said Walinsky, who wrote many of Kennedy's campaign speeches. "They were tracking and monitoring delegates. They were really, in today's terms, 'political analysts.'"[24] Dun Gifford, who supervised the Boiler Room, agreed, saying that title would "do more justice to the responsibilities and talents of the young women who ran the operation." "But back in the 1960s, the title 'secretary' was not considered a demeaning term as it is today," he explained. "To be a 'Kennedy secretary' was something special, and the Boiler Room Girls were the 'go-to' people for Bobby's campaign."[25] Handpicked for their discretion, intelligence, loyalty, and good-natured humor under stressful circumstances, the young women were accorded significant freedom to act. Their exceptional ability to stay ahead of fluctuating intelligence on delegates allowed them to negotiate deals on RFK's behalf, to travel with him when necessary, and even to offer their opinions when they had the best working knowledge of a situation. The Boiler Room Girls were so highly regarded that one Kennedy staffer noted, "People brought them coffee."[26]

Of all the Boiler Room Girls, Mary Jo was the most outstanding according to Gifford. "She was the most 'political' and astute of anybody in the boiler room," he recalled. "Had Bobby won the election, Mary Jo would have been rewarded with a very significant job in his administration."[27] Barbara Coleman, another member of RFK's staff, recalled that Mary Jo was "a bright girl who had come into her own" during the campaign and that the other Boiler Room Girls were "not as good."[28] In fact, Kopechne became the "key Washington contact in the boiler room," according to Kennedy biographer Burton Hersh. "She kept track of every map, every pin, everything in critical Indiana and Pennsylvania, as well as Kentucky and the District of Columbia." Robert Kennedy valued her so much that "she was often consulted by him," added Hersh.[29]

Some writers claim that the relationship between Kopechne and Kennedy became more intimate during his presidential campaign. According to C. David Heymann, author of *Bobby and Jackie*, RFK began an affair with Mary Jo in the early spring of 1968. Heymann quotes Senator George Smathers, Kopechne's former boss, as warning her against traveling with Kennedy on the campaign plane:

> I knew Bobby, and I knew he would take advantage of the situation. And that's precisely what happened. It didn't matter if Ethel was also on the plane. They'd check into hotels at night and Mary Jo would be given her own room. It didn't take Bobby much time to excuse himself from a strategy meeting for a few minutes and go visit Mary Jo in her room. Nobody was the wiser for it. It reminded me of Jack [Kennedy] when he campaigned for the presidency in 1960, except that Jackie wasn't around most of the time.[30]

Heymann also referred to the alleged affair in an earlier book, titled *RFK*. According to Heymann, Doris Lilly, a high-society columnist for the *New York Post* who had known Kopechne since 1965, had been planning an article about RFK after his death. During one of their meetings, Mary Jo supposedly "admitted that she'd been in love with him and that they'd had an affair during the early months of 1968." "This didn't surprise me," Lilly admitted. "Bobby wasn't exactly the choirboy that everybody thought he was. He had dozens of affairs, some longer-lived, some shorter. And Mary Jo had all the prerequisites: youth, vibrancy, intelligence."[31]

Jerry Oppenheimer, another Kennedy biographer, supported Heymann's allegation. Oppenheimer wrote that "Bobby not only considered Mary Jo invaluable as his assistant," but he was also "sexually drawn to her" and "took advantage of her trust in him, and her being somewhat naïve and not really sophisticated," according to "insiders." He also wrote that Kennedy was attracted to Mary Jo's "fresh-faced look, her cute ways, her pert body," qualities in which she "resembled his wife, Ethel." RFK, according to Oppenheimer, also knew that Mary Jo was "completely trustworthy, a young woman who would keep everything between them confidential."[32]

However, the reputations of these tabloid-style writers cast serious doubt on their allegations of an affair between Mary Jo and Robert Kennedy. Heymann was often criticized for factual errors as well as for his "use of single rather than multiple sources and his reliance on hearsay accounts by people not directly involved in the incidents he was describing."[33] Similarly, Oppenheimer, who has written several unauthorized biographies, has been accused of being "biased and mean-spirited" and criticized for "relying heavily on unnamed and un-enumerated sources."[34] The testimonials and accounts of those family, friends, and coworkers who knew Kopechne do not support the allegations of an affair with Robert Kennedy. According to Wendell Pigman, another legislative aid with whom Kopechne worked for two years, Mary Jo was "chosen to work on the '68 presidential campaign because she was extremely competent, period."

"Of all the girls who worked in the office, she was the least likely to have an affair or to be involved in any scandal. Mary Jo was modest almost to the point of being prim. She almost scowled at hearing a dirty word."[35] For as much as Mary Jo idolized RFK, she was just as fiercely devoted to her Catholic faith. Together with her strict moral code, her strong religious convictions would have prevented her from committing adultery, especially with a married man like Robert Kennedy. "If she had an affair with the senator," said Jeannie Main, "I'd say she must have been the greatest dissembler of all time because none of the staff ever suspected it."[36]

By the summer of 1968, the Kennedy campaign was running full tilt. The Vietnam War was dividing the country, and the assassination of Martin Luther King Jr. ignited race riots in major cities nationwide.[37] Many Americans believed RFK was the only person who could unite the country. "He was both an idealist and realist," said Peter Edelman, a legislative aide and campaign adviser. "He was tough and determined, and he had a record to show for it. But he was soft and sweet and dreamy, too, especially in his last years, and a real comfort when he saw someone's need for support."[38] Those seemingly antithetical qualities enabled Kennedy to transcend ideological and generational differences among Democratic voters. After winning primaries in Indiana, Nebraska, South Dakota, and California, Kennedy's staffers genuinely believed that he would go on to win the party's nomination and, later, the presidency against Republican Richard Nixon.[39] But their hopes were shattered in the early morning hours of June 5, when

Bobby was shot in a kitchen passageway at the Ambassador Hotel in Los Angeles after winning California.

The assailant was a twenty-four-year-old Palestinian, Sirhan Sirhan, who was supposedly angered by Kennedy's support for Israel in the June 1967 Six-Day War.[40] After several minutes, medical attendants arrived, lifted the senator onto a stretcher, and rushed him first to Los Angeles's Central Receiving Hospital and then to the city's Good Samaritan Hospital. Despite extensive neurosurgery to remove the bullet and bone fragments from his brain, Kennedy was pronounced dead at 1:44 a.m. on June 6, nearly twenty-six hours after the shooting.[41]

Ted Kennedy was devastated by his brother's assassination, much as Bobby had been over the death of JFK. "I'd never seen a man in as much agony," recalled press secretary Frank Mankiewicz, who spotted Ted Kennedy in a hospital bathroom after the announcement of RFK's death. "His face was contorted. His body was bent over."[42] Some of Bob's advisers worried that he wouldn't be able to "pull off the eulogy" he was to deliver two days later at Saint Patrick's Catholic Cathedral in New York.[43] Instead, Ted summoned the strength to deliver a stirring testimony to his brother's life and political career, concluding with some of the most memorable words associated with the Kennedy family:

> My brother need not be idealized, or enlarged in death beyond what he was in life; to be remembered simply as a good and decent man, who saw wrong and tried to right it, saw suffering and tried to heal it, saw war and tried to stop it. Those of us who loved him and who take him to his rest today, pray that what he was to us and what he wished for others will some day come to pass for all the world. As he said many times, in many parts of this nation, to those he touched and who sought to touch him: *Some men see things as they are and say why. I dream things that never were and say why not.*[44]

Nor did Ted hide himself from the passengers on a private funeral train that carried his brother's body from New York to Washington DC to be buried in Arlington National Cemetery. The 225-mile journey that would normally have taken four hours ended up lasting more than eight hours as mourners came out by the hundreds of thousands to line the tracks and say farewell to Robert Kennedy.[45] But there was also tremendous pressure on Ted to pick up the fallen standard for his deceased brothers.

Even before RFK was buried, Kennedy acolytes and party leaders began to pressure Ted to run in his brother's place for the good of the country. Just a few years earlier, it was unthinkable that Ted would run for the Oval Office. Of the three Kennedy brothers who entered public service, Ted had the least desire to become president. He was the one who loved to socialize most, to make others laugh. He enjoyed the back-slapping, handshaking, and bantering that defined life on Capitol Hill, but he certainly did not possess the intelligence of Jack or the driving passion of Bobby to run the nation. Everyone in the Kennedy family loved Teddy, the youngest child, but they also expected the least from him. Now, with the death of RFK, Ted, at age thirty-six, was thrust into the spotlight as the great hope of the Democratic Party as well as the head of nation's most glamorous political dynasty. And he wasn't ready for it. When Jack died, Ted could still rely on Bobby, but with Bobby gone Ted had no one he could fully trust.[46] "Nineteen-sixty-eight was Bobby's year," he admitted years later. "I just didn't have the stomach to run. I didn't feel I was personally equipped for the race. And I thought it was too great a burden to place on my family at the time."[47] Instead, Ted, to strengthen his position among Senate colleagues, ran for Majority Whip and was elected to the position over the incumbent, Russell Long of Louisiana. He also spent more time at the family compound in Hyannis with his bedridden father and assumed the role of a surrogate father for his thirteen nephews and nieces.[48]

Bobby's death was also a serious blow to Kopechne, who remained in his senatorial office for the next two months sorting and packing files. "Mary Jo was one of the most grief-stricken staff members," recalled Joe Gargan, a cousin, adviser, and confidant of Senator Ted Kennedy's who supervised the shutting down of the Boiler Room.[49] But she also found comfort by being around other coworkers, who made the process of mourning more tolerable. "All of us were devastated by the Senator's death," recalled Judith Cromwell, who was working on the campaign in northern California but returned to Washington after

RFK's death. "Cleaning out the office was the most natural thing for us to do. Besides, we didn't want to leave each other."[50]

To ease the pain, Gargan and Gifford arranged a three-day trip for the Boiler Room Girls to Cape Cod. The vacation began at Gifford's house on Nantucket. The following day the young women were invited to Ted Kennedy's house at Hyannis for cocktails. Although Ted was too distraught to attend the event, his wife, Joan, proved to be a welcoming hostess. A cookout followed at Joe and Betty Gargan's home, just a few miles away. The next morning the party swam out to Ted's sixty-foot sloop, the *Mira*, anchored in the harbor. With Gargan and Gifford at the helm, the party set sail for a daylong cruise. In the evening, they docked at Nantucket and enjoyed dinner at Thirty Acres restaurant. Sailing back to Hyannis the next day, the Boiler Room Girls stayed one more night at the Gargans' before returning to Washington.[51] Dun Gifford and Dave Hackett threw a second party for the Boiler Room Girls in Washington in January 1969. According to Nance Lyons, Mary Jo's roommate, the event was called a "Bachelors' Ball" and was intended "to marry off the Boiler Room Girls." "There had to be two bachelors for every girl." Kennedy attended the affair and was so overcome with emotion that he broke down. "I think it's the first time he cried in public," said Lyons in a 2008 interview. "There was a special relationship between the boiler room girls and Teddy. He was comfortable with us, and I thought afterward that maybe it was good that he was able to show his emotions."

A third reunion followed in June, although Kennedy did not attend that one.[52] Gifford, who helped arrange the parties, said that the gatherings were meant to help the Boiler Room Girls during the grieving process. "There was an incredibly intense feeling of sadness among the staffers," explained Gifford. "It's hard to remember sometimes, how passionate that group of people was. The bonding that went on between us was intense. We all felt an awful absence after Bobby's death. There were also feelings of remorse over what was lost, over what might have been. We all had to deal with that emptiness. It was a real tragedy. Mary Jo and the others who worked in the Boiler Room spent a lot of time together. It was part of the healing process."[53]

There was also value in staying in contact with the Boiler Room Girls in the event that Ted Kennedy decided to launch his own bid for the White House sometime in the future.[54] But Judith Cromwell, Kopechne's closest friend on RFK's staff, insisted that Mary Jo would have rejected an offer to work for Ted Kennedy, either in his Senate office or on a presidential campaign. "It would've been impossible for Mary Jo, or for me, to switch allegiances to Ted Kennedy," she said. "It would've been too traumatic. Our allegiance was strictly to Bobby. We never felt as if we were working for the Senate or for a Senator's office when we were on the Hill. We were working for Robert Kennedy, the person. We were committed to him because of his values and his commitments. When he was gone, that was it. Besides, there was a kind of jealousy between the two staffs. Few of Bobby's female staffers would've considered working for Ted."[55] Cromwell's remarks were not completely accurate, though.

Ted Kennedy had recruited Maryellen and Nance Lyons to work for RFK's Boiler Room, and at least one of RFK's female staffers—Melody Miller—went on to become Ted's press secretary.[56] Where Cromwell's statement does appear to be accurate is in her insistence that Mary Jo would *not* have considered working for Ted Kennedy and that there was an uneasy relationship between the respective Senate staffs of the Kennedy brothers. RFK biographer Larry Tye contends that "there was a competition between the two staffs." Bobby's staff members were "very ambitious and disdainful of Ted's staff," which was "more effective in the fundamental work of the Senate" and "resented the way they were treated by RFK's staff."[57] Whether Mary Jo entertained any animosity toward Ted Kennedy or his staff is unclear, but after RFK's death she told her parents that she "didn't want to work for him."[58] A few months later, Kopechne admitted to a former college professor that she could not return to Capitol Hill because she "felt Bobby's presence everywhere" and that she "can't go back because it will never be the same again."[59]

After closing RFK's office on August 5, Mary Jo headed to Chicago for the Democratic National Convention, where she volunteered for George McGovern's campaign. The following month she was hired by the Southern Political Education and Action Committee, a tax-free, nonpartisan voter registration organization, to survey Dade County, Florida, for unregistered potential voters.[60] But Kopechne's desire to return to Washington DC was too strong to remain with the organization. Former colleagues teased her about suffering from "Potomac fever," or the "burning desire to do more work for less pay." Instead of returning to Capitol Hill, however, Mary Jo joined Matt Reese Associates, a campaign consultant firm based in the city.[61]

Kopechne's first assignment sent her to Denver, where she assisted former Colorado governor Steve McNichols in his bid to unseat Republican senator Peter Dominick. Michael Bonafede, who worked with Kopechne on the campaign, said Mary Jo "was an extremely intelligent person with a delightful sense of humor." "There were about ten to fifteen of us on that campaign, including McNichols's sons, who went to college together, and Mary Jo fit in beautifully," he said. Assigned to supervise a group of telephone operators who solicited volunteers, Kopechne's efforts yielded eleven thousand unpaid workers. "She worked seven days a week, twelve- to fifteen-hour days," said Bonafede, who went on to become assistant attorney general of Colorado. "Mary Jo was so busy that she didn't have much time to dwell on Robert Kennedy's death."[62]

During Christmas break, Mary Jo told a former college professor that she "liked her job with Matt Reese Associates" and was "sufficiently over the shock of Robert Kennedy's death."[63] Mary Jo had also put some distance between herself and the Boiler Room Girls. Although she attended another reunion in January, Kopechne was now circulating among a group of young intellectuals who resided in Georgetown and in the Foggy Bottom area, where the State Department was located. While the women in this group worked in government or business, most of the men were in Foreign Service, including "a young man she hoped to marry," according to her mother, Gwen.[64] "Mary Jo's personality was *always* bright and her spirit gay," recalled Reynold Reimer, who dated her during the last year of her life. "She had become more adventuresome. She loved clothes and dressed in a nice, modern way. She loved to dance and was good at it. But Mary Jo also remained a very decent and introspective person. She read deeply about the racial crisis and while she was a devout Catholic she was less ready to accept all the Church's precepts."[65]

Mary Jo was happier and more confident than ever before. She found a young man she loved and was ready to marry.[66] She enjoyed her job with Reese Associates and was highly respected by her new colleagues. Her boss, who had tremendous confidence in her abilities as well as her potential as a political consultant, offered her a full-time job with the firm. "Mary Jo was vitally interested in the nuts and bolts of how politics actually works—the 'whys' as well as the issues," said Reese. "And she was very good at it, too. She got along with people and got them to do the things that needed to be done, got them done right, on time, and with very little fuss." Kopechne also refused to compromise her morality. When Reese considered taking on the campaign of an old-time politician who didn't meet her ethical standards, Mary Jo told him, "If you take him, I won't work on his campaign!"[67] When her father heard the story, he said, "Mary Jo has reached the pinnacle. She's got what she wants, and she knows it."[68]

In spring 1969 Mary Jo returned to her home state of New Jersey as Reese's second-in-command for a primary election involving Jersey City's mayor, Thomas J. Whelan. According to Gwen Kopechne, when Reese asked Mary Jo to return to Jersey City in June to manage the subsequent runoff election, "she agreed on the condition that he pay her plane fare back to Washington each weekend so she could be with the young foreign service officer she wanted to marry." Reese agreed. Mary Jo continued to work on the Whelan campaign, and he won the election by sixty-one thousand votes.[69]

In early July, Kopechne returned to Washington to work on a fundraising event to pay off debts from RFK's presidential campaign. She and the other Boiler Room Girls volunteered their services, insuring the success of the event. An invitation for a fourth reunion was also extended by Joe Gargan. It would be held on Martha's Vineyard the weekend of the Edgartown Regatta from July 18 to 20. Mary Jo did not make a commitment to attend the reunion, however, because Reese had scheduled her to begin working on another campaign, this one in South Carolina.[70]

When she returned to work, Kopechne desperately tried to find a replacement for the South Carolina assignment so she could attend the reunion. Perhaps she had become nostalgic about her days in the Boiler Room or inspired to share with old friends the Apollo moon landing, an event that would represent JFK's vision to "put a man on the moon before the decade is out." Kennedy's vision would be realized on July 20, when *Apollo 11* landed on the moon and astronaut Neil Armstrong became the first human to set foot on it.[71] That thought was not far from Mary Jo's mind when she went to work on Wednesday morning, July 16, the day NASA launched the Saturn V booster rocket into orbit.

"Have you ever seen that picture of the earth hanging in space, looking from the moon?" she asked April Reese, her boss's teenaged daughter, who was interning at the office. When the teen nodded, Kopechne offered the following insight: "Just imagine someone took a picture of the whole world. Everything is there. . . . The [Vietnam] war, prejudice, everything. And we're just hanging in the blackness of space. One wrong move and it would be the end. It's frightening."[72]

It was a profound and sobering remark, considering all of the historic events that were taking place at the time—Vietnam, civil rights, the nuclear arms buildup, and the Space Race with the Soviet Union. There must have also been some personal regret since Mary Jo once believed that Robert Kennedy, her political hero, would have solved those same problems had he lived to become president. Whatever the case may have been, Kopechne was determined to attend the Edgartown reunion and, at the last minute, found a replacement. "She was so excited about going to Cape Cod," recalled April Reese. "Everyone in the office was very excited for her and told her to have a good time."[73]

On Thursday night, July 17, before she left for Martha's Vineyard, Mary Jo made two phone calls. The first call was to Cathy Reynolds, Matt Reese's administrative assistant, to ask off for the following Monday so she could remain in Edgartown on Sunday to watch the moon landing with her friends.[74] The second phone call was to her parents, Joseph and Gwen. "Mother, I've made three decisions," gushed Mary Jo when Gwen answered the phone. "First of all, I'm going to accept an offer from Matt Reese to work full-time." Gwen remembers being "delighted" by the news because Reese was offering to pay her daughter $15,000 a year, double what she made working for RFK, and because "there was great potential in the job." When her husband picked up the other receiver to listen in and hear the good news, the conversation went in another direction.[75]

Mary Jo never told them what her other two decisions were. She never saw the moon landing. Never returned to Washington. Never married. Never fulfilled her dream of having a family of her own.

5 Chappaquiddick

Chappaquiddick is a tiny island of brushwood and sand located a ferry ride away from the small resort of Edgartown on Martha's Vineyard off the coast of Massachusetts. "Chappy," as the locals refer to the three-mile-wide by five-mile-long island, belongs to one of the most picturesque areas of Cape Cod, a summer playground for the rich and famous. The island was isolated, with no stores or gas stations and just seven families who lived there year-round. Even when summer residents arrived, the population was fewer than five hundred. Chappy was a quiet, uneventful place, and those who lived there preferred it that way.[1] But on the weekend of July 18–20, 1969, when the Edgartown Yacht Club sponsored its annual regatta, Chappaquiddick would be thrust into the national spotlight. Afterward, the island would be known infamously as the place where Senator Edward M. Kennedy lost any hope of becoming president of the United States.

For Ted Kennedy the annual regatta had not only become a summer highlight but a valued ritual, as his family had competed in the event for many years. Sailing was also an important release for the senator allowing time for personal reflection. Never before did Kennedy need such an escape from the political pressures of Capitol Hill as much as he did on this mid-July weekend.[2] Still grieving over the death of his brother Bobby, the Massachusetts legislator looked forward to the three-day recess from Congress. He "planned to sail" the *Victura*, a blue-hulled Wianno he inherited from his brother John, "in the annual regatta" and host a group of aides, associates, and former campaign workers for a series of cookouts in the evenings after each race.[3]

On Wednesday, July 16, Jack Crimmins, Kennedy's part-time chauffeur, drove the senator's 1967 Oldsmobile down from Boston to make reservations for the Boiler Room Girls at the Katama Shores Motel

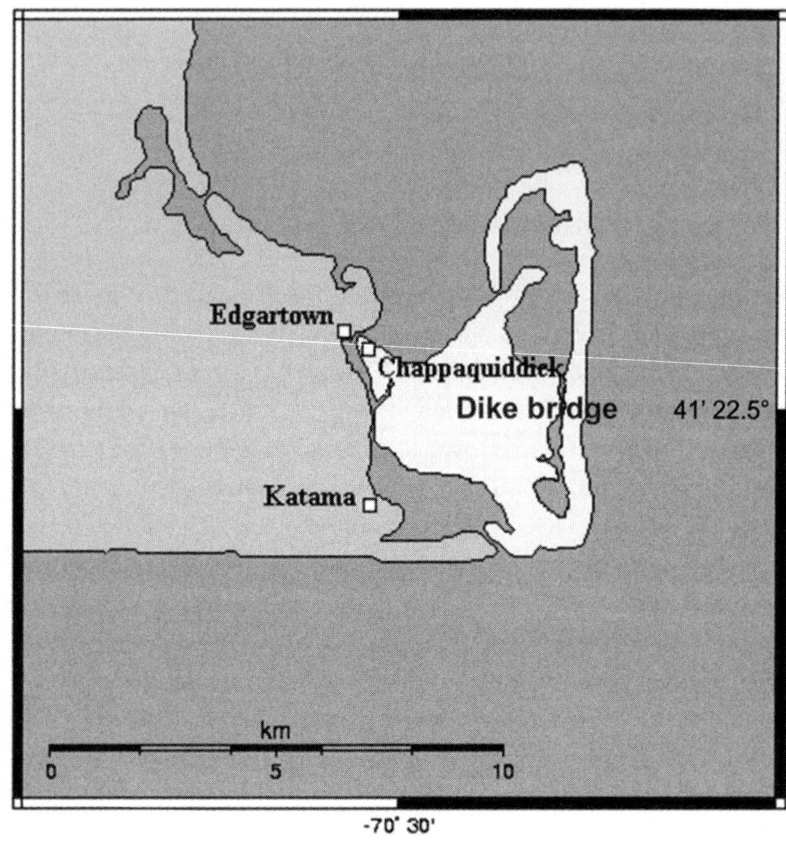

21. Area of detail, Chappaquiddick Island. Wikimedia Commons.

near Edgartown.[4] He also "purchased the liquor used at the cookouts," which consisted of "three half-gallons of Vodka, four fifths of Scotch, two bottles of rum and several cases of canned beer."[5] The following day, Joe Gargan, Kennedy's cousin and cohost of the party, sailed the *Victura* from Hyannis Port to Edgartown. A month earlier Gargan had rented a small cottage on Chappaquiddick for eight days. He planned to vacation there with his wife and children in mid-July. But those plans were scuttled when his mother-in-law was rushed to the hospital for surgery. Instead, the cottage would be used for the Friday night cookout.[6]

Located two miles from the ferry landing, the cottage, with weather-beaten shingles and yellow shutters, was owned by Sydney Lawrence, a resident of Scarsdale, New York. When he wasn't vacationing on the Island, Lawrence rented the place for $200 a week, a bargain when Edgartown guesthouses rented rooms for $35 to $40 a day. Known by the locals as Lawrence Cottage, the bungalow consisted of two small bedrooms, each with twin beds, and a bathroom that was adequate for a family of four. A large twelve-by-twenty-foot room held a galley kitchen with an ample refrigerator and small stove at one end and a fireplace and daybed at the other. The living-room space and kitchen were divided by a built-in counter with four high stools.[7]

Lawrence Cottage would be an ideal bathhouse and cookout site for the Kennedy entourage: six men (five of whom were married), and six younger unmarried women who were being hosted by the senator. In addition to Kennedy (age 37) and Gargan (39), the men included Paul Markham (38), a former U.S. attorney for Massachusetts; Ray LaRosa (41), a Kennedy campaign worker; Charles Tretter (30), head of the Boston Redevelopment Commission and a Kennedy campaign aide; and Jack Crimmins (63), Kennedy's part-time chauffeur and the only bachelor. The six women were Boiler Room Girls: Rosemary Keough (age 23), Mary Jo Kopechne (28), Maryellen Lyons (27), Nance Lyons (26), Esther Newberg (26), and Susan Tannenbaum (24).[8] On the surface, a gathering of young single women and older married men might be interpreted as inappropriate, if not scandalous, even by the flexible moral standards of the 1960s. But according to *Time* magazine, "none of the young women [were] strikingly attractive, and as a group they were hardly the sort that older men would invite for a weekend of dalliance." Instead, *Time* identified the Boiler Room Girls as "uniformly bright, efficient, fascinated by politics and cultishly pro-Kennedy."[9] Like their host, the young women were also grief-stricken over RFK's death and still searching for ways to channel their professional ambitions and personal ideals. Thus the Chappaquiddick reunion was intended to be a friendly, relaxing, and therapeutic event for everyone involved.[10]

On Friday, July 18, Kennedy took a late morning flight from Washington to Boston with House Speaker Thomas "Tip" O'Neill, who held the congressional seat once occupied by JFK. The two legislators were close friends, but O'Neill later recalled that Ted was "not talkative" and looked "tired as hell."[11] Indeed, Kennedy was preoccupied by his future and the burden of carrying the torch for his dead brothers. Not only was he the head of the nation's most influential political dynasty, but Ted was also the frontrunner for the Democratic presidential nomination in 1972.[12] That prospect frightened his children and their thirteen cousins, all of whom were relying on Ted's counsel and guidance. His father was paralyzed from a stroke, his mother was still grieving the violent death of her favorite son, and his beautiful wife, Joan, had turned to drinking, unable to cope with the demands and pressures of being a high-profile senator's wife. Ted had also begun to drink more heavily.[13] On a recent flight back to Washington from Alaska, where he had attended a hearing on Alaskan Native education, reporters were shocked by his raucous behavior, the result of too much alcohol.[14] At one point on the flight, Ted even expressed his fear that if he were to run for president "they'd shoot [my] ass off the way they shot off Bobby's." While the incident was not reported at the time, the journalists who covered the Massachusetts senator realized that he was beginning to buckle under the pressure. Near the end of his life, Kennedy admitted that "in the months and years after Bobby's death, I tried to stay ahead of the darkness." "I drove my car at high speeds," he explained. "I drove myself in the Senate; I drove my staff; I sometimes drove my capacity for liquor to the limit. I might well have driven Joan deeper into her anguish."[15]

Shortly after 1:00 p.m., Kennedy arrived on Martha's Vineyard on a charter flight from Boston. Crimmins met him at Edgartown and the two men drove to the ferry that carried them across the 150-yard seawater channel to Chappaquiddick. During the four-minute crossing, the chauffeur, a foul-mouthed bachelor and former policeman, voiced displeasure about his responsibilities for the weekend. Not only would he have to spend his nights at Lawrence Cottage—a place he referred to as a "fucking dump"—but he was also expected to drive the Boiler

Room Girls wherever they wanted to go. Crimmins told Kennedy that he resented the presence of the women and wanted nothing to do with them. But the senator, accustomed to his chauffeur's gruff language and contrary attitude, dismissed the complaints.[16]

When they arrived at Lawrence Cottage, Kennedy changed into a bathing suit and had Crimmins drive him to the beach. There he joined the Boiler Room Girls for an hour-long swim, which seemed to rejuvenate him. Later that afternoon, Kennedy, with Gargan and Markham as crew, sailed the *Victura* in the annual regatta. Conditions were poor, "being hot and humid with very little wind," according to Gargan. Ted, who consumed "a beer" during the race, finished a disappointing ninth. After, he joined Ross Richards, a sailing friend and the winner of the race, aboard his vessel, *Bettawin*, for a congratulatory toast. According to Stan Moore, another contestant who was on the boat, Ted downed three rum and cokes. He then excused himself and had Gargan drive him to his room at the Shiretown Inn, where he changed clothes for the cookout.[17] Crimmins then chauffeured Kennedy to Lawrence Cottage.

Arriving at 7:30 p.m., Ted undressed and soaked in a hot tub for twenty minutes to ease his chronically aching back and nursed another rum and coke. Gargan, who arrived at 8:15 p.m., immediately began baking frozen hors d'oeuvres and stoking the charcoal in a small grill to prepare the steaks. Another aide, Ray LaRosa, took a rented car to pick up the Boiler Room Girls at Katama Shores.[18] They had returned to their motel after the race to shower, nap, and change clothes. As a result, they did not arrive at Lawrence Cottage until almost 9:00 p.m.

Dinner would be served late. The barbeque grill was so small, only two steaks could be grilled at a time. Nor had the potatoes been baked or a salad prepared. The cheese and sausage hors d'oeuvres would have to suffice as the partygoers mingled with each other.[19] Kennedy labored to be a good host. Gargan later testified that he saw the senator "on a couple of occasions with a glass in his hand," but he expressed uncertainty over whether the "dark fluid" he observed in the glass was rum and coke or simply Coca-Cola.[20] Regardless of how much alcohol the senator consumed, it was clear to Charles Tretter that Ted was "not having a hell of a good time."[21] To brighten the dismal mood, Tretter and Cricket Keough returned to the Shiretown Inn in Edgartown to borrow a radio. When they returned, some partygoers danced, while others continued to talk until dinner was served. The drinking was moderate, according to all of the testimony given at the inquest into Kopechne's death six months later.[22] Foster Silva, a fire captain who lived just a hundred yards from the cottage, had a different recollection of the party, though.

"There was a lot of singing and laughing coming from that house," said Silva, who had been watching television that evening. "They were damned loud." He went to bed about midnight but was unable to sleep because of all the noise. "By 1:00 a.m., I was pretty damn well fed up with the whole thing," added Silva. "It was a farce at that hour of the morning. If they kept it up much longer, I would've called the police." Although the party quieted down around 1:30 a.m., it continued for another hour.[23]

By that time, Kennedy had been long gone from Lawrence Cottage. According to his court testimony, the senator left the party at 11:15 p.m. When he was about to leave, Mary Jo asked him if he "would be kind enough to drop her back at her hotel." Kopechne, who felt ill because of too much sun, told no one that she was leaving with him, according to Kennedy's testimony, and left her purse and hotel key at the party. Instead of asking Crimmins to drive them, EMK got behind the wheel of his 1967 black Oldsmobile with Mary Jo beside him. When asked at the inquest why Crimmins did not drive them back to Edgartown, Kennedy explained that his chauffeur, along with some of the other guests, "were concluding their meal, enjoying the fellowship and it didn't appear to be necessary."[24]

When Kennedy left Lawrence Cottage he drove north on School Road in the direction of the ferry landing. But when he reached Chappaquiddick Road, the blacktopped drive that headed west to the ferry slip, Kennedy, according to the statement he wrote for police chief Dominick "Jim" Arena, veered east onto a bumpy gravel lane called Dike Road that led to the beach.[25] A half mile down was a narrow, hump-backed wooden bridge that curved off the dirt road in a sharp,

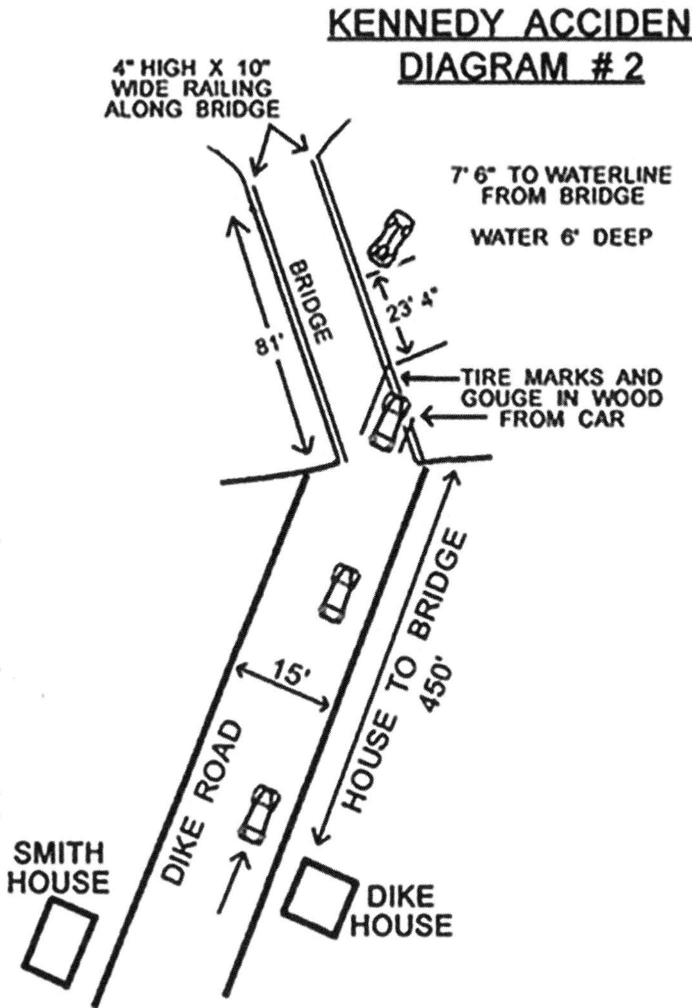

22. Kennedy Accident Diagram 2. Edgartown District Court, *Inquest into the Death of Mary Jo Kopechne.*

twenty-seven-degree angle to the left. Since there were no artificial lights or signs, the structure was difficult to see that late at night. Nor did Dike Bridge have any guardrails—just timber rub rails that were four inches high and ten inches wide on each side. If a driver was traveling faster than ten miles per hour, he could easily lose control of his vehicle and plunge into the small channel below. Kennedy, according to his testimony, was driving at "approximately twenty miles an hour." Unable to navigate the twenty-seven-degree turn, he lost control of the Oldsmobile as it plunged off the right side of the bridge and landed on its roof at the bottom of Poucha Pond in the ten-foot-deep channel.[26]

Somehow the senator escaped from the vehicle and was carried to the shore by the current. Kopechne remained trapped inside the car.[27] Kennedy, according to his court testimony, attempted to rescue Mary Jo "seven or eight times" but finally gave in to exhaustion. "For fifteen or twenty minutes," the senator lay on the bank coughing up water. Then he returned to the party, "walking, trotting, jogging and stumbling as fast as [he] possibly could." But at no time during the journey did he stop at any house to seek help. When asked at the inquest why he failed to do so, Kennedy said he "never saw a cottage with a light on."[28]

When Kennedy arrived at Lawrence Cottage, he explained his predicament to Gargan and Markham, both of whom followed the senator back to the bridge and made another unsuccessful attempt to rescue Mary Jo. Gargan and Markham, both lawyers, insisted that Kennedy report the accident immediately, then drove him to the ferry landing. When the car reached the slip, Gargan and Markham "reiterated that [the accident] has to be reported," according to the senator's testimony. Kennedy further stated that he realized that the accident "had to be reported" and that he had "full intention of reporting it." "You take care of the [Boiler Room] girls," he told his two friends, and "I will take care of the accident."[29]

When asked later why he gave those instructions, Kennedy, in court testimony, stated that he "felt strongly that if those girls were notified that an accident had taken place and that Mary Jo had in fact drowned" that it would "only be a matter of seconds before all of those girls, who were dear friends of Mary Jo's, [would] go to the scene of the accident to rescue her." "I felt there was a good chance that some serious mishap might occur to any one of them," he added.[30]

Since the ferry shut down at midnight, Kennedy, according to his testimony, swam across the five-hundred-foot channel back to Edgartown and returned to his room at the Shiretown Inn "sometime before

2 o'clock." He also stated that he was "very conscious of a throbbing headache, of pains in [his] neck, of strain on [his] back, but what [he] was even more conscious of [was] the tragedy and loss of a very devoted friend," Mary Jo Kopechne. Unable to determine whether it was morning, afternoon, or nighttime, Kennedy changed into a clean jacket and slacks, left his room, and, spotting Russell Peachey, a hotel clerk, "standing under the light off the balcony, asked what time it was." Peachey informed him that it was 2:30 a.m., and the senator returned to his room and went to sleep.[31]

Kennedy rose early the next morning, bought a newspaper, and joined his friends Ross Richards, his wife, Marilyn, and Stan Moore for breakfast on the second-floor porch of the Shiretown Inn. Richards, in a statement he later gave to police, noted that there was nothing unusual about the senator. He was dressed neatly and showed no discomfort. Suddenly, Gargan and Markham, both sweaty and agitated, interrupted the gathering. Gargan demanded to see Kennedy privately. The senator excused himself and the three men went to his room. When they returned, Richards observed that EMK was clearly distraught and rushed off without even saying goodbye.[32] When Gargan and Markham confronted him, Kennedy was forced to admit that he "hadn't reported the accident." According to his court testimony,

> They asked, had I reported the accident, and why I hadn't reported the accident; and I told them about my own thoughts and feelings as I swam across the channel and how I always willed that Mary Jo still lived; how I was hopeful even as that night went on and as I tossed and turned that night that somehow . . . Mary Jo was still alive. I told them how . . . I just couldn't gain the strength within me, the moral strength to call Mrs. Kopechne at 2:00 o'clock in the morning and tell her that her daughter was dead.[33]

Kennedy, Gargan, and Markham rushed to the ferry and crossed over to Chappaquiddick. "I picked the senator up on the Edgartown side that morning and brought him with two other men over to Chappy," recalled Steve Ewing, a ferry operator. "The senator walked off the ferry and over to the ferry shed where there's a pay phone and he was in there for quite a while. You could tell something was building. There was a little bit of tension."[34] While Kennedy used the phone to call family members and his lawyer, Burke Marshall, a tow truck arrived and headed in the direction of Dike Bridge. Gargan, having spotted the truck, realized that the overturned Oldsmobile had been discovered. He interrupted Kennedy and snapped: "You've got to do what I've been saying right along. Get over there [to Edgartown] and report [the accident] as fast as possible."[35]

It was about 9:30 a.m. when EMK finally hung up the phone. Gargan insisted that Markham accompany Kennedy to the police station. Determined not to take the blame for the accident, Gargan knew that Ted was clinging to the hope that "someone else" would admit to driving the car. He also knew that he was the most logical candidate because of EMK's lifelong reliance on him—something that was reinforced whenever Kennedy half-jokingly quipped, "Old Joey will fix it!" Gargan's instincts would soon prove to be correct.[36]

As Kennedy and Markham boarded the ferry for Edgartown, Gargan got into a Plymouth Valiant he rented for the weekend and headed back to Lawrence Cottage. About a quarter mile down Chappaquiddick Road, he came across LaRosa, Crimmins, the Lyons sisters, and Newberg, who were walking toward the ferry slip. Gargan stopped the car and told them to get in. Sensing that something was wrong, Nance Lyons asked, "What's happened?"

"The senator's been in an accident," replied Gargan. "He's okay, but we can't find Mary Jo." Now he was bombarded by questions that he refused to answer due to his limited knowledge of the details.

When the group arrived at Lawrence Cottage, Crimmins and LaRosa cleaned up, making sure to dispose of all empty wine bottles and beer cans. The young women gathered their belongings. Nance Lyons, who found Mary Jo's handbag next to hers under a chair in the living room, continued to badger Gargan for more information.

"Can't you do something?" she asked. "Isn't there some way we can have somebody else as driver of the car?"

"That would be impossible," Gargan snapped.

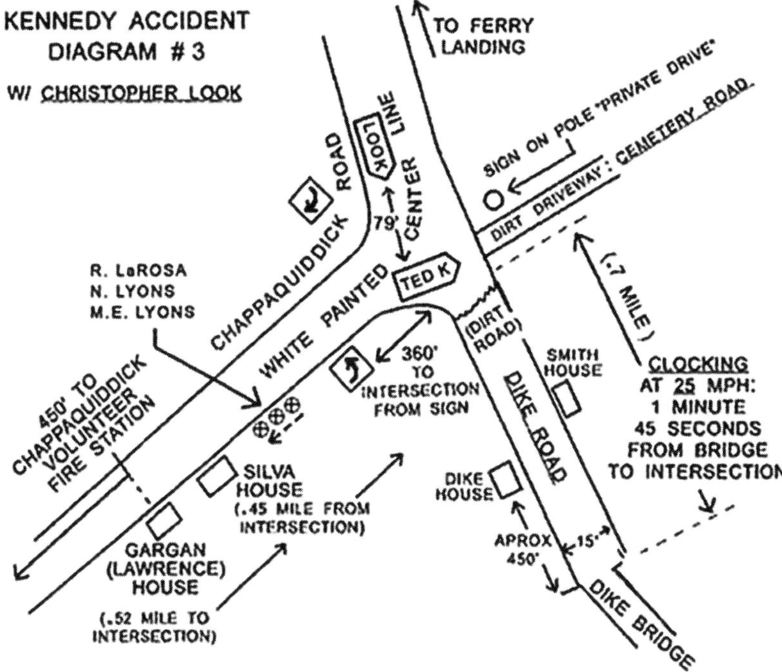

23. Kennedy Accident Diagram 3. Edgartown District Court, *Inquest into the Death of Mary Jo Kopechne*.

"I don't know why *you* couldn't be driving the car?" Lyons suggested as she continued to hound him.

"Of course not," Gargan shot back, incredulously.

"Can't someone else take the blame?" Lyons persisted.

"We can't, that's all," he barked, putting an end to the discussion. "The Senator was driving."[37]

The heated exchange reflected the conflicting emotions Ted Kennedy had created for his friends. At one end of the spectrum was Nance Lyons, whose unconditional loyalty to the senator placed his political ambitions—and perhaps her own—above any other consideration. It was the kind of blind loyalty the Kennedys had expected of their employees and campaign volunteers. On the other hand, Joe Gargan had drawn a line that he refused to cross. All his life, he was expected to cater to Ted, to resolve the problems his cousin created for himself, or at the very least to cover for him. Until now, Gargan had been a good soldier and a loyal friend. But he was adamant about his refusal to take the fall for an accident he did not commit. He might have been an "honorary Kennedy," but he did not enjoy the same wealth, power, influence that went along with that surname. In other words, if Gargan assumed responsibility for the accident by saying he was the driver, he would certainly spend time in jail for manslaughter. Ted would have to assume responsibility for himself this time.

By the time the partygoers returned to their Edgartown hotels, packed, and departed from Martha's Vineyard, the scene of the accident had become the focus of a police investigation. About 7:30 a.m., two boys fishing on Dike Bridge discovered the submerged Oldsmobile. They ran to the nearest house, one hundred feet from the bridge, and asked Sylvia Malm, a renter, to phone the Edgartown police. Just after 8:30 a.m., Chief Jim Arena arrived at Pouch Pond. Borrowing a bathing suit, the six-foot-four, 230-pound police chief attempted to enter the overturned car. "I tried to go under to see if I could get into the car, but each time I did, the tide swept me along, so I gave up," said the police chief in a 2009 interview. "I boosted myself up and stayed on the car. Sitting there, I had an inner feeling that somebody's in there." Arena called in to the Registry of Motor Vehicles to find the name of the car's owner. To his amazement, he learned that the license plate—L78207—had been registered to Edward M. Kennedy.[38]

Arena was soon joined by John Farrar, captain of the search and rescue division of Edgartown's volunteer fire department. Already dressed in dive gear, Farrar adjusted an oxygen tank across his back and swam toward the overturned car with a safety line. Handing one end of the line to Arena, the fire captain placed the oxygen tube in his mouth and dove underwater. He peered through the driver's side open window and saw that the front seat was empty. Circling to the back of the car, Farrar looked through the top righthand corner of the rear window and saw two feet clad in sandals. Returning to the driver's side of the car, he pushed himself through the open window. He could now see the body more clearly. It was a female. Her head was cocked back, with the face pressed into the foot-well of the floor and hands gripping the edge of the backseat. "By holding herself in such a position she could avail herself of the last remaining air in the car," explained Farrar, months later at the inquest hearing. He also noted that his experience showed that persons trapped underwater had survived as much as five hours by breathing in a pocket of air and that he could have had Mary Jo out of the car alive in twenty-five minutes had he been called immediately.[39]

When Farrar reached out to extricate the body, his fingers touched her cold, hard thigh, and he knew she was dead. To prevent the body from being swept away by the current, the diver fastened the safety line around her neck and pulled the body out of the car and up to the surface.[40] He hoisted the corpse onto Arena's lap. Usually a calm, collected individual, the police chief became visibly shaken. He scrutinized Mary Jo's pale, lightly freckled face as expressionless eyes stared at him through partially closed lids. Rigor mortis had already set in. Her mouth was open and teeth gritted. Dressed in a long-sleeve white blouse with navy blue slacks, Mary Jo wore a ring on her left hand and two gold bracelets on her wrist. Arena noted that "there were no injuries," that "everything was in place," and that "if the body hadn't been wringing wet it would appear as if she was about to go to work, or to a party."[41]

At 9:30 a.m. Donald R. Mills, the Dukes County associate medical examiner, arrived to inspect the victim's body. Mills looked for any sign of bruising and found none. Convinced that it was a case of "accidental drowning," he dismissed the need for an autopsy. He then reported the fatality to District Attorney Edmund Dinis, who okayed the decision to forgo an autopsy. Then, Mills issued a death certificate and released the body to the Massachusetts State Police laboratory for analysis.[42]

As Mills conducted his examination, Farrar dove underwater again to check the rest of the car. He recovered the chain belt that had broken free of the victim's body when he removed her from the automobile. He also found a woman's handbag on the front passenger seat. Inside was a wallet containing two keys for room 56 at the Katama Shores Motor Inn, a Virginia driver's license, and a U.S. Senate identification card bearing the name of Rosemary Keough. When Farrar surfaced to report his finding, Arena told him to check downstream to see if there were other bodies that might have been in the automobile. He then called in to the police station to send someone to locate Ted Kennedy. Instead, the police chief learned that the senator was already waiting for him at the station and hurried back to Edgartown.[43]

While waiting in Arena's office, Kennedy, sometime between 9:00 and 9:30 a.m., mustered the moral courage to phone the Kopechnes and inform them of their daughter's death. When Gwen Kopechne answered the phone at the couple's home in Berkeley Heights, New Jersey, the senator identified himself and asked for her husband. After learning that he was unavailable, Kennedy said, "Mary Jo has been in an accident."

"Was she killed?" Gwen blurted out.

"Yes," he replied.

Gwen went numb and hung up the phone. "All I remember is that I started screaming," she said many years later. "'Mary Jo! Mary Jo's been killed!' I kept screaming." A neighbor heard the blood-curdling sound and rushed over to see if Gwen was all right. But she was so hysterical that the neighbor had to slap her across the face several times to restore some semblance of calm. Another neighbor located her husband, Joe, and told him the news every parent dreads: that his only child was dead. Not until six hours later, when a *Boston Globe* reporter contacted them, did the Kopechnes get any details about who was driving the car, when it happened, or how it happened. When the reporter read Kennedy's police statement, which had just been released by Arena, Joe said, "Now I don't know what to think."[44]

When Arena arrived at the police station, Carmen Salvador, the receptionist, informed him that the senator, accompanied by Markham, was in his office using the phone. Arena entered, and Kennedy came around the desk to shake his hand. "I'm sorry about the accident," said the police chief.

"Yes, I know," replied Kennedy. "I was the driver."

Stunned by the admission, Arena had assumed that the victim had driven the car off the bridge. "Nothing in my prior career as a police officer prepared me for standing in a wet bathing suit and shaking hands with a United States Senator—and a Kennedy," he later recalled.

"Do you know where Rosemary Keough is from so we can notify her next of kin?" Arena asked.

"It isn't 'Cricket' Keough; it's Mary Jo Kopechne," Kennedy said. "I've already notified her parents. What would you like for me to do. We must do what is right or we'll both be criticized for it."

"The first thing we have to do is to have a statement from you about what happened," replied Arena.

"Would it be all right if I wrote it out?" the senator asked, requesting privacy to prepare the statement.

The police chief agreed and led the two men to an unoccupied office, where Kennedy dictated the following statement to Markham, who wrote it down:

> On July 18, 1969, at approximately 11:15 p.m. in Chappaquiddick, Martha's Vineyard, Massachusetts, I was driving my car on Main Street on my way to get the ferry back to Edgartown. I was unfamiliar with the road and turned right onto Dike Road, instead of bearing hard left on Main Street. After proceeding for approximately one-half mile [800 m] on Dike Road I descended a hill and came upon a narrow bridge. The car went off the side of the bridge. There was one passenger with me, one Miss Mary Jo [Kopechne], a former secretary of my brother Sen. Robert Kennedy.
>
> The car turned over and sank into the water and landed with the roof resting on the bottom. I attempted to open the door and the window of the car but have no recollection of how I got out of the car. I came to the surface and then repeatedly dove down to the car in an attempt to see if the passenger was still in the car. I was unsuccessful in the attempt. I was exhausted and in a state of shock. I recall walking back to where my friends were eating. There was a car parked in front of the cottage and I climbed into the backseat. I then asked for someone to bring me back to Edgartown. I remember walking around for a period and then going back to my hotel room. When I fully realized what had happened this morning, I immediately contacted the police.[45]

It took more than an hour for Kennedy to compose the statement, which said nothing about a party or the alcohol that was consumed at it. Nor did the statement include Ted's signature. When he finally completed it, the senator requested that Arena not release the statement until he gave the okay, presumably because he wished to consult with his lawyers. Arena agreed to hold the statement but wanted to ask some questions, principally, why it took so long for Kennedy to report the accident. Markham intervened, assuring the police chief that the senator "will answer questions after he has consulted his attorney." But the police chief continued to press. When he asked to see the senator's driver's license, Kennedy said he didn't have it with him because he lost his wallet. Arena then asked if the license had been "properly renewed," and Kennedy assured him that it had. With that, the senator departed.[46]

Arena was left behind to deal with the dozens of newspaper and television reporters who had descended upon Edgartown to report the story. Overwhelmed by the pressure to release Kennedy's statement, the police chief struggled mightily to keep his promise to the senator that he would hold off until further notice from him.

"It was quite obvious that Jim Arena was a small-town sheriff," recalled Liz Trotta, who was covering the story for NBC-TV. "Suddenly he was talking to a network television crew, and I caught a sense of that because he seemed so overwhelmed by our presence. It was clear that he was on the spot because a U.S. Senator was involved."[47] To cover his own public relations, Kennedy called in his press secretary, Dick Drayne. Drayne, who had traveled with RFK's 1968 presidential campaign and was popular among reporters due to his irrepressible sense of humor. The press also respected him because of his acute political sense and his thorough understanding of the sometimes conflicting needs of the media and his political employer.[48] "Dick Drayne was an expert at being completely relaxed, laughing and joking with the press," said Trotta. "At Chappaquiddick he just hung out with reporters and shot the breeze but never told us anything at all."[49]

One of the other phone calls Ted Kennedy made that morning was to Dun Gifford, a trusted aide who had a summer residence on nearby

Nantucket. Kennedy asked Gifford to fly to Chappaquiddick and obtain the necessary papers to have Kopechne's body released from the Martha's Vineyard funeral home where it had been transported from Dike Bridge and flown back to northeastern Pennsylvania for burial. He would remain there with her parents, Gwen and Joe Kopechne, to assist them in making funeral arrangements and to advance for the senator, who planned to attend the service.[50] Although there were suspicions that Gifford rushed the body off the Cape to avoid an autopsy, he flatly denied such an insidious motive. "I had a clear impression of my job from the very beginning," he said in a 1994 interview. "My job was to make it as easy as possible for Mr. and Mrs. Kopechne. To get the paperwork straightened out and do so above board and in the best possible way. The senator was totally on the high road. It was his and my decision to do it right."[51] Nor did the Kopechnes believe that Gifford had any ulterior motive. "Dun Gifford was very generous," said Joe Kopechne. "He helped us a lot, but he never forced himself on us. He let us answer our phone. He never made any suggestions one way or another as to how we should handle ourselves. You have to respect somebody like that because he was a Kennedy man."[52]

On Sunday, July 20, as the nation anticipated the *Apollo 11* space mission's moon landing, Chappaquiddick became the top story in most newspapers.[53] The headline of Kennedy's hometown *Boston Globe* read, "Ted Kennedy Escapes, Woman Dies as Car Plunges into Vineyard Pond." The three stories that followed were all sympathetic to the Massachusetts senator, portraying the accident as the latest in a series of personal tragedies to beset the Kennedy family. The Apollo moon landing, scheduled to be the headline, was bumped to the bottom of the front page.[54]

The following day, police chief Jim Arena filed in district court a formal complaint charging Edward Kennedy with leaving the scene of an accident after causing personal injury, a misdemeanor punishable by two months in prison. Under Massachusetts state law, the charge was a more serious offense than reckless driving but far more lenient that the charge of manslaughter or negligent homicide. The police chief told the press that he was "firmly convinced that there was no negligence involved" in the accident. But there was, in his opinion, "a violation of leaving the scene" because of the nearly ten-hour period "that elapsed after the accident."[55]

Meanwhile a crisis management team of advisers assembled at the Kennedy compound in Hyannis Port. Among those assembled were Robert McNamara, JFK's secretary of defense and then president of the World Bank; Ted Sorensen, JFK's speechwriter; Milton Gwirtzman, Ted's speechwriter; and Richard Goodwin, JFK's adviser on Latin America.[56] These were ambitious politicians who had attached themselves to the Kennedy family to advance their careers. Now they feared that their own futures as well as the restoration of a Kennedy presidency might come to an abrupt halt. "I was a very reluctant participant," Ted Sorenson admitted in a 2006 interview. "I didn't want to be there, but I thought, as a lawyer, when somebody is in need and asks for some advice that is at least quasi-legal advice, I felt I had some duty to offer that advice. At the time, July '69, I was thinking about the possibility of running for office myself. I obviously felt very sorry for Ted and wanted to help, but that was not a great place to be for anybody who had a [political] future."[57]

Others who gathered at the Kennedy compound were Ted's close friends, Paul Markham and Joe Gargan and family members, including his mother, Rose, sisters, Eunice, Pat, and Jean, and brothers-in-law, Sargent Shriver and Stephen Smith. Smith, who had run RFK's campaign, took charge. Smith was a master at troubleshooting, having strong connections to the highest levels of business and politics in Massachusetts. Accordingly, he hired nine lawyers to help navigate the complicated legal issues involved in the case. Burke Marshall, who had been RFK's most trusted legal adviser at the Justice Department, and Edward Hanify were the most prominent of the attorneys being senior partners in the prestigious Boston firm of Ropes and Gray. One of the first measures taken was to implement a gag rule. Marshall, Hanify, and Smith ordered that "neither Ted himself, nor anyone on his staff, nor anyone who had been present at the party . . . speak either publicly or privately about any aspect of the accident." Smith, in particular, insisted on "complete and lasting silence."[58] And that's exactly what the press received from Kennedy beginning on Saturday, July 19, when it first learned of the accident, until Friday evening of July 25, when the senator appeared on national television to give his version of the story.

During that week, Esther Newberg was the only member of the Kennedy entourage who violated the gag rule. During a four-day period, Newberg gave interviews from her Washington home to reporters from the *New York Times*, *Chicago Tribune*, and *Worcester (MA) Gazette*. In those interviews, Newberg, when asked what time Kennedy and Kopechne left the cottage, said that nobody was paying any attention to time and that her watch was not working so she was unable to tell when they left. Insisting that "nobody's trying to hide anything," the Boiler Room Girl said that there wasn't much drinking, "at most, one or two drinks apiece," and that the party was simply a quiet, reflective gathering of people who worked for RFK. Newberg also dismissed the death of Kopechne as "an accident." "What can you do about an accident," she added. "Mary Jo is dead and there isn't anything we can do."[59]

Kennedy struggled to remain silent during his self-imposed seclusion at the family compound. But his political instincts quickly took control, and he insisted on delivering a nationally televised speech to provide the voters with his own version of the accident, an idea that was initially rejected by some of his advisers. "The speech had both legal and political implications and consequences," recalled Ted Sorensen. "At one point I called my senior partner, Arthur Lyman, one of the best lawyers in my law firm . . . and asked about the possible consequences of a speech before the formal hearing."[60]

Some Kennedy biographers contend that EMK considered resigning from the Senate and promising to never seek the presidency but that Eunice Shriver talked her younger brother out of those plans. She assisted Ted Sorensen in writing a carefully crafted statement to help him salvage his political career. "If I have anything to say about it," snapped Hanify, "he'll never make that speech.[61] Consequently, the only statement issued from Hyannis Port in the immediate aftermath of the accident addressed Mary Jo Kopechne's dedicated service to the Kennedy family, and it came from RFK's widow, Ethel Kennedy: "Mary Jo was a sweet wonderful girl. She worked for Bobby for years and she was in the Boiler Room, the phone room used for delegate counts during the campaign. Only the great ones worked there and she was just terrific. She often came out to [Hickory Hill] and she was the one who stayed up all night typing Bobby's speech on Vietnam. She was a wonderful person."[62] "That was all we got," recalled Liz Trotta of NBC News. "There was no information about the accident from the Kennedys. It was a stone wall."[63]

Mary Jo's funeral was held on July 22, 1969, at Saint Vincent's Catholic Church in Plymouth, Pennsylvania, an old coal mining town of about ten thousand residents. A few days before, her body had been flown from Chappaquiddick to the Wilkes-Barre/Scranton Airport and then transported by car to the Kielty Funeral Home in Plymouth. Almost immediately the funeral home was surrounded by the national and international press. Television cameras were everywhere. "Our telephone rang constantly," recalled Helen Kielty, wife of the funeral director. "My husband finally had to put the phone on answering service and he became a master sergeant during the viewing, admitting only those he knew. We also got bags of the weirdest mail, some mean, some threatening, others just curious."[64]

The remaining Boiler Room Girls attended the viewing and burst into tears upon seeing Mary Jo reposed in an open bronze casket, dressed in a blue peignoir, her hands clasping a rosary. Floral tributes surrounded her, but one stood on a pedestal, separate from the others. It was a bouquet of yellow roses sent by Ted and Joan Kennedy.[65]

The morning of the funeral was hot and muggy, but that did not discourage locals from turning out by the hundreds. "I could understand the crowds," said Joe Kopechne. "The Kennedys were coming and nothing this big has happened around here since 34 settlers were killed by Indians during the Revolutionary War."[66]

Ted Kennedy attended the service with his wife, Joan, who was pregnant with their third child, his sister-in-law, Ethel, and two of his closest friends, Rep. John V. Tunney of California and Rep. John C. Culver of Iowa, both of whom would later be elected to the U.S. Senate. The Kennedy party flew out of Hyannis at 6:30 a.m. and arrived in Wilkes-Barre at 8:50 a.m.[67] The entourage arrived at the church in a white Buick at 9:25 a.m. Kennedy, dressed in a dark blue suit, white dress shirt, and black tie, stepped out of the car first. His head was erect due to a thick, white cervical collar he wore for an injury reportedly suffered in the accident. Monsignor William Burchill and his assistant, Reverend Arnold Smith, met Ted, Joan, and Ethel and escorted them into the rectory, where they met with Joe and Gwen Kopechne. After introductions were made, Burchill drew the shades of the front parlor and excused himself so they could have privacy. Gwen was heavily sedated. She wept inconsolably as she leaned on the arm of Dun Gifford; one hand held a white handkerchief to her mouth. Ted tried to tell the Kopechnes that he wished that he, not Mary Jo, had died in the accident. But Joe Kopechne said that Kennedy was "so broken up, I could hardly understand him."[68]

Ethel Kennedy, a devout Catholic, was more empathetic, having lost her husband a year earlier. "She talked about faith, and how it helped her and how it could help us," recalled Joe.[69] Several minutes later, just before the funeral mass began, the Kennedys left the rectory via a back door and entered the church through a side door that led to the sacristy. Seven hundred people crowded into the church that sat five hundred, with several hundred more spilling out the door and onto the sidewalk and street. Ted, Joan, and Ethel took their seats in a front pew and later joined Joseph and Gwen Kopechne at the altar to receive Holy Communion. Burchill celebrated the low requiem mass but did not deliver a eulogy. Instead he simply read, "In baptism, she died with Christ, in death may she have her resurrection."

When the service ended, the Kopechnes left out the front doors following their daughter's casket, while the Kennedys departed through the same side door by which they entered. A twenty-two-car procession wound its way through the town and up a winding road to the parish cemetery in neighboring Larksville. Police cordoned off the gravesite, so onlookers appropriated nearby headstones as seats. At the gravesite, the Kopechne family sat on folding chairs beneath a faded green canopy while Kennedy, visibly distressed, stood nearby with his wife at his side. When the gravesite service ended, the Kennedys attended a post-funeral buffet and then returned to Hyannis Port.[70]

The press was waiting for EMK when his plane landed on Cape Cod at 2:15 p.m. He turned away the first wave of reporters who questioned him. "This is the day of the funeral," he said. "This isn't an appropriate time. But I will make a full statement at the appropriate time." Most of the reporters trailed off, leaving Kennedy alone. But Liz Trotta of NBC-TV was determined to get a statement. "There has been some question as to what effect this will have on your political career," she said, chasing after him.

The remark hit Kennedy like a gut punch. Whirling around to confront his inquisitor, he snapped: "I've just come from the funeral of a very lovely young lady. And this is *not* the appropriate time for such questions! I am *not* going to have any other comment to make!"[71]

Shortly after the confrontation, a Kennedy aide made a threatening call to NBC News, demanding that Trotta be removed from the story. "I was led to believe that my job was at risk," she said in a recent interview. "I was told by the vice president at NBC News that the Kennedy people had in fact contacted the network and very strongly suggested that I be taken off the story. It was naked power reaching out, saying, 'Lay off,' 'Take the fall.'"[72] But NBC refused to be intimidated, and Trotta continued to cover the story.

Three days later, on July 25, Kennedy, accompanied by one of his lawyers, Richard McCarron, appeared before Judge James A. Boyle at the Dukes County Court House in Edgartown and pled guilty to leaving the scene of an accident with personal injury.[73] Surprisingly, Boyle never asked Kennedy why he hadn't reported the accident sooner. Instead, the judge, after hearing a partial statement of the facts, asked police chief Jim Arena if there had been "a deliberate attempt to conceal the identity of the defendant." Arena replied, "Not to my knowledge, Your Honor," and he was immediately excused from the witness stand.[74]

Although Kennedy could have been charged with involuntary homicide and given significant jail time, his attorneys suggested that any jail sentence should be suspended, and the prosecutors agreed, citing Kennedy's age, character, and prior reputation. After hearing their request, Boyle sentenced the senator to two months' incarceration, the statutory minimum for the offense. He then immediately suspended the sentence, citing Kennedy's "unblemished record" and stated his opinion that Ted had "already been, and will continue to be, punished far beyond anything this court can impose."[75] The entire proceeding took just seven minutes.

At 7:30 p.m., Kennedy appeared in the library of his parents' Hyannis Port home to explain what had happened. The crisis management team he had assembled at Hyannis in the wake of the accident had prepared a statement for him to deliver.[76] A crew from WHDH-TV was there to produce the national broadcast that was televised on all three major networks. More Americans tuned in than had watched Neil Armstrong take man's first step on the moon five days earlier.[77]

Seated at a table, dressed in a dark blue suit, Kennedy began by offering an explanation for his week-long silence. "Prior to my appearance in court it would have been improper for me to comment on these matters," he said. "But tonight I am free to tell you what happened and say what it means to me." Although he held the pages of the speech in his hand, Kennedy was actually reading cue cards held beneath the television camera. He was calm and articulate, but his presentation was at times mechanical, his expression distant.

Next he addressed his friendship with Kopechne. Speaking of her dedication to the Kennedy family, Ted called Mary Jo a "devoted campaign secretary" and "a gentle, kind and idealistic person." "There is no truth, no truth whatever to the widely circulated suspicions of immoral conduct that have been leveled at my behavior and hers regarding that evening," he said, addressing the rumors of a sexual tryst. "There has never been a private relationship between us of any kind." Kennedy went on to insist that he was "not driving under the influence of alcohol" and described his repeated attempts—and those of Gargan and Markham—to rescue Kopechne.

In addressing the nearly ten-hour time lapse in reporting the car crash, the senator admitted that he "regarded as indefensible the fact that I did not report the accident to the police immediately." He did offer an alibi, though. "My conduct and conversation during the next several hours [after the accident], to the extent that I can remember them, make no sense to me at all," he explained. "Although my doctors informed me that I suffered a cerebral concussion as well as shock, I do not seek to escape responsibility for my actions by placing the blame either on the physical, emotional trauma brought on by the accident or on anyone else." He also wondered whether "some awful curse actually did hang over all the Kennedys." Finally, Ted placed the papers he had been holding on the table, looked directly into the camera, and appealed to the people of Massachusetts to help him decide whether he should resign from office. "If at any time, the citizens of Massachusetts should lack confidence in their Senator's character or his ability, with or without justification, he could not in my opinion adequately perform his duties, and should not continue in office," said Kennedy. "The opportunity to work with you and serve Massachusetts has made my life worthwhile. So, I ask you tonight, the people of Massachusetts, to think this through with me. In facing this decision, I seek your advice and opinion. In making it I seek your prayers."

"Whatever is decided, whatever the future holds for me," he concluded, "I hope I shall be able to put this most recent tragedy behind me and make some future contribution to our state and mankind whether it be in public or private life."[78]

EMK appeared to win over public opinion, initially. The *Boston Globe* reported that the phone calls they received were "two-to-one in favor of Kennedy." Many Senate colleagues, including Thomas McIntyre of New Hampshire and Edmund Muskie of Maine, expressed their "trust" in Ted's version of the story. Even Gwen Kopechne told reporters that she was "satisfied with the senator's statement" and that she "hopes he decides to stay in the Senate."[79] Members of the press were more skeptical. While Steve Kurkjian of the *Boston Globe* admitted that Kennedy delivered a "very compelling statement" and "opened up to show his pain," the speech "left more questions than it answered."[80] Liz Trotta of NBC was more direct when asked about the speech decades later.

> We were being called upon to be super indulgent about the senator and what happened in that car. . . . By the time the television speech occurred there were expectations that questions would be answered. That surely they could not hold out this long. That they

> had to give a coherent story to satisfy all these questions—the car, the girl, what time she was in the car, what his movements were, what happened at the party, why he didn't report the accident immediately—we thought that some of these questions would be answered by the television speech. Of course, all the speech did was to further occlude the events and only add to the confusion and certainly to a deep skepticism that this thing was being rigged.[81]

Just as troubling was Kennedy's attempt to spin the story as another family tragedy. His reference to an "awful curse . . . over all the Kennedys" and his concluding remark about "putting this most recent tragedy behind me," sounded as if he was assuming the role of victim instead of offender. In addition, the brief mention of Mary Jo at the beginning of the speech was made in the larger context of her service to the Kennedy family and how he was offended by the rumors of a "personal relationship" between them. Never did Ted acknowledge that she was the victim of his poor judgment and irresponsibility. When that point was mentioned to Dun Gifford many years later, he dismissed it, emphasizing that the speech was a "political" one. "Ted Kennedy is a politician and a very good one," he explained. "It was a speech to his electorate. And if you understand that it was a political speech, then you have to admit that it was a good one."[82] If Gifford was correct, than he reinforced the popular suspicion that Kennedy's political survival was more important than any other consideration, including Kopechne's life.

Despite Ted Kennedy's attempts to put the Chappaquiddick affair in the past, rumors of foul play increased. The failure to conduct an autopsy gave rise to many of those suspicions. Stung by the criticism and facing reelection on the Democratic ticket, Edmund Dinis, district attorney of the Southern District of Massachusetts requested on July 31 an inquest into the death of Mary Jo Kopechne. Judge Boyle granted the request and originally set the date for September 3 but later postponed the inquest until January 5, 1970. In the interim, Dinis sought to have Mary Jo's body exhumed from its grave in Luzerne County, Pennsylvania.[83] But Joe and Gwen Kopechne refused to allow the exhumation and retained the legal services of Joseph Flanagan, a local attorney, to fight it.

"The Kopechnes were devout Catholics," recalled Flanagan in a 2010 interview. "They did not want the body exhumed for religious reasons. Gwen said many times that she and her husband would not have opposed an autopsy before the body was released in Massachusetts. But after the burial took place they didn't want Mary Jo's grave to be disturbed."[84]

On October 20–21, 1969, a Luzerne County Common Pease Court under presiding judge Bernard Brominski held a hearing on Dinis's request. Brominski eventually ruled against the exhumation, saying that there was "no evidence" that "anything other than drowning had caused the death."[85] Ten days later, the Massachusetts Supreme Court consented to the request of Kennedy's attorneys, barred the press and public from the inquest hearing, and ordered all documents pertaining to the Chappaquiddick accident impounded until after all possible prosecution against the senator ended.[86]

The inquest convened at Edgartown on January 5, 1970. It was not a criminal trial but rather a "fact-finding procedure" based on the remarks of the twenty-seven individuals who were called to give testimony. Among those who testified were Senator Kennedy, the five remaining Boiler Room Girls, Joe Gargan, Paul Markham, Charles Tretter, Jack Crimmins, John Farrar, Dr. Donald Mills, police chief Jim Arena, and his deputy, Christopher "Huck" Look.[87] Only Judge Boyle, who had also presided over the July 25 hearing in which Kennedy pled guilty to leaving the scene of an accident, or District Attorney Dinis could recommend that the case be reopened. At the end of the four-day inquest, Boyle stated the following conclusions in his report:

1. The accident occurred "between 11:30 p.m. on July 18 and 1:00 a.m. on July 19."
2. "Kopechne and Kennedy did *not* intend to drive to the ferry slip and his turn onto Dike Road had been intentional."
3. "A speed of twenty miles per hour as Kennedy testified to operating the car as large as his Oldsmobile would be at least negligent and possibly reckless."

4. "For some reason not apparent from [Kennedy's] testimony, he failed to exercise due care as he approached the bridge."
5. "There is probable cause to believe that Edward M. Kennedy operated his motor vehicle negligently . . . and that such operation appears to have contributed to the death of Mary Jo Kopechne."

It is important to note that Judge Boyle did *not* find Kennedy guilty of a crime, stating that there was only "probable cause" to believe he had acted negligently.[88] Although Boyle found no reason to pursue criminal proceedings, a Dukes County grand jury assembled on April 6, 1970, in a special session to investigate Kopechne's death. Judge Wilfred Paquet, who presided over the session, instructed the members of the grand jury that they could consider only matters brought to their attention by the superior court, the district attorney, or their personal knowledge. Nor was the grand jury permitted to see the evidence or Boyle's report from the inquest, which were still impounded. Frustrated by the restrictions, the grand jury called four witnesses who had not testified at the inquest. Their testimonies, conducted over a two-day period, took a total of twenty minutes. After considerable deliberation, Leslie Leland, the foreman, informed the judge, "We, the grand jury, have no presentments."[89]

"We were stymied by our inability to call important witnesses and to be allowed to read the inquest report," recalled Leland in a 2010 interview. "Today, the grand jury would have been able to subpoena everyone at the Kennedy party. Hard questions would have been asked. There wouldn't have been an inquest, especially a secret one. There would have been an open investigation. But at that time, Kennedy's people were able to change the rules. They made it a secretive hearing, when it was supposed to be an open one. It was a cover-up from beginning to end."[90]

Leland was not alone in his belief of a conspiracy to cover up the death of Mary Jo Kopechne.

6 Unanswered Questions

The inquest into Mary Jo Kopechne's death raised more questions than it answered because of the many inconsistencies in Senator Edward M. Kennedy's testimony. Those inconsistencies led more than a dozen writers to conclude that there was a conspiracy to cover up Kennedy's irresponsible behavior on the late night of July 18, 1969.[1] While the impulse behind such conspiracy theories is understandable, it does not mean that a conspiracy actually occurred. In fact, there is a difference between a *conspiracy* and a *conspiracy theory.*

According to *Black's Law Dictionary*, a conspiracy occurs when two or more persons join for the purpose of committing an unlawful or criminal act and it must be proven. But a conspiracy theory is an *unproven proposal* about a premeditated scheme. In other words, a conspiracy theory may or may not be true but can still result in hard measures to prevent potential criminal activity. Nor are conspiracy theories necessarily accurate. In fact, conspiracy theorists are often motivated by personal gain and extremely inflexible when new evidence surfaces to disprove their theory.[2] Based on this understanding, what happened at Chappaquiddick on July 18–20, 1969, was *not* a conspiracy. Nor did any of several conspiracy theories surrounding the events of that weekend ever prove to be accurate. Nevertheless, there are still questions about that weekend that have never been answered and probably never will.

Were Mary Jo Kopechne and Senator Edward Kennedy Having an Affair?

In the aftermath of Chappaquiddick, the tabloid press capitalized on the opportunity to increase sales by contending that Kopechne and Kennedy were romantically linked. Even some mainstream outlets made the same suggestion.[3] "There was absolutely nothing decent reported about our daughter," recalled Gwen Kopechne in a 1989 interview. "Her name was dragged through the mud."[4] Those scandalous impressions were reinforced over the next fifty years by many other writers as well as individuals who were involved in the Chappaquiddick tragedy.[5] On the twenty-fifth anniversary of the event in 1994, for example, the British Broadcasting Corporation produced a documentary titled *Investigative Reports: Chappaquiddick*. The film producers interviewed detective Bernie Flynn, who investigated the events of July 18, 1969. When asked for his opinion about the timeline of those events, Flynn said that Kennedy and Kopechne left the cottage before midnight because the senator "wanted to make love to Mary Jo." The detective supported his belief by pointing out that it was "over an hour from the time EMK left the party to 12:45 a.m. when his car was spotted by deputy sheriff, Huck Look on Cemetery Road, known by locals as 'Lovers' Lane.'"[6]

The BBC also interviewed Rosemary Keough, one of the Boiler Room Girls. Although Keough insisted that the relationships between the married men and single girls at the party were "not that way," she also contended that Mary Jo was "not a saint" but rather "a normal, red-blooded American girl like the rest of us." But she never explained what the difference was between a "saint" and a "normal, red-blooded American girl," leaving the suggestion that such a girl was the polar opposite of a saint.[7] Keough's ambiguity seemed to give credence to popular suspicions that there was an inappropriate relationship between Kennedy, a married man, and Kopechne, an unmarried woman.

In 2009 K. Dun Gifford, a Kennedy aide who assisted Gwen and Jo Kopechne in planning their daughter's funeral, seemed to suggest a third possibility. In a documentary produced by the *Boston Globe*, Gifford admitted that while he did not attend the gathering, he "certainly knew about partying with those who did" because he was the "head dog of the Boiler Room." That experience led Gifford to conclude that the party "wasn't like a bunch of nuns and priests, but it wasn't an orgy, either."[8] The response suggests that no one at the party or even those who knew both Kennedy and Kopechne well could with any certainty confirm or deny that they were having an affair.

On the other hand, Kennedy's wife, Joan, who was pregnant at the time of the event, called Chappaquiddick "the beginning of the end for

Ted and me." Until that point in their marriage, Joan genuinely believed that Ted had been faithful to her. But the events of the mid-July weekend confirmed, in her own mind, the rumors of her husband's infidelity. "I really tried telling myself that it didn't matter," Joan confessed to Marcia Chellis, author of *Living with the Kennedys*. "But I couldn't help wondering who might be with him. It hurt my feelings and it went to the core of my self-esteem."[9] What is unclear, however, is whether Joan was referring to the possibility of a sexual liaison between her husband and Mary Jo Kopechne or the *actual* affair he was having with Helga Wagner, a voluptuous, Austrian-born blonde who studied art at the Du Pont Royal Academy in Paris. One of the first phone calls Kennedy made after the accident was to Wagner, who was separated from a wealthy shipping tycoon and belonged to the international jet-set entourage that followed him at the time.[10]

"Ted Kennedy had such a reputation as a womanizer that the mere fact that he was alone with a woman in a car late at night on an isolated island would lead to the inevitable conclusion of an affair," wrote Laurence Leamer in his 2004 book *Sons of Camelot*. "But Ted could never raise the excuse that he was in love with Helga Wagner, and that Mary Jo was unlike the women to whom he was generally attracted." Kennedy, according to Leamer, "liked stunning, sexy women, and that was not Kopechne." Mary Jo had the "fresh good looks of a high school prom princess, pretty but not beautiful, educated but not sophisticated."[11] Leamer's belief is supported by another Kennedy biographer, Burton Hersh, who insisted that the straitlaced Kopechne "wasn't Ted's kind of girl." She was, according to Hersh, "pastier and tougher, intimidating in a quiet way," not at all like the kind of girl "Ted would hope to drag behind a dune and out in time for the midnight ferry."[12]

Even those within Kennedy's immediate circle claimed that an affair between the senator and Mary Jo was highly unlikely. "Mary Jo was not Edward Kennedy's type," insisted Melody Miller, who worked for both RFK and his younger brother. "She was not a glamour queen. She was not someone men would hit on." Miller even confessed that the women who worked for RFK gave Mary Jo the nickname "office virgin" and felt that the idea that Kopechne and Ted Kennedy were "going off to the beach for a tryst" was "absurd."[13]

Mary Jo's strong moral code and devout Catholic faith seem to corroborate these statements. She called herself a "novena Catholic," which meant that she was very devout in the practice of her faith, which considered adultery a mortal sin. Her friends testified to the fact that she was a young woman who was almost prudish in her rejection of obscene language, suggestive humor, and sexual impropriety. In addition, Kennedy did not even know her last name at the time of the accident; he referred to her simply as "Mary Jo" in his police statement and left the surname blank.[14] In fact, Kennedy could only recall speaking at length with Kopechne twice. He really did not know much about her.[15] Thus EMK's court testimony that he "never in [his] life had any personal relationship with Mary Jo Kopechne" appears to be accurate.[16] As far as Kennedy's case was concerned, however, it really didn't even matter if he was having an affair. The presumption of fornication would not be as damaging as the implication that he had so little regard for Mary Jo's life that he left her behind underwater to drown to eliminate the suggestion of intimacy with her.

Why Would Kopechne Leave Her Purse at Lawrence Cottage If She Was Returning to Her Edgartown Motel for the Night?

According to Kennedy's court testimony, he and Kopechne left the party about 11:15 p.m. to return to Edgartown on an evening ferry. Mary Jo, feeling ill because of too much sun, requested a ride from the senator, and he agreed since he was also calling it a night.[17] If that was true, why then did Kopechne leave her purse, including her driver's license and the key to her motel room, at Lawrence Cottage?

The inconsistency was one of many that haunted Joe and Gwen Kopechne for years after their daughter's tragic death. Ultimately, they chose to believe that Mary Jo, who seldom stayed up late, "left the party early and fell asleep in the back seat" of the Oldsmobile and that "she was not noticed at first by Kennedy and another woman from the party, who swam to safety after the accident."[18] The other female passenger was subsequently identified by Chappaquiddick conspiracy theorists as

Rosemary Keough, another Boiler Room Girl.[19] Keough's presence in the car was based on the fact that her pocketbook was retrieved from the front seat by diver John Farrar. The theory is also supported by Deputy Sheriff Huck Look's testimony that there were "two, possibly three people" in the Oldsmobile, which he spotted parked on Cemetery Road at 12:45 a.m.[20]

Speculation about her presence in the car must have caused enough embarrassment for Keough that she felt compelled to defend herself publicly over the years. On the first anniversary of the tragedy, she visited Mary Jo's grave in Larksville, Pennsylvania, bearing a basket of daisies, and told reporters, "My friend Mary Jo just happened to be in the wrong car at the wrong time with the wrong people." The word "people" suggested that Kennedy and Kopechne were not the only ones in the car that night. Keough repeated the remark four years later to the *Boston Globe* but refused to elaborate. According to Don Nelson, author of *Chappaquiddick Tragedy*, Keough's remark was "intentional." "She wished to confirm that Mary Jo was an unwilling, unintended, and unobserved passenger who happened to be sleeping off too much to drink in the rear seat when Kennedy's car plunged into Poucha Pond," Nelson argued.[21]

Keough, as mentioned earlier, gave an interview to the BBC in 1994 in which she appeared to discount her presence in the Oldsmobile. But she continued to insist that "whatever happened [happened] innocently in terms of people's intentions" and that she was speaking out because she hoped to "give Mr. and Mrs. Kopechne assurance" in their advancing years. Curiously, Keough also appeared to contradict her statement about "innocent intentions" when she remarked in that same interview that Mary Jo was "not a saint" but rather "a normal, red-blooded American girl like the rest of us."[22]

But James Lange and Katherine DeWitt reject the theory of a third passenger in their book *Chappaquiddick*, pointing out that if Mary Jo was asleep in the back seat, she would not have been visible to deputy sheriff Look. Nor did Keough have any injuries to confirm her presence in the front passenger seat, where she would have suffered abrasions if not open cuts from shattered glass. Most damning, why would Kennedy leave himself open to charges of manslaughter if a witness existed who could confirm his innocence? All of these factors, according to Lange and DeWitt, "tend to support Kennedy's version of the events."[23]

Was Kennedy Drunk When He Left the Party with Mary Jo?

Kennedy told the *Boston Globe* that he drove off Dike Bridge not because he was intoxicated but because he was confused. He thought he was driving in the direction of the ferry, not away from it. There were no lights or signs to alert a nighttime driver to the bridge, which was at an odd angle to the road. By the time EMK knew what was happening, it was too late.[24] Kennedy's court testimony indicated that his drinking was limited to one beer and four rum and cokes before the party actually started at 9:00 p.m. Joseph Gargan's testimony appeared to corroborate Kennedy's. Gargan admitted that during the party he saw the senator "on a couple of occasions with a glass in his hand," but he expressed uncertainty over whether the "dark fluid" he observed in the glass was rum and coke or simply Coca-Cola. In addition, those present at the party insisted that the "drinking was moderate" with the women having a total of nine or ten drinks among the six of them, and the men, including Kennedy, having a total of just six drinks among them.[25]

But these testimonies do not square with the account of Foster Silvia, who lived just a hundred yards from the cottage and was disturbed by loud noise, which often accompanies heavy drinking. Silvia told Les Leland, the grand jury foreman, that the partygoers were "damned loud" and that "by 1:00 a.m. he was so disturbed by all the noise" that he was "ready to call the police."[26] Nor is the court testimony of the partygoers consistent with the actual amount of alcohol that was consumed that evening.

Indeed, there was considerable alcohol at Lawrence Cottage that night. Jack Crimmins, Kennedy's chauffeur, admitted in court that he "purchased . . . three half-gallons of Vodka, four fifths of Scotch, two bottles of rum and several cases of canned beer." After the party, Crimmins said he removed two bottles of vodka, three of scotch, and the beer.[27] Based on the court testimony, Lester David, author of *Good Ted, Bad Ted*, calculated that "a half gallon of vodka, a fifth of scotch and two bottles of rum were consumed" by the partygoers, or a "total of 93.8 drinks with an average of 7.8 drinks per person." If the average drink contained 1.5 ounces of alcohol," than the twelve partygoers consumed a total of 140.8 ounces of liquor that evening. That leaves 77.9 drinks or 116.8 ounces of liquor unaccounted for, if the court testimony of the partygoers is to be believed.[28]

If Ted Kennedy was drunk when he got behind the wheel of his 1967 Oldsmobile, then the accident at Dike Bridge was the result of intoxication, which is a crime. But we will never know if Kennedy was drunk when he left the party because he did not appear at the Edgartown Police Station until ten hours after the accident. Even if he took a breathalyzer test at that time, the results would have been inconclusive because alcohol expires from the body at the rate of 1.5 ounces every two hours. It would also be difficult to determine if Kennedy's judgment and his ability to function was impaired by the amount of alcohol he did consume. Body weight, tolerance, and food consumption before drinking are all significant factors in determining the effects of alcohol on a drinker. In 1969 Massachusetts law considered a reading of 0.15 percent blood alcohol evidence of driving while intoxicated. For Kennedy, who weighed 220 pounds and had a high tolerance for liquor, the percentage necessary for him to become intoxicated was probably much higher than 0.15.[29]

On the other hand, Mary Jo, who weighted just 110 pounds and had an extremely low tolerance for alcohol because she rarely drank, would be considerably affected by the amount of alcohol she consumed. When Dr. John J. McHugh, the Massachusetts state police chemist, tested the alcohol content of Kopechne's blood after the accident, it measured 0.09 percent. That level of alcohol "would be consistent with about 3.75 to 5 ounces of 80 to 90 proof liquor within one hour of death," according to McHugh's court testimony. Under these circumstances, Mary Jo would not only have been intoxicated, but her inhibitions lower and her decision making and judgment severely impaired.[30]

Was Mary Jo Driving the 1967 Oldsmobile When It Crashed?

Kopechne's high blood-alcohol level led Jack Olsen, the first writer to publish an account of the Chappaquiddick tragedy, to propose the theory that Mary Jo—not Ted Kennedy—was driving the car when it crashed into Poucha Pond. Olsen, in his 1970 book *The Bridge at Chappaquiddick*, argues that Kennedy panicked when deputy sheriff Look spotted him and Kopechne on Cemetery Road. To avoid the appearance of an affair, the senator got out of the car, directed Mary Jo to drive on and circle back to pick him up. Kopechne, tipsy and unfamiliar with the geography as well as the car, drove off Dike Bridge.[31]

This theory was given credibility by David Guay, an undertaker's assistant who embalmed Kopechne's body. According to Guay, the body bore "no cuts or bruises, no puncture wounds, no lacerations, no broken bones, no broken teeth, no broken finger nails."[32] The observation is significant because if Kopechne was the front seat passenger instead of the driver, she would have sustained severe injury according to Robert DuBois, a crash analyst who was interviewed by the BBC in 1994. "The right hand passenger seat was the worst place for [Mary Jo] to be in that car because everything would be landing on her at once from a number of different directions," said DuBois. "The fact that her body had no superficial injuries is just remarkable to me because the window on the passenger side breaks into 'popcorn-sized' pieces of glass shards which will result 'dicing,' or deep cuts." Because Kopechne's body was unscathed, DuBois concluded that she "had to be somewhere else other than the front passenger seat" and that it was "conceivable that she could escape injury if she was the driver."[33]

But Lange and DeWitt also discredit this theory, insisting that EMK was the driver. They explain that "the pressure of the water acted on Kennedy, next to the open driver's side window, like pressure of carbon dioxide on the cork of a champagne bottle, forcing him through the window." Kennedy's physical injuries, including a concussion, combined with the action of being washed out of the car, according to the authors, "explain why he maintained he didn't know how he got out of the car." There is also the issue of logic: "Why would Kennedy say he was driving the car when he could have contended that he got out and let Mary Jo drive?" Under those circumstances, she would have been responsible for her own death and he would have avoided any penalty.[34]

Would Mary Jo Have Survived If Kennedy Had Reported the Accident Immediately?

Donald R. Mills, the associate medical examiner for Dukes County who examined Kopechne's corpse, does not believe she would have survived if Kennedy had reported the accident immediately. His ruling that she died of drowning was supported by Arthur Little, Inc., a New England consulting firm hired by Kennedy to do a "physical factors" study of the accident.[35] Using a car similar to Kennedy's 1967 Oldsmobile, the firm concluded that breathable air drained quickly from the car and that Kopechne could not have remained conscious more than four minutes, nor lived for more than fourteen minutes. Several writers agree with this conclusion, contending that Mary Jo drowned almost immediately after the car plunged into Poucha Pond.[36]

But John Farrar, the scuba diver who recovered Kopechne's lifeless body, insists that she did not drown but managed to find an air pocket in the back wheel well of the Oldsmobile and slowly suffocated over the course of "three or four hours."[37] In an August 20, 1969, interrogation by Lt. George Killen of the Massachusetts State Police in advance of the inquest, Farrar, according to his measurements, contended Kennedy's Oldsmobile skidded thirty-six feet before dropping eight feet into Poucha Pond, hitting the water at a forty-five-degree angle. "The momentum flipped the car over, bringing it to settle upside down in the water," he explained. "On impact, the water would have gushed through the two right windows. However, due to the vertical settling of the car, a large amount of air would have initially been trapped underneath the floor of the car."

Farrar pointed to a diagram (fig. 24), which shows "a possible water level based on the way the car entered the water and settled." The sketch also shows that the air pocket was large enough to have sustained life for a while. According to Farrar, the position of Mary Jo's body in the right rear seat wheel well suggested that she may have been trying desperately to take advantage of the last air. "With respect to the seat,

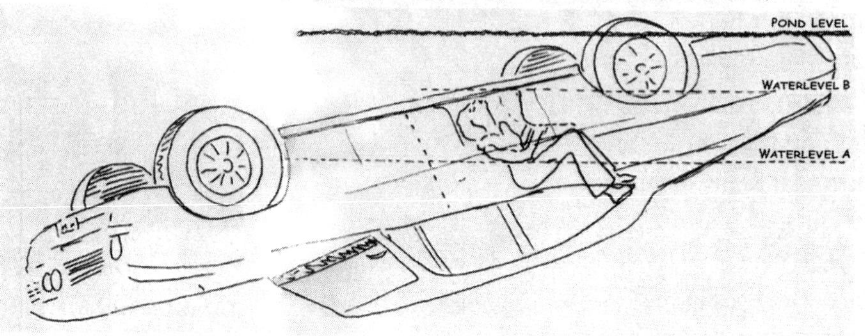

24. Water levels in submerged car, according to diver John Farrar, who retrieved Kopechne's body. Diagram 14. Edgartown District Court, *Inquest into the Death of Mary Jo Kopechne*.

she was upside down," recalled the diver. "With respect to the water, she was right side up. Her head was cocked back, her face pressed into the foot well. This is where the air bubble likely would have formed."

Farrar believed that Mary Jo's position in the submerged car was "consciously assumed," and was "indicative of a person who was consciously aware" while trying to "obtain her last breath of air." The fact that air bubbles emanated from the car when the tow truck driver removed it from Poucha Pond—two hours after Farrar extricated Kopechne's body—and the fact that there was a large air void and lack of water in the car's trunk ten hours after the accident led the diver to the conclude that he "could have had her out of that car [in] 25 minutes" if he had received a phone call.[38] Despite Farrar's belief that Kopechne could have been saved, we'll never know for sure.

Why Didn't Kennedy Stop at One of the Four Cottages along the Route Back to the Party to Call for Help?

When asked at the inquest why he failed to stop at any house to seek help on his return journey to Lawrence cottage from the scene of the accident, Kennedy said that he "never saw a cottage with a light on."[39] But his testimony was challenged by Sylvia Malm, who resided about 450 feet away from Dike Bridge. Once out of the water, Kennedy could have reached the Malm house in a matter of seconds. Sylvia Malm, who was seventeen at the time, recalled in a 1994 interview that there was in fact a night light on downstairs in the living room that was visible from the bridge side of the house. She also stated that the family had two dogs that would have barked if anyone knocked on the front door. But Sylvia and her parents heard nothing until 8:30 a.m. the following morning, when the two fishermen knocked of their door to have them report the accident.[40]

In addition, the Chappaquiddick fire station, located near Lawrence Cottage, was lit all night. Even if Kennedy was so disoriented from the accident that he could not see the fire station's light, Gargan and Markham, who returned to the accident scene and attempted to rescue Kopechne, surely would have noticed it.[41] But Gargan, in court testimony, claimed that he didn't even think of seeking help because he "felt there was only one thing to do and that was to get into the car and as quickly as possible, because I knew if I did not, there wasn't a chance in the world of saving Mary Jo."[42]

Why Did Kennedy Fail to Report the Accident until Saturday Morning, Nearly Ten Hours after It Occurred?

The question of timing is the most critical factor in determining the truth about the Chappaquiddick tragedy. According to Kennedy's court testimony, he left Lawrence Cottage at 11:15 p.m. on the evening of Friday, July 18, to drive himself and Kopechne to the ferry; he mistakenly turned right onto Dike Road and headed in the direction of the beach, instead of bearing hard left on Main Street to return to the ferry; and after proceeding for approximately one-half mile on Dike Road, he descended a hill, came upon the narrow Dike Bridge, and inadvertently drove the car off the bridge into Poucha Pond.

If the accident occurred between 11:30 p.m. and 11:45 p.m., the senator gave the following account of the next two hours and forty-five minutes. He insisted that after surviving the accident he spent fifteen minutes trying to rescue Mary Jo and another fifteen minutes laying exhausted on the bank before returning to Lawrence Cottage, which was at least a fifteen-minute walk. Kennedy then testified that he returned to the scene of the accident in the rented Plymouth Valiant with Joe Gargan and Paul Markham, who spent another forty-five minutes in another unsuccessful attempt to rescue Kopechne. After, the three men drove to the ferry landing where, according to Markham, there was a ten-minute discussion. Then Kennedy decided impulsively to swim across the channel to Edgartown, which took another ten minutes. When he reached the shore, he testified that he walked around for another fifteen minutes before returning to his hotel room. EMK estimated that it took him thirty minutes to change clothes and rest before going downstairs to ask the desk clerk Russell Peachey for the time, which was 2:30 a.m.[43]

But Kennedy's court testimony is at odds with that of Deputy sheriff Huck Look, who spotted a car matching the description and license plate of the senator's 1967 Oldsmobile parked in Cemetery Road at 12:45 a.m.[44] That would place the accident about 1:00 a.m. Thus Kennedy's accounting of the next two hours and forty-five minutes would place his conversation with Peachey about 3:45 a.m., making it clear that some of the events he described could not have taken place within the time frame he established in court.

Even if the accident occurred within Kennedy's timetable, which would be about 11:45 p.m., why did it take him ten hours to report it to police chief Jim Arena sometime between 9:45 and 10:00 a.m. the following morning? "I was exhausted and in a state of shock," Kennedy explained in his seventeen-minute, nationally televised speech on July 25:

> My doctors informed me that I suffered a cerebral concussion as well as shock. Instead of looking directly for a telephone, after lying exhausted in the grass for an undetermined time, I walked back to the cottage where the party was being held and requested the help of two friends, my cousin Joseph Gargan and [Boston lawyer] Paul Markham, and directed them to return immediately to the scene

> with me—this was sometime after midnight—in order to undertake a new effort to dive down and locate Miss Kopechne. Their strenuous efforts, undertaken at some risk to their own lives, also proved futile.

Over the next ten hours, Kennedy recalled fighting a terrible inner tumult, wondering "whether the girl might still be alive somewhere out of that immediate area, whether some awful curse did actually hang over all the Kennedys, whether there was some justifiable reason for me to doubt what had happened and to delay my report, whether somehow the awful weight of the incredible instant might in some way pass from my shoulders. I was overcome by a jumble of emotion—grief, fear, doubt, exhaustion, panic, confusion, and shock." Not until the next morning, "with my mind somewhat more lucid," did Ted report the accident at the police station.[45]

If Kennedy was suffering from a concussion, why didn't Gargan and Markham report the accident to the Edgartown police? Both were members of the Massachusetts bar and understood the legal necessity of reporting an accident with bodily injury. Both must have realized that Kennedy had suffered a concussion, that he was not thinking clearly, and that he was unable to report the accident himself. If nothing else, did they not feel a moral obligation to report the accident? "I can't envision any three people who can go to bed and sleep for five or six hours knowing that there's a dead body floating around in a car in that pond," said detective Bernie Flynn, who investigated the accident for Dukes County district attorney Edmund Dinis.[46]

Why Didn't Police Chief Jim Arena Detain Kennedy When He Discovered the Senator Did Not Have His Driver's License?

According to Leo Damore, the author of *Senatorial Privilege*, Kennedy, in "failing to produce a license, was in clear violation of the law." Massachusetts law required every driver to have possession of a license or easy access to one. Failure to comply allowed police to arrest the offender without warrant and keep him in custody for twenty-four hours. In addition, Arena was "bending enforcement to a breaking point by not pressing the charge" as well as by letting Kennedy go without explaining his delay in reporting the accident, something the statement did not do.[47]

Nor did Arena ever ask Kennedy about his consumption of alcohol. He didn't even know about the party until he read about it in the newspapers on Sunday, July 20. Arena also admitted he never questioned any of the guests at the party, learning after the fact that the five remaining Boiler Room girls had been registered at the Katama Shores Motor Inn in Edgartown and that they had hurriedly checked out on Saturday morning, July 19.[48] "Nobody asked me to come in and talk," recalled Rosemary Keough, who corroborated that fact in a 1994 interview. "Nobody asked me to answer any questions. I think people were informed of where we were and I think people were also informed that we were leaving." As a result of all these oversights, Damore concludes that the Edgartown police chief was out of his depth, handling the matter like "a routine traffic case."[49]

Why Was No Autopsy Performed on the Body of Mary Jo?

Donald Mills, the medical examiner, could not provide a clear answer for this question. According to Massachusetts law, an autopsy must be conducted in cases where death is obviously not the result of natural causes. In fact, John Farrar, the diver who retrieved Kopechne's body, anticipated that Mills would do an autopsy because "there were so many questions as to the cause of death." Similarly, Eugene Frieh, director of the Martha's Vineyard Funeral Home, who released Mary Jo's body to her family, "expected an autopsy to be done because of the type of accident, the people involved and the insurance."[50] There were also indications that Mills himself expected to do an autopsy. According to Farrar, after the physician examined Kopechne's body for bruises or cuts and found none, he turned to the diver and remarked, "It looks like a simple drowning, John, but I wouldn't worry because the autopsy will tell."[51]

However, when Mills phoned Edmund Dinis, district attorney for the Southern District of Massachusetts, to ask for permission, Dinis, torn between his legal duty and his sympathy for Ted Kennedy, discouraged the autopsy. Mills, according to his colleague Dr. Robert

Nevins, explained that Dinis instructed him to "be a good guy and don't obstruct the Kennedys. . . . Play the game and you won't have any problems." But Mills "felt that an autopsy was in order and that certain inevitable questions were going to be asked that could be answered more appropriately by an autopsy."[52]

Instead, Mills released a statement to the press saying that he was "fully satisfied with my diagnosis of accidental drowning" and that he "notified the district attorney's office that no autopsy was necessary."[53] The statement would later return to haunt Mills as rumors of a conspiracy and the suggestion that Mary Jo was pregnant surfaced shortly after she was laid to rest on July 22.[54] Public pressure on Dinis became so intense that he launched an investigation to eliminate any question of foul play. As part of that investigation, Dinis petitioned the Common Pleas Court of Luzerne County, Pennsylvania, where Mary Jo was buried, to exhume her body so an autopsy could be performed.[55]

Initially, Mary Jo's parents were in favor of the exhumation, believing that it was "the only way to clear their daughter's reputation." They had been inundated with "snide remarks" from anonymous phone callers and "vicious mail" attacking their daughter for an alleged affair with Ted Kennedy and ruining his chance to become president. Devastated by the hurtful accusations and salacious innuendo, Joe Kopechne retreated inward, preferring to be alone. But Gwen was insulted by the rumors that her daughter was pregnant and insisted on an autopsy to disprove that notion. "I know there are a lot of sick people in the world and we should expect a little bit of vicious mail," she told the *Evening News* of Newark, New Jersey, on July 24. "But we don't know how to handle it. If an autopsy is the only way to clear my daughter, than I would like to have it performed."[56] Two days later, however, Gwen did an about-face. After listening to Kennedy's nationally televised account of the Chappaquiddick tragedy and its impact on his future, she abandoned her wish for the autopsy. Instead, she stated that she was "satisfied" with the senator's statement, appreciated the fact that the Kennedy's had treated her daughter like "a member of the family," and saw no need for the exhumation or the autopsy.[57]

In August the Kopechnes hired attorney Joseph Flanagan, a partner in the Kingston, Pennsylvania, legal firm of Flanagan, Doran, Biscontini, and Shaffer, to block Dinis's motion for exhumation. "There were religious reasons for their decision," recalled Flanagan in a 2010 interview. "Gwen and Joe Kopechne were devout Catholics. They said many times that they would not have objected to the autopsy before the body was released in Massachusetts. But after the burial took place they did not want her grave to be disturbed."[58] Gwen Kopechne told Suzanne James of *McCall's Magazine* a slightly different story, though. She explained that the couple would have still agreed to the exhumation if they believed that "foul play had been the cause of Mary Jo's death" and that "an autopsy would yield new evidence." Ultimately, the Kopechnes' decision was based on the "thought of [exhumation] being grossly offensive to us." "It would have been like a second funeral," Gwen added.[59]

On October 21, 1969, a Luzerne County Common Pleas Court under President Judge Bernard C. Brominski ruled against the exhumation, saying that there was "no evidence" that "anything other than drowning had caused the death."[60] Twenty years later, the Luzerne County judge acknowledged the conspiracy theories that emerged in the intervening years and that some even accused him of a cover-up to save Ted Kennedy's political career. But he insisted that "based on the facts that were presented to me at the time, I felt quite comfortable then, as I do now, that I made the proper adjudication."[61] Brominski's ruling came as a relief to the Kopechnes. "This means that I can go back to [Pennsylvania] and visit my daughter," Gwen told the press. "I could not face going to the cemetery if I had known the grave had been disturbed."[62]

There are two individuals who still believe that the Kopechnes were manipulated into abandoning the autopsy. Donald McFadden, the special investigator retained by the couple's lawyer, claims that the "Kennedy circle closed ranks after Mary Jo's body was discovered." "Dun Gifford, an aide to Ted Kennedy, made sure no autopsy was conducted by having the body flown to the Kielty Funeral home in Plymouth, [Pennsylvania], where he remained two full days before the burial," he explained. "Other members of Kennedy's inner circle skirted many of the legal procedures that must be done once a body is discovered. It was all damage control." At the end of his investigation, McFadden concluded that "everything Kennedy and his aides did the night of the accident and in the days immediately after was a cover-up to preserve his chances of becoming president."[63] Leslie Leland, the foreman of the grand jury for the inquest, supports McFadden's conclusion:

> After Mary Jo's body was returned to Pennsylvania, Dun Gifford, an aide to Ted Kennedy, descended on the Kopechne home and took charge. He claimed that he was there to help them through the tragedy, but he was actually there to control all communication with friends, neighbors the media and anyone else who tried to contact the couple. Not only did Gifford shield them from every contact, but monitored every phone call. He manipulated all the information supplied to Gwen and Joe relating to the accident, going so far as to keep them from reading the newspapers. They were purposely kept in the dark. And he made sure that the Kennedy team knew everything that was going on. It was damage control.[64]

Naturally, Dun Gifford rejected any notion that he manipulated Gwen and Joe Kopechne in the days after their daughter's death. Gifford insisted that his role was to "help Mary Jo's parents get through a very difficult time in whatever way I possibly could." When asked about the couple's change of mind on having an autopsy, Gifford said that it was "a matter of religious conviction, personal conviction and moral judgement." "I know how strongly they felt about not doing the autopsy because I listened to them talk about it many times," he explained. "They came to the decision that what was done was done. Nothing was going to bring their daughter back, and the best way to handle it was to leave it in God's hands."[65]

Even if Gifford was telling the truth and McFadden's and Leland's allegations of a conspiracy are baseless, it is still unclear why Mills did not conduct the autopsy in the first place. Was he strong-armed by District Attorney Edmund Dinis, as his colleague Dr. Robert Nevins suggested? If so, why would Dinis, who wanted to protect Kennedy, change his mind and petition the Luzerne County Court to exhume

Kopechne's body if there was even a remote possibility that an autopsy would reveal foul play?

Why Wasn't Ted Kennedy Charged with Manslaughter?

Massachusetts law requires a hearing whenever a person is killed in an accident. State law also requires the prosecution to bring an action for criminal manslaughter in those cases.[66] Edgartown police chief Jim Arena was aware that a manslaughter charge was mandatory. Special prosecutor Walter Steele was also aware of that fact. But Steele, in a 1994 interview, admitted that he was "going to be very careful" and "not seek criminal complaints that could not be substantiated with evidence." He also made an important distinction by explaining that in 1969 manslaughter "required willful, wanton and reckless conduct, not *after* the accident, but at the time of the accident." In other words, if Kennedy had been driving while intoxicated and at a speed of ninety miles per hour in a congested area, the manslaughter charge would have been pursued. But Steele insisted that the prosecution did "not have the evidence to prove those conditions," so the "highest complaint appropriate was leaving the scene of an accident with bodily injury."[67]

On July 25 Kennedy appeared in Dukes County Court in Edgartown and pled guilty to leaving the scene of an accident involving bodily injury. After hearing a partial statement of the facts, Judge Boyle asked police chief Jim Arena if there had been "a deliberate attempt to conceal the identity of the defendant." Arena replied, "Not to my knowledge, Your Honor," and was immediately excused from the witness stand. Boyle never asked Kennedy why he hadn't reported the accident sooner. Nor did he charge the senator with involuntary manslaughter, which carried a jail sentence of up to twenty years.[68] Instead, Boyle accepted Kennedy's plea to leaving the scene, sentenced him to two months' incarceration (the statutory minimum for that offense), and granted the request of EMK's attorneys that any jail sentence should be suspended due to Kennedy's age, character, and prior reputation.[69]

Within days of the ruling, there was public pressure on District Attorney Edmund Dinis, a Democrat up for reelection, to pursue a full inquest into the death of Mary Jo Kopechne. The media also descended on Leslie Leland, a twenty-nine-year-old Edgartown pharmacist, to ask him if he intended to exercise his right as foreman of the grand jury to call for an investigation. Leland contacted Dinis to ask about his responsibilities as foreman and to request that the district attorney take the lead in the investigation. But Dinis stalled until August 8, when Judge Boyle scheduled the inquest hearing for September 3. He promised to keep Leland informed but emphasized that he did not want to involve the grand jury.[70] Years later Dinis admitted to the *National Enquirer* that there was "no question in [his] mind that the grand jury would have brought an indictment against Ted Kennedy for manslaughter if I had given them the case."[71]

Leland believes that Dinis wanted not only to insure his own reelection but also to protect Kennedy. "Calling for an inquest was not the proper course of action," he said in a 2010 interview. "A hearing is automatic. Walter Steele, the prosecutor, was obligated to bring action against Kennedy for criminal manslaughter because Mary Jo was killed in the accident. The law is clear on that point. Instead, Dinis circumvented the law by calling for an inquest, which is nothing more than a fact-finding mission." Leland also insists that Kennedy's circle of lawyers controlled the timing as well as the actual proceeding of the inquest. That is why Judge Boyle postponed the hearing until January 5, why the Massachusetts Supreme Court "barred the press, the grand jury, the public and even the Kopechnes from the inquest hearing," and why the transcript and other court documents were "impounded until all possible prosecution against Kennedy ended."[72] Apparently, Dinis was not the only one who wanted to protect Kennedy.

A few days after the accident, police chief Jim Arena and prosecutor Walter Steele had a private meeting with Leland and registered the following three points: 1) Kennedy risked his life to rescue Kopechne after the crash; 2) the accident was yet another stroke of misfortune for a family that has given great service to the nation; and 3) every aspect of the accident was covered in the investigation and everyone came to the same conclusion that it was an accidental drowning. "It was obvious that they wanted to impress upon me that there was no reason for any further investigation," said Leland, "absolutely no reason whatsoever for the grand jury to get involved."[73]

During the inquest hearing in January 1970, Judge Boyle also protected Kennedy. Not only did Boyle refuse to challenge any part of the Massachusetts senator's testimony despite obvious inconsistencies, but he also attempted to undermine Deputy Sheriff Huck Look's identification of EMK's car the night of the accident and to disallow testimony related to the speed of the car and the possibility that Kopechne suffocated rather than drowned. Interestingly, Boyle resigned from his judgeship on February 19, 1970, the day after he filed his report of the inquest with the Superior Court of Suffolk County. Although he did not offer a reason for his decision to resign, Boyle, just sixty-three years old and in good health, was "embarrassed" by his ruling, according to Don Nelson, author of *Chappaquiddick Tragedy*. The judge's protection of Kennedy by "disallowing, even expunging testimony" was "so inconsistent with his reputation for fairness and honesty" that it can "only be understood as resulting from phoned threats from Boston" (i.e., the Massachusetts Supreme Judicial Court). Thus Boyle's decision to resign, claims Nelson, was a matter of "shame" for "failing to follow his own expressed duty of issuing process against anyone likely guilty of negligence."[74]

Unsettled by the haunting belief that "Kennedy was treated with kid gloves" by local law enforcement, Leland requested the reconvening of the grand jury. Between the time of his written request on March 17, 1970, and the reconvening of the grand jury on April 6, 1970, the Edgartown pharmacist received two anonymous phone calls threatening the lives of his wife and children if he pursued any further inquiry into the Chappaquiddick tragedy.[75] Despite the fact that Massachusetts state law empowers the grand jury to ask questions, call any witnesses it desires, and view any documents, impounded or not, Judge Wilfred J. Paquet told the jurors they were not allowed to subpoena any of the twenty-six witnesses who had already testified at the earlier inquest hearing.[76] Those witnesses included Kennedy, Gargan, Markham, and the five surviving Boiler Room Girls who attended the Chappaquiddick party. When they were denied, the jurors requested to see the transcripts of the witnesses' testimony from the inquest, but Paquet denied that request as well. Dinis, who served as the grand jury's legal counsel, refused to challenge either of judge's decisions.[77]

Due to these obstacles, the jurors only heard the testimonies of four witnesses: Stephen Gentle, owner and manager of the Edgartown airport; Nina Trott, reservations manager at the Shiretown Inn where Kennedy stayed; Benjamin Hall, who lived across the street from the Shiretown Inn and might have seen Kennedy return to the hotel after he supposedly swam across the channel; and Robert J. Carroll, a former Democratic selectman who was rumored to have flown Kennedy off the island in the early morning after the accident to his summer home at Hyannis Port on Cape Cod, and then flown him back to Martha's Vineyard. None of the witnesses offered any relevant testimony over the course of the two-day session. Having reached no presentments, the jurors were dismissed, and the case was officially closed.[78]

"It was a cover-up from beginning to end," Leland insisted. "There was never a chance to try Kennedy for manslaughter. We were stymied by our inability to call important witnesses, and to be allowed to read the inquest report. All the jurors felt the same way. It wasn't just me." He confessed many years later, "Throughout the ordeal, I did a lot of soul searching and my thoughts always went to Gwen and Joseph Kopechne. Mary Jo was their daughter. Their only child. And I felt badly for them. Then my thoughts went to Ted Kennedy, who was only trying to protect his political career. I was never able to understand how the sympathy for him and his loss of a chance at the presidency could have overshadowed the sad tragedy of a young lady who lost her life when it might possibly have been saved."[79]

Broken Hearts 7

To outlive one's child by more than thirty years is not only a painful anomaly but the cruelest fate a parent can experience. Most children, in adulthood, validate the love and selfless commitment parents invest in their upbringing by establishing successful careers, raising families of their own and caring for their parents in old age. But Mary Jo Kopechne was taken from her parents so early in life that they were robbed of those precious rewards. The loss was especially difficult for Joe and Gwen because they had been fully active in their daughter's upbringing and remained extremely close to Mary Jo after she left home. Brokenhearted, the couple tried desperately to hold themselves together in the weeks and months following their daughter's death.

Initially, Gwen suppressed her grief with Valium. Mary Jo's death was more than she could bear. Nothing spared her. Even sleep did not offer much of a refuge because when she awoke, the hard reality of her daughter's death immediately returned to haunt her. "I was completely out of it," she admitted in a 1989 interview with *Ladies' Home Journal*. "My husband was the one who had to cope."[1] While Joe tried mightily to be strong for his wife, he was just as devastated by Mary Jo's death. Unlike most fathers of his generation, Joe had participated in her education, spiritual development, and recreational activities. Like Gwen, Joe loved his daughter unconditionally and was proud of her every achievement. But Gwen was a strict disciplinarian, while Joe was easier on his "little girl." As a result, father and daughter had a special affinity for each other. After Mary Jo's death, Joe seemed to lose interest in life. Haunted by Chappaquiddick, he was unable to sleep, lost considerable weight, and became physically ill for several years.[2]

What was truly unconscionable, however, was the additional suffering the couple were forced to endure at the hands of journalists who made

Ted Kennedy the victim of the Chappaquiddick tragedy and Mary Jo the offender. She was slandered as an adulteress who cost the Massachusetts senator the opportunity to become president of the United States.[3] The lies and innuendo were not limited to the tabloid press, either. In the weeks following Chappaquiddick, the mainstream press treated Kopechne just as unfairly. Nationally syndicated columnist Jack Anderson wrote that Kennedy "invited pretty, young Mary Jo to join him for a midnight swim and they set out on a nocturnal adventure not uncommon on Martha's Vineyard."[4] Rowland Evans and Robert Novak, also syndicated Washington columnists, made Kennedy a victim, blaming Kopechne for destroying his chance at becoming president.[5] James Reston, editor of the *New York Times*, went even further, calling Ted Kennedy's July 25 televised speech to the nation "a kind of tragic profile in courage."[6] In fact, of all the major newspapers, the *Times* published editorials that were the most sympathetic toward Ted Kennedy, emphasizing the tragedy narrative.[7]

At the same time, there were also ugly rumors that Mary Jo had been estranged from her parents. That Gwen and Joe did not want an autopsy because they had something to hide. That the couple received a considerable financial windfall from Ted Kennedy after Mary Jo's death. That Joe, now set for life, quit his job, and that the couple took an extravagant vacation to Bermuda and were building an expensive home in the Pocono Mountains of northeast Pennsylvania.[8] The rumors resulted in a steady flow of malicious letters.[9]

Some of these letters were mailed to the Kopechnes in the late summer and autumn of 1969, others in 1970, and a few on the anniversary of Chappaquiddick in 1971 and 1972. What is so astonishing about the letter writers is that they had no apparent association with Mary Jo or her parents, choosing instead to base their opinions and advice on the innuendo surrounding her relationship with the Kennedy family in general and Ted Kennedy in particular. One writer, who identified himself as "a Boston native," insisted that there was a conspiracy to kill Mary Jo because she "was pregnant" and "threatened Kennedy that she would tell his wife." To prevent that, the senator "sent the car into the water, jumping out before it went off the bridge." The writer considered Kennedy a "lying skunk" and pleaded with the Kopechnes to "let them do an autopsy" and "put him where he belongs—in jail."[10]

Others accused the Kopechnes of accepting hush money from Kennedy. A writer from New Bedford, Massachusetts, called the couple "the most despised persons in the country" for accepting "that mighty Kennedy dollar."[11] "Did you get money?" asked another writer, who strongly suggested that the Kopechnes were paid off. "Then shame on you!"[12] An anonymous writer from Evansville, Indiana, asked, "Do you really believe the blood-stained money Kennedy is paying you will ever make you happy? If anyone else killed your daughter they would be in jail, but the Kennedy money talks!"[13]

Still other letters were addressed specifically to Gwen and accused her of being a negligent mother. "I have read so much about Mary Jo that it breaks my heart to think how you as her mother can still say, 'no autopsy,'" began a letter from Sturbridge, Massachusetts. "Did it ever occur to you that Mary Jo would want you to have [the autopsy]?"[14] Another letter absolved Kennedy of any wrongdoing and suggested that Gwen should have been a better mother by preventing Mary Jo from leading a promiscuous lifestyle:

> Mrs. Kopechne:
>
> I was really "floored" by your latest remarks that you want Ted to explain. Explain what? It was just an accident. Aren't you a little late concerning yourself about Mary Jo? Why was she allowed to lead her life freely with no parental supervision? Couldn't she have been at home and employed there? Do you know who she was with—who was in her life—before Ted drove her that night? You are not only casting aspersions on Ted, but also on your daughter's morals, too. Let your daughter rest in peace. Do not destroy her memory.
>
> A Mother[15]

Joe and Gwen struggled with the hate mail as well as with the rumors about Mary Jo and the many questions that remained unanswered about her death. They had hoped the inquest hearing would end their doubts, but it didn't. Instead, the media pressured the couple to speak out publicly, offering significant financial remuneration to do so. But the couple remained silent until September 1970, when they agreed to speak with Suzanne James of *McCall's Magazine*, which later published the six-page interview. In that interview, the couple revealed the following points:

The stories about a sexual relationship between Mary Jo and Ted Kennedy were "just plain silly" and that she "got to know him only after Robert Kennedy's death; and even then she rarely saw him."

Mary Jo was "emotionally involved with the problems of unfortunate [i.e., disadvantaged] people" and she "loved politics and her political education."[16]

Mary Jo was "never overly impressed by . . . her professional closeness with the Kennedys."[17]

Mary Jo was not estranged from her parents; rather she "called [them] two or three times a week from wherever she was and told them everything" and she "spent every holiday with [them]."

The Kopechnes initially wanted an autopsy "because they thought it was a matter of routine" and because of all the "disturbing stories they were hearing." But after being reassured by Ted Kennedy in his nationally televised speech that there was "no foul play" they abandoned the idea because it was "grossly offensive to [them], almost like a second funeral."

The Kennedys "offered to pay for Mary Jo's funeral," but the Kopechnes turned down the offer because they "felt it was [their] responsibility."

The Kopechnes "believed that [Ted] Kennedy went off the bridge accidentally, and that he did all he could to save Mary Jo by diving down to the car."

The Kopechnes believed that Ted Kennedy was "in shock" after the accident and that if his "judgement had not been impaired he would have tried to seek help at one of the homes along the way" back to Lawrence Cottage.

> The Kopechnes blamed Joe Gargan and Paul Markham for not reporting the accident immediately because "Senator Kennedy was in shock, but they *surely* weren't."

Initially, the Kopechnes held Ted Kennedy blameless. "Recriminations are pointless; we cannot live with anger and hate," Gwen concluded in the published interview. "Mary Jo is gone and a million accusations won't bring her back." Instead, the Kopechnes found solace in their belief that their daughter was "with God and that one day we will all be reunited."[18] They also gained support from the more than eight hundred condolence letters they received from across the nation in the years following May Jo's death. Many of the letters came from people they did not know but who felt a genuine sympathy for their loss. Others were sent from their daughter's friends and colleagues who had worked for RFK or Matt Reese.[19]

Although the Kopechnes could have taken legal action against Kennedy, they refused to do so, believing that "people would think we were looking for blood money."[20] While there is no evidence that the Massachusetts senator paid the couple for their silence, the Associated Press reported in 1976 that the Kopechnes did receive a payment of $90,904 from the Massachusetts senator and an additional $50,000 from his insurance company.[21] Joseph Flanagan, the Kopechnes' lawyer, corroborated those figures in a 2010 interview. According to Flanagan, Kennedy paid the couple a total of $140,923, which included $50,000 in damages from his insurance company, the maximum allowable under Massachusetts law for an auto accident death in which pain and suffering is not proved. "The total amount was based on an insurance actuary's calculation of Miss Kopechne's earnings potential had she lived," explained Flanagan. He also said that after his fee for representing the Kopechnes at the 1969 exhumation hearing, the family netted about $100,000. This figure included the remuneration from *McCall's Magazine* for the interview, which Flanagan also negotiated. But that figure was "not consistent with the money the couple paid to build a new home in the Poconos and the lot on which it was located." Instead,

Flanagan speculated that most of the money for the new home and the lot came from their life savings and a nest egg they had accumulated to pay for Mary Jo's wedding.[22]

In addition to the $140,923 Kennedy and his insurance company paid the Kopechnes, Ted may have also funded a scholarship in Mary Jo's name. On August 14, 1969, Caldwell College, Kopechne's alma mater, announced that a "group of businessmen in the Boston vicinity" established the scholarship, being "impressed by her idealism."[23] But Sister Rita Margaret Chambers said in a 2009 interview, "Many of the sisters at the college believed that the money came from Senator Kennedy himself."[24]

In 1971 the Kopechnes mustered the strength to visit Chappaquiddick. There they went to the scene of the accident, where they met with John Farrar, the scuba diver who recovered Mary Jo's body. Until that time, they believed that their daughter died immediately after Kennedy's car capsized into Poucha Pond. But then Farrar revealed his belief that Mary Jo did not drown but suffocated to death and that he could have saved her life if the accident had been reported sooner. Then the Kopechnes began to question Ted Kennedy's innocence. In fact, the notion that Mary Jo would still be alive if Kennedy had had the moral courage to report the accident immediately after it occurred haunted Joe so deeply that his health declined, and within a few years he developed stomach cancer. Although Joe would eventually recover, both he and his wife mourned the loss of their only child for the rest of their lives.[25]

Chappaquiddick also took a toll on Ted Kennedy, both professionally and personally. When he returned to the Senate three weeks after the accident, Kennedy, according to Sylvia Wright of *Life* magazine, "seemed devastated." "He walked and moved slowly. His massive body had grown thin, the jowls which always made him look like a caricature of himself were barely noticeable. The ashen face was melted down. The tortured eyes looked out tentatively, seeking signs of loyalty or defection, then were cast down again."[26] The remorse he felt was for letting down his Senate colleagues, some of whom were not so forgiving.

In January 1971 Kennedy lost his position as Senate Majority Whip when several colleagues withdrew their support and voted for Senator Robert Byrd of West Virginia, the final vote coming in at 31–24. Although Kennedy later told Byrd that the defeat was a blessing in disguise as it allowed him to become chair of the Senate subcommittee on health care and play a leading role in the creation and passage of the National Cancer Act of 1971, the rebuff indicated that Kennedy now had enemies in the Senate who would be inclined to vote against legislation he sponsored in the future.[27] Ted made other political enemies, too.

Immediately after learning of the Chappaquiddick accident, J. Edgar Hoover, the director of the Federal Bureau of Investigation, and President Richard Nixon joined efforts to ruin Kennedy's political career. Hoover, who once worked for and disdained JFK and RFK, had begun a file on Ted after he was first elected to the Senate in 1962. John Dean, then assistant to deputy attorney general Richard Kleindienst, said that the Justice Department was "anxious to learn anything it could about Kopechne and her relationship with Ted Kennedy." In a June 2010 interview, Dean, who later became White House counsel to Nixon and was implicated in the Watergate break-in that forced Nixon's resignation in 1974, also admitted that "Nixon had a lot of interest in Kennedy." Nixon, according to Dean, thought "Teddy was going to run against him in 1972, so he was constantly looking for any information on him of a negative nature."[28] In fact, Nixon hired his own private detectives to investigate the accident. One of those detectives was Tony Ulasewicz, who along with FBI agents descended on Martha's Vineyard, where they wiretapped journalists, interviewed residents, and buttonholed Edgartown police and legal officials in order to gain intelligence on Kennedy's behavior during the July 18–20 weekend.[29]

Ulasewicz, later known as the "Bag Man" during the Watergate scandal because he would deliver hush money, went to the Katama Shores Motor Inn, where the Boiler Room Girls were staying, late Saturday morning and found that they'd been whisked off Martha's Vineyard. Then he visited the Edgartown Police Station and saw on the blotter that Rosemary Keough's handbag had been recovered. "I asked about [the handbag] and learned that a few minutes before I arrived a man in a dark blue suit had claimed it."[30] That man was later identified as Charles Tretter, one of the partygoers.[31]

Nixon also considered destroying Mary Jo Kopechne's reputation. According to a recently released White House memorandum from administration member Jack Caufield, Mary Jo likely died after performing an "immoral act." The memo went on to state that since Kennedy fled the scene a priest was not able to read the victim her last rites. As a result, wrote Caufield, "the victim's afterlife might have been impacted by her and Kennedy's actions that night." In addition, Caufield suggested that Nixon would be able to use this information against Kennedy, who "enjoys hard core unswayable support from devout Roman Catholics, particularly Irish and Slavic elements in all parts of the country."[32]

Nixon's detectives and FBI agents also discovered that Mary Jo roomed with Carole Tyler, a girlfriend of Senate secretary Bobby Baker. Since Baker was a sexual rogue on Capitol Hill, the association damaged Mary Jo's reputation and tied Kennedy to the risqué lifestyles that were rampant on the Hill. Another informant tipped off the FBI that Rosemary Keough's purse was found in the front seat of Kennedy's car. After that, the FBI leaked the story to the tabloids that Kennedy and Keough escaped the Oldsmobile, neither aware that Kopechne was asleep in the back.[33]

But the most damning evidence came from a private investigator named Albert S. Patterson.[34] Recently declassified FBI files reveal that Patterson, in a series of letters to Senator John Stennis, then the chairman of the Select Committee on Standards and Conduct, and to Benjamin Fern, then chief counsel for the committee, accused Kennedy of committing perjury at the January 1970 inquest.[35] Patterson, in a fifty-eight-page manuscript titled "All Honorable Men (and Women)—or Perjury at Edgartown," claims that Kennedy lied six times during his testimony at the inquest:

1. Kennedy initially said that the driver's side window was closed and later claimed that the window was open.
2. Kennedy testified that he was driving "approximately 20 m.p.h." when the car's skid marks of thirty-six feet indicate that he was driving at an "estimated 26½ m.p.h."

3. Kennedy stated that at "no time after he turned on to Dike Road did [he] realize he had made a wrong turn." But he also admitted that he knew the road from Lawrence Cottage to the ferry was paved and that he had become "generally aware sometime while on Dike Road that it was unpaved." Thus he had to know that he wasn't on his way to the ferry.
4. Kennedy relied strongly on darkness to support his alibi, especially when the car capsized in Poucha Pond and he said it was "pitch black" underwater. But the "headlights remained on for several minutes after the plunge" creating "quite a bit of underwater illumination."
5. Kennedy, in earlier testimony, insisted that he had been upside down immediately after the car ran off the bridge, but the passenger side window shattered indicating that the car landed on its side initially.
6. Kennedy claimed that he made several attempts to rescue Kopechne, but that the current was running too fast for him to succeed in the rescue. But the tide was low and there was no current at all at 11:30 p.m. on Saturday, July 18, 1969, the time Kennedy claimed the accident occurred.[36]

Kennedy also began to receive death threats after Chappaquiddick, referring to his role in Mary Jo Kopechne's death. The threats continued for the remainder of his political career, often around the anniversary of the tragedy.[37] Nor was the damage confined to Ted's political career. Chappaquiddick had a severe impact on Kennedy's family, too. After the accident, EMK returned to Hyannis to tell his father of the ordeal and to ask for his forgiveness. Joe Kennedy Sr., bedridden and confined to his Cape Cod estate, had held fast to the hope that his youngest son would one day become president.[38] It was the only reason the patriarch fought to stay alive after the deaths of his three elder sons. Ted knew it, too. Ascending the staircase of the family home, the heir to the Kennedy political dynasty timidly entered his father's bedroom. He felt like a little boy who realized that he had done something wrong and was about to be punished for it. "Dad, I'm in some trouble," he began, gently placing a hand on old Joe's shoulder. The patriarch, noticeably pleased to see his son, tilted his head forward so he could hear better.

"There's been an accident," Ted explained, gathering the courage to continue. "There was a girl in the car and she drowned."

The news hit the old man like a gut punch. His head fell back in disbelief.

"You're going to hear all sorts of things about me from now on," Ted added. "Terrible things . . ." His voice trailed off, unable to say anything more than, "I'm sorry, Dad. I've done the best I can." Joe mustered the strength to pat his son's arm with the one hand he was still able to move. Then he closed his eyes and motioned for his son to leave the room.[39]

Rita Dallas, the old man's personal nurse, noticed a rapid deterioration in his condition after that. "After the deaths of John and Bobby, he eventually bounced back," she recalled. "But after Chappaquiddick, he just couldn't bounce back."[40] With nothing left to live for, Joseph P. Kennedy, once among the wealthiest and most influential men in America and the patriarch of its most glamorous political dynasty, died on November 18, 1969.[41] According to Burton Hersh, a Kennedy biographer, Joe Kennedy believed that "the family had been completely disgraced by Chappaquiddick." "The old man just didn't have anything to live for," and after the patriarch died "Ted told me, 'I killed my father.' Ted carried that [belief] to his grave."[42]

Kennedy's wife, Joan, was also shattered by Chappaquiddick. Pregnant with the couple's third child at the time of incident, she had flown to Plymouth, Pennsylvania, in late July to attend Mary Jo's funeral. Despite doctor's orders not to fly, Joan made the plane trip in a public show of support for her husband, but she paid the price a month later when she suffered a miscarriage. "After Chappaquiddick, my drinking became worse," she admitted to Laurence Leamer in a 1994 interview. "For a few months everyone had to put on this side show, and then I just didn't care anymore. I just saw no future. That's when I truly became an alcoholic."[43] Joan's drinking increased as Ted's infidelities continued. At home, her two sons were struggling with health issues. Patrick, the younger son, suffered from severe asthma attacks, and in 1973 Ted Jr. lost a leg to cancer and underwent a difficult two-year experimental drug treatment.[44] The pressures became so severe by the mid-1970s that Joan entered treatment for alcoholism and emotional strain.[45] In 1977 Ted and Joan separated, although they continued to make some public appearances together. Four years later, in 1981, they filed for divorce.[46]

Despite his professional and personal difficulties, Kennedy appeared to retain the loyalties of the voters. Before Chappaquiddick, national polls indicated that a large majority of Americans expected Ted not only to run for the presidency in 1972 but to be the frontrunner for the Democratic nomination.[47] After the accident, polls showed that Kennedy could still win the nomination if he tried, despite his declaration that he would not run in 1972. But there were other factors that discouraged a bid. For years, Richard Nixon, then incumbent president, had feared a challenge by the Massachusetts senator and tried to destroy his political career after Chappaquiddick by sending his own agents to investigate the accident and by wiretapping Kennedy. Ted knew it. But he also realized that Nixon's approval rating was almost at 70 percent due to a strong economy and his foreign policy successes, including a trip to China and the potential for peace in Vietnam.[48] As a result, EMK stood his ground. Declining to run, Ted claimed that he needed "breathing time" to gain more experience and to "take care of [his] family."[49] Even then, he was recruited at the convention by the Democratic nominee, George McGovern, as his vice presidential running mate.[50] Massachusetts's voters also continued to support Kennedy, reelecting him to the Senate in 1970 with 62 percent of the vote against Republican candidate Josiah Spaulding.[51]

Determined to become a better senator, Kennedy renewed his efforts for national health insurance, pushed for campaign finance reform and traveled to the Soviet Union where he met Premier Leonid Brezhnev and advocated a full nuclear test ban as well as a relaxed emigration policy. He also got revenge against Nixon in 1973 by stage managing the Watergate hearings behind the scenes. Although the Senate Select Committee on Presidential Campaign Activities was headed by Senator Sam Ervin of North Carolina, Kennedy played a huge role on the committee by knowing what kinds of questions to ask and who to subpoena. Ted's involvement played a significant role in forcing Nixon to resign on August 9, 1974.[52]

Nixon's humiliating resignation appeared to open the door for Kennedy not only to run in 1976 but to win. His reputation in the Senate had improved considerably over the previous seven years and was viewed as the only Democratic candidate who could unite the traditional and progressive wings of the party. Ted also had the advantages of the Kennedy name, the wealth and the same progressive legacy as his older brothers. But again, Chappaquiddick proved to be his undoing. On October 29, 1974, the *Boston Globe* published the findings of a two-month investigation completed by their Spotlight team. Although Ted was interviewed extensively for the story and continued to cite his exhaustion as the reason he failed to report the accident and denied allegations of a cover-up, Spotlight identified more than one hundred discrepancies in the senator's testimony given at the 1970 inquest hearing.[53] It was clear that Chappaquiddick was not going to be forgotten. When he was approached by Democratic Party leaders to run for the presidency in 1976, he announced that for family reasons he would not run and that his decision was "firm, final and unconditional."[54]

If Ted planned to make a presidential bid in the future, he apparently intended to do so with his own staff since he distanced himself from Bobby's Boiler Room Girls, whom he once tried to cultivate. Instead, the five young women became successful in their own right. Susan Tannenbaum went to work for New York's representative Allard Lowenstein, one of the architects of the 1968 "Dump Johnson" movement. She later married a Washington lawyer and became a lobbyist. Esther Newberg went to work for the vice president of the Urban Institute in Washington and later became a successful New York City literary agent and executive. Rosemary Keough went to work for the Kennedy family foundation for children with intellectual disabilities and later became a partner in a Lincoln, Massachusetts, law firm with her husband, Paul Redmond. Maryellen Lyons became a practicing attorney in Boston.[55] Her sister, Nance, was the only one who returned to her old job working for Ted, but she admitted that she "was not made to feel welcome":

> Even though I returned to work within ten feet of [Senator Kennedy's] office, he never, never, never asked how I was doing; or said how sorry he was that I and the other women were subjected to such [media] scrutiny. I certainly didn't feel welcomed back by this staff. Still, he never mentioned Mary Jo to me. No call during each year's anniversary scrutiny. No thank you for supporting him during these trying times. To me this was unbelievable and I have not forgiven him for that insensitivity. Frankly, I believe he set up my departure. He knew I wanted to leave. I was offered a job in New York through one of his associates. It took me a while to understand the ploy, but I did move on to New York.[56]

Although Nance Lyons never discussed publicly the particular details of that weekend at Chappaquiddick in July 1969, she admitted in a 2008 interview that it "changed my life." She and the other young women who had once held significant responsibility in RFK's presidential campaign were "humiliated by the press," which "portrayed [them] as girls of no significance—even as party girls." Then for the next ten to twelve years on each anniversary of the tragedy, the women were "pursued by the press, subjected to hate mail and veiled accusations about [their] moral rectitude." Some lost jobs. Others didn't get jobs for which they were qualified.[57] Nor did Ted Kennedy intervene on their behalf. His treatment of Gwen and Joe Kopechne was even more reprehensible.

After Mary Jo's funeral on July 22, 1969, Kennedy promised the couple he would meet with them privately to discuss the events surrounding their daughter's death. Ted kept his promise to meet with the Kopechnes on two occasions, both times at his home in McLean, Virginia. But each time, Gwen and Joe didn't learn anything more than what they already knew. "They were really ridiculous meetings," Gwen recalled twenty years later in an interview with *Ladies' Home Journal*:

> He led us to believe he was going to explain what really happened. But when the time came, he just told us he didn't know which way he was heading when he left the cottage. Everything was so damn disappointing. I didn't hear anything new; nobody told me any-

> thing, and I didn't even know what to ask. I don't believe anything I've heard so far, either.
>
> I want [the senator] to tell me what happened. Can't he relieve us of this? Isn't there something he could tell me that would lift this heavy burden from my heart? I don't think he was upset either time we saw him, and I don't remember him saying I'm sorry.[58]

But Kennedy, in his autobiography *True Compass*, published after his death in 2009, insisted that he delivered "many apologies to the Kopechne family" and that he "gave them the best account of [Chappaquiddick] in [his] power." Ted also admitted that he remained silent on the matter after 1970 because he "refused to respond to false gossip and innuendo" and because his "public discussion of that terrible night would only have caused the Kopechnes more pain."[59]

In 1976 Joe Kopechne, age sixty-three, retired, and the couple relocated from Berkeley Heights, New Jersey, to Swiftwater, a small town in the Pocono Mountains of Pennsylvania, where they had built a modest ranch-style house. Located in a quiet cul-de-sac, the three-bedroom house was surrounded by trees. A "Wilkum" sign hung near the front door. Seashells from the shores off Chappaquiddick could be found adorning the backyard stoop. Although Mary Jo never lived there, her presence could be seen throughout the home: her college portrait hung over the piano in the living room, her worn teddy bear and other favorite stuffed animals occupied a corner of the guest room, and in the family room hung a framed photograph of JFK that he had autographed for Mary Jo a week before his assassination.

To stay busy, the couple cared for their home and gardens, attended church functions, and traveled regularly to California and Florida to visit friends and relatives. In addition, Gwen belonged to a coffee and cake club with her neighbors. Joe played tennis, was active in a town watch group, and delivered food to shut-ins. They also enjoyed visits from family members, especially their young nieces and nephews, and hosted the family Memorial Day party each year.[60]

But those who knew the couple well could tell how heartbroken they were over the death of their only child. "One look in their eyes told you that they were just waiting to follow Mary Jo," said Georgetta Potoski, their niece and the executor of the Kopechne estate. "It was as though their hearts had already gone ahead. There was a bone-deep sorrow within each one that simply never left."[61]

In April 1980 Kennedy contacted the Kopechnes to inform them that he would be returning to Luzerne County that month to campaign for the Democratic presidential nomination against incumbent Jimmy Carter. At the time, Gwen Kopechne felt that Kennedy called them simply to "find out how bitter we are and whether we were going to be cooperative. If I wasn't in shock when he called, I would have said to him, 'Did you go up to my daughter's grave?'" "Hell," snapped Joe, referring to the phone call, "you could see right through it. He just cared about himself and his political career. We could've said some nasty things about him during that campaign, but we didn't."[62]

When Kennedy arrived in Wilkes-Barre on April 16, he attracted hundreds of supporters who braved the wind, cold, and the occasional snow flurry to greet him. Not everyone came to cheer the Democratic candidate, though. Before Ted's visit, local television stations ran Carter campaign ads that showed voters speaking directly to the camera about Kennedy and Chappaquiddick, insisting "I don't trust him" and "I don't believe him."[63] Those ads made a deep impression with some voters, who formed an unruly mob and confronted EMK on his way to a press conference at the city's Bicentennial Building. One disgruntled man held a sign that asked, "Senator Kennedy, can you do that trick in the Susquehanna River?" It was a reference to Chappaquiddick, and the sign bearer wanted to know if Kennedy could have escaped if he had driven a car into the nearby Susquehanna. Journalist David Espo of the Associated Press, who covered Kennedy's 1980 presidential campaign, was shocked by the scene:

> It was one of the most frightening days of the entire campaign. I will never forget it. People were yelling and screaming obscenities at Kennedy because Mary Jo Kopechne was from northeastern Pennsylvania. The crowd was blue-collar, conservative, anti-abortion Democrats, and Catholics. I've never seen anything quite like it

> since, in any campaign that I've covered. It was so visceral. They were so angry, and they weren't angry over a policy or a war or the economy. It was more personal. The Secret Service was genuinely troubled by it and had to figure out how to get the Senator into the building for the press conference and then how to get him out later.[64]

By 4:00 p.m., when Kennedy was scheduled to speak on Public Square, the mob had dispersed and was replaced by enthusiastic supporters. Men and women, young and old, surged toward the podium to greet the Democratic candidate. Children were hoisted atop of the shoulders of parents who had once embraced Kennedy's martyred brothers, John and Robert. But the rooftops of the surrounding buildings were taken over by the Wilkes-Barre police and U.S. Secret Service agents, who hoped to prevent another nasty incident like the mob that had assembled earlier.[65]

Although polls showed EMK ahead of Carter by a two-to-one margin when he decided to run in August 1979, the electorate rallied around the president during the Iranian hostage crisis, which began on November 4, and the Soviet invasion of Afghanistan on December 27, knocking Kennedy's campaign out of the headlines.[66] Nor did the Massachusetts senator help his own cause. Kennedy proved to be an ineffective campaigner.

Perhaps his biggest gaffe occurred shortly after he announced his candidacy on November 7, 1979, when Roger Mudd of CBS News asked him, "Why do you want to be president?" Kennedy initially froze, then rambled on, unable to give a coherent response:

> Well, I'm—were I to make the announcement, and to run, the reasons I would run is because I have a great belief in this country. That it is—there's more natural resources than any nation in the world; the greatest education population in the world; the greatest technology of any country in the world; the greatest capacity for innovation in the world; and the greatest political system in the world.
>
> And yet I see at the current time that most of the industrial nations of the world are exceeding us in terms of productivity and are doing better than us in terms of meeting the problems of inflation; that

> they're dealing with their problems of energy and their problems of unemployment. It just seems to me that this nation can cope and deal with its problems in a way that it has in the past.
>
> We're facing complex issues and problems in this nation at this time and that we have faced similar challenges at other times. And the energies and resourcefulness of this nation, I think, should be focused on these problems in a way that brings a sense of restoration in this country by its people in dealing with the problems that we face: primarily issues on the economy, the problems of inflation, and the problems of energy.
>
> And I would basically feel that—that it's imperative for this country to either move forward; that it can't stand still or otherwise it moves backward. And that leadership for this nation can galvanize a—a—an effort with a team to try and deal with these problems that we're facing in our nation, and can be effective in trying to cope with the problems that we'd face. And I think that'd be the real challenge in—in the 1980s. I think it's a watershed period in our country, from a variety of different points, primarily from an energy point of view and from an economic point of view.[67]

The answer was unprepared, obtuse, and disconnected. It also raised questions over whether Ted genuinely wanted to be president or if he was simply doing what was expected of him as the last surviving Kennedy brother. Chappaquiddick also continued to haunt him.

As the campaign unfolded, Chappaquiddick became a major handicap for Ted. After Kennedy lost the Iowa caucus and lost again in New Hampshire, he was asked if he could blame voters for having misgivings about whether he could be trusted not to panic in an emergency. "That was a tragic automobile accident," he replied attempting to draw a clear distinction between the two. "But that's a good deal different from whether I can perform in the office of the president. I've worked in the public life for some seventeen years, he added, suggesting that he could in fact handle the pressures of executive office."[68] But the press didn't buy it. Several newspaper columnists and editorials criticized him for his inability to clarify the many questions that still existed about his involvement in the affair.

The issue came to a head during the key Illinois primary in March when assassination threats forced Kennedy to wear a bulletproof vest during Chicago's Saint Patrick's Day parade. As EMK plunged into the crowd to shake hands, one heckler cried out, "When are you going to learn to drive?" Another one asked, "Where's Mary Jo?"[69]

Kennedy lost the Illinois primary. With polls showing a likely defeat in the New York primary, he considered withdrawing from the race until he staged a last-minute upset, winning New York by a 59–41 percent margin. Carter counterattacked by running another series of ads on Chappaquiddick, but EMK still managed a narrow victory in the April 22 Pennsylvania primary. Although Carter appeared to clinch the Democratic nomination in May by winning eleven of the twelve primaries that month, Kennedy rebounded again in the June 3 Super Tuesday primaries by winning California, New Jersey, and three smaller states out of the eight contests. Heading into the Democratic National Convention in August, Carter, who had won twenty-four primaries to Kennedy's ten, had enough delegates to capture the nomination. Ted made a last-ditch effort, trying to have a rule passed that would free delegates from being bound by primary results and opening the convention. But the attempt failed on the first night, and Kennedy withdrew. The next evening, he delivered the most passionate speech of his career, concluding with the words: "For me, a few hours ago, this campaign came to an end. For all those whose cares have been our concern, the work goes on, the cause endures, the hope still lives and the dream shall never die."[70]

Ultimately, Mary Jo Kopechne's death and Kennedy's failure to properly deal with the accident, along with numerous discrepancies in his account of what happened, damaged his national reputation, and cost him the 1980 Democratic nomination. Ted considered running again in 1984 and 1988, but he declined each time, citing his desire to remain in the Senate and to care for his family.[71] In fact, the end of EMK's presidential aspirations probably came as a relief.

Liberated from the expectations of his father and the legacy created by his late brothers, Ted forged his own legacy as the "Lion of the Senate" during the conservative Republican administrations of Ronald Reagan

(1981–88), George H. W. Bush (1988–92), and George W. Bush (1999–2008). What made Kennedy unique was his ability to retain a broader ideological commitment while also practicing the art of compromise. He was a masterful legislator, instinctively knowing when to stand firm and when to cut a deal. As an indispensable dealmaker, Kennedy was able to reach across the aisle in a GOP-controlled Congress to achieve a long list of legislative accomplishments:

Title IX (1972): Prohibits schools from discriminating against women in the classroom and on the athletic field.

Meals on Wheels Act (1972): Insures that senior citizens unable to leave their homes will receive nutritious meals.

Women, Infants, and Children Nutrition Program (1972): Provides low-income women and their children with access to food and nutrition and health services.

Individual with Disabilities Education Act (1975): Mandates that all children with a disability have access to free public education that meets their needs.

Americans with Disabilities Act (1990): Prohibits discrimination against a job applicant or employee for having a disability.

Health Insurance Portability and Accountability Act (1996): Protects the health insurance of Americans who change or lose their jobs.

State Children's Health Insurance Program (1997): Provides insurance for children whose family incomes are too high to qualify for Medicaid but too low to afford private coverage.

No Child Left Behind Act (2001): Established requirements and benchmarks for every public school in America to qualify for federal funding.

Expansion of Medicare (2003): Kennedy, a longtime chair of the Senate's Committee on Health, Education, Labor and Pensions, called for extending Medicare coverage to all Americans, medical coverage for the uninsured and modernizing health care systems by using new technologies to cut costs. He also proposed to implement a rule that would require every American to have some form of health insurance, a point which became one of the

> key points of contention between Democrats and Republicans. Although not all of his proposals were adopted, Kennedy did succeed in expanded Medicare to include prescription drug benefits, making it the largest expansion of the program in its history.[72]

Kennedy's unrivaled success as a legislator enabled him to influence nearly every major bill passed by the Senate in the second part of the twentieth century. Thus while the presidency eluded him, Ted Kennedy, during his four decades in Congress, contributed more to American liberalism than either of his brothers. But he was never able to distance himself completely from Chappaquiddick.

On the twentieth anniversary of the event, Kennedy issued a prepared statement insisting that he had "told everything [he knew] about the accident." He also expressed his "remorse and responsibility to [his] own family, to the Kopechne family and to the people of Massachusetts."[73] But the Kopechnes were unconvinced and agreed to a third and what would be their final interview to tell their side of the story.

Published by *Ladies' Home Journal* on July 25, 1989, the interview revealed how bitter the couple had become in the years since their daughter's death. Gwen Kopechne was adamant that the senator had not apologized for his role in the accident. She also vented her anger at the Boiler Room Girls. "Why haven't they said anything?" Gwen asked. "I think there was a big cover-up and that everyone was paid off." Her husband was more objective. Joe admitted that he constantly reminds himself that Mary Jo's death was "not in vain" because it "kept the Senator from becoming president." Nevertheless he, like Gwen, was haunted by the thought of what their daughter might have accomplished if she had lived. "Mary Jo made her mark in the world," said Joe, "but she could've done a lot more." "If she were alive she'd be married and have about a dozen kids," Gwen chimed in. "I'd be a grandmother."[74]

In November 1989 the Kopechnes called for a further investigation of their daughter's death after reading Kenneth Kappel's 1989 book *Chappaquiddick Revealed*. Based on previously unexamined photographic evidence, Kappel argued that a drunken Kennedy crashed his car into trees near Dike Bridge. Believing that he killed Mary Jo, the senator staged a cover-up to avoid a manslaughter charge.[75] "We are not experts in matters of criminal investigation," said Gwen, speaking for the couple, "but we believe that Mr. Kappel presents a persuasive argument that Senator Kennedy's car was involved in a second unreported accident and it has changed our minds regarding what happened the night our daughter died. We believe that in order to clear up a mystery that troubles us every day of our lives, Senator Kennedy should respond to the new evidence presented in this book."[76] But the Massachusetts senator never did respond. Instead, his office issued a brief statement calling Kappel's book "preposterous and absurd" and saying that the senator was "not going to comment on it any further."[77] Thus the Kopechnes never learned anything more about their daughter's death than what they knew in the immediate weeks and months after it occurred. Worse, the anxiety of not knowing, not being able to bring closure to Mary Jo's life, took a punishing physical toll on them.

Gwen, age seventy-one, had recently had surgery for suspected cancer. Although she was given a clean bill of health by the doctors, she admitted that the "stress [was] getting too much for [her]." "You go to bed at night and you think and think and rehash everything," said Gwen. "You can't go to sleep because your mind is running like a movie camera." It was especially stressful during each anniversary of the event because of the media's obsession with Chappaquiddick. "I get too upset just having to talk about it. We've been bothered with people on the property. We don't answer the phone. It's ridiculous."[78]

Joe's health was worse. At age seventy-six, he was a cancer survivor, having lost half his stomach, all of his spleen and gallbladder, and part of his pancreas to the disease. But he admitted that he had to learn to "let go of the grief" or he "would die" and that he could "not bear to leave Gwen alone." Therefore, Joe kept up appearances, insisting that he was "still going better than he ever did." But Gwen knew that her husband had been depressed ever since Mary Jo's death. "She was his whole life," she confessed.[79]

Not wanting to be a burden on their Swiftwater neighbors, whom they had increasingly come to rely on, the Kopechnes sold their home in 2001 and moved to Stroud Manor, an assisted living facility in nearby

East Stroudsburg, Pennsylvania. Joe died there at age ninety on December 24, 2003. Shortly after, Gwen relocated to Valley Crest Nursing Home in Plains Township to be closer to her nieces, Georgetta Potoski and Ruth Bader, both of whom managed her affairs in the last years of her life. Gwen died at the age of eighty-nine on December 20, 2007. The couple was laid to rest with Mary Jo at Saint Vincent's Cemetery on Larksville Mountain.[80]

Ted Kennedy lived another two years, until 2009, before succumbing to brain cancer.[81] But Chappaquiddick had continued to haunt him for the remainder of his days. As a Catholic, he tried to find solace in personal atonement for Mary Jo's death, which he admitted was "a process that never ends." "I had suffered many losses during my life," he admitted in his autobiography, *True Compass*. "I had lost all my brothers and my sister, Kathleen. My father had been lost to me in many respects because of his debilitating stroke." But Chappaquiddick was different because "I myself was responsible." He wrote, "I was driving. Yes, it was an accident. But that doesn't erase the fact that I had caused an innocent woman's death."[82]

When Edward Kennedy died on August 25, 2009, he would have to confront a more powerful judge than James A. Boyle. Only God knows if he was forgiven.

8 Mary Jo's Legacy

"In many ways, Mary Jo Kopechne's life was just beginning at the time of her death," wrote Sally Quinn of the *Washington Post* a week after the Chappaquiddick tragedy. "She was, at 28, a late bloomer. When she came to Washington six years ago, she was like thousands of small town girls who come to make their way on Capitol Hill—unsure of herself in a world of glamour, but irresistibly drawn to it."[1] While that may be true, Mary Jo possessed the strength of character to live in that "world of glamour" without becoming part of it. Those who knew her predicted that she would have eventually left Capitol Hill to marry, raise a family, and pursue a career in college teaching.[2] Not in her wildest dreams, however, could Mary Jo have predicted that her life and legacy would, for better and worse, be forever bound to the Kennedy brothers and their pursuit of the U.S. presidency.

"For the Kennedys, it's either the White House or the shithouse," Joseph P. Kennedy Sr. predicted before he was felled by a stroke in December 1961.[3] Thanks to the patriarch, the Kennedy brothers were financially independent and able to pursue the only ambition that had eluded their father. It was a mixed blessing. John and Robert were genuinely concerned about the welfare of the nation, and their efforts added immeasurably to civil rights, the space program, and U.S. foreign policy. But in their ruthless quest for the White House, the two brothers sometimes flirted with the proverbial "shithouse" and paid for it with their lives.[4]

JFK, after serving in Congress for more than a decade, exploited the public optimism of the 1960s to win the presidency. His youth, good looks, cool style, and tough-minded rhetoric were attractive to both male and female voters, who were lulled into believing that the seemingly strong, vigorous military hero was the kind of president the country needed to combat Cold War Communism.[5] These qualities as well as his idealism and Catholic faith inspired Mary Jo, as a student at Caldwell College, to volunteer for his presidential campaign. Kennedy's growth as president endeared him to her even more.

JFK's early Cold War challenges compelled him to reevaluate U.S. foreign policy. His failure to overthrow Cuban dictator Fidel Castro in the 1961 Bay of Pigs invasion, his flirtation with nuclear Armageddon in the 1962 Cuban Missile Crisis with the Soviet Union, and the growing numbers of American casualties in Vietnam convinced him of the need to take a more dovish approach in foreign policy. To that end, Kennedy initiated the Nuclear Test Ban Treaty of 1963. There are also indications that he planned to withdraw American forces from Southeast Asia after being reelected in 1964.[6]

At home, JFK placed the United States on the path of space exploration, which improved our understanding of the universe as well as the quality of life in America.[7] He inspired a generation of young people to pursue public service and established the Peace Corps as a vehicle to improve the U.S. reputation abroad.[8] While JFK was reluctant to move forward on the momentous issue of civil rights, his brother Robert, who served as U.S. attorney general, convinced him of the necessity to protect the rights of African Americans, as well as the need to draft legislation that would insure those rights in the future.[9]

But JFK was also reckless. His extramarital affairs with East German–born Ellen Rometsch, a high-class call girl rumored to be a communist spy, and with Judith Exner and other prostitutes supplied by organized crime figures threatened to compromise national security.[10] In addition, there are those historians who argue that JFK took unnecessary risks in staring down Soviet premier Nikita Khrushchev during the October 1962 Cuban Missile Crisis and in signing off on a covert operation by the Central Intelligence Agency to assassinate Fidel Castro.[11] Still others argue that those risks resulted in JFK's own assassination at the hands of the CIA and the mob.[12]

For Mary Jo Kopechne—who knew nothing of JFK's private life and would choose not to believe it if she did—the president's transformation from hawk to dove, his challenge to the young to serve their country, and his eventual support of civil rights inspired her to pursue public service, first as a teacher in the Deep South and later as a secretary on Capitol Hill. She had her sights set on working in the White House until JFK was assassinated. Afterward, Kopechne, like many Americans, was devastated and viewed his presidency as a golden age in politics. RFK eventually picked up the fallen standard JFK left behind.

Once viewed as a ruthless protector of his older brother and a fierce prosecutor of organized crime, Bobby reinvented himself as the champion of a new kind of liberalism: "compassionate yet strong, supportive but not indulgent."[13] After campaigning for and winning election to the U.S. Senate, RFK began a crusade to improve the plight of blacks in urban America, the exploitation of Hispanic farm workers, the poor in Appalachia and on Native American reservations.[14] Bobby also challenged President Johnson's decision to escalate American involvement in the Vietnam War, admitting his own responsibility for the failure to pull out of Southeast Asia during his brother's administration.[15] But like his older brother, RFK had also made enemies in his dogged effort to destroy organized crime and in his unwelcome interference in CIA affairs as U.S. attorney general. Those enemies made him pay with his life.[16]

RFK was Mary Jo's political hero. He embodied the qualities she valued most: compassion for the underprivileged, social idealism tempered by political realism, and a fierce devotion to just causes. These were the same virtues Kopechne aspired to in the contributions she made as a secretary to his Senate office and later as a political operative for his presidential campaign. But her contributions and the ideals that imbued them represent only a part of Mary Jo's legacy. Unwittingly, she exercised a more significant influence over Edward Kennedy's political career.

Martyrdom endeared John and Robert Kennedy to the American people, and the two brothers still continue to exercise a strong hold on the Baby Boom generation, who voted them into office.[17] Ted was different. Like his brothers, Teddy genuinely cared about the future of the nation and made many meaningful contributions during his nearly half century in the U.S. Senate. Unlike JFK and RFK, however, the youngest Kennedy brother never seemed to want the presidency. Instead, he was compelled to pursue it by their legacies and his father's expectations.

It would be easy to scapegoat Mary Jo as *the* reason for Ted's inability to win the presidency. However, the failure was his and his alone. The Chappaquiddick accident, Ted's negligence to report it in a timely manner, and ultimately Mary Jo's death were unconscionable acts, the antithesis of how his brothers would have behaved under the same circumstances. In fact, any other individual that acted so recklessly would have been charged with involuntary homicide and given significant jail time. Although Ted Kennedy escaped that fate, Mary Jo's death did cast a shadow over him for the rest of his life. Even when EMK made his one—and only—bid for the presidency in 1980, he did so halfheartedly. Unable to articulate his reasons for seeking the presidency, Ted stumbled through the campaign. His speeches lacked the passion of a politician who genuinely believed he could solve the problems that confronted the nation. Ultimately, the American electorate rejected him, not because of Chappaquiddick, but because of their belief that he was not up to the job. The accident was not forgotten, though.

For many years after Chappaquiddick, a steady stream of books on the incident appeared, reminding the American electorate of Edward Kennedy's recklessness and irresponsibility. While Mary Jo's death triggered those sensationalist accounts, the books did more to prevent Ted's bid for the White House than she did. Initially, the authors focused on the scandalous: a high-profile, married man alone with a single young woman; rumors of a sexual affair, possibly a pregnancy; death by drowning at night off a barren road.[18] By 1980 writers were less concerned about the accident itself or how it happened. Instead, they raised the possibility of a cover-up initiated by the Kennedy family to protect Ted's political future.[19] Leo Damore resurrected the popular suspicion of a conspiracy in 1988 with *Senatorial Privilege*. Damore, a dogged and thorough researcher who was working for the *Cape Cod News* in July 1969, interviewed several of the local law enforcement officials involved in the investigation. His muckraking account offered readers a spellbinding tale of death, intrigue, obstruction of justice, and corrupt politics, allegedly provoking the wrath of the Kennedy family.[20] But the Kennedys and their sycophants were sorely mistaken if they thought they could salvage another shot at the White House with Ted.

Conspiratorial accounts of Chappaquiddick continued throughout the 1990s and 2000s.[21] Revisionist interpretations of JFK's presidency, which began in the 1970s, also increased. John Kennedy was portrayed as a risk-taking, mediocre chief executive with few achievements and a private life wracked by poor health and extramarital affairs.[22] In addition, several "kiss-and-tell" accounts of the Kennedy family by "insiders" tarnished the once-impeccable reputation of America's most glamorous political dynasty. According to the muckraking authors, the Kennedys were at best cursed and at worst masters of deception who exploited the American public to acquire and exercise political power.[23]

More recently, historians and journalists have portrayed the Kennedy brothers as neither saints nor sinners but simply human, with many of the same foibles, fears, and shortcomings.[24] This is especially true of the Hollywood film *Chappaquiddick* (2018), directed by John Curran and written by Taylor Allen and Andrew Logan, who based their screenplay on the official records and inquest testimonies of those who were there. Although Allen and Logan insist that the movie is "neither pro-Kennedy nor anti-Kennedy," they do reveal the moral ambiguity and emotional vulnerability of Ted (played by actor Jason Clarke) as he finds himself caught between doing what is right and protecting his family legacy as well as his own political career.[25]

At the same time, the screenwriters did justice to Mary Jo Kopechne, played by Kate Mara. "It was important for us not to portray her as a damsel in distress," Logan said. "We wanted to show, even in a time of great crisis, she was poised. And she was somebody who had great courage and who had a lot of promise ahead of her."[26] Mary Jo's character is based in part on a self-published ebook of letters and remembrances titled *Our Mary Jo*, written by a first cousin and childhood friend, Georgetta Potoski, and Potoski's son, William Nelson.[27] "Maybe now Mary Jo will be brought to the forefront and remembered not just for how she died but for who she was," Potoski told *People* magazine shortly after the film was released.[28]

Indeed, Mary Jo Kopechne's life and legacy are much greater than her death at Chappaquiddick and the cottage industry of sensationalist accounts that followed for the next half century. Mary Jo should be celebrated for her *positive* impact on Ted Kennedy. After Chappaquiddick, the Massachusetts legislator forged a respectable reputation in the U.S. Congress as a hardworking senator and the leader of the Democratic Party's progressive wing. He became not only an inspirational leader but the bulwark of some of the most important measures on civil rights, education, and health care passed by Congress in the last half century.

If Kennedy truly believed that "atonement is a process that never ends," then perhaps he did his penance by championing such meaningful legislation.[29] If so, Mary Jo Kopechne inspired those achievements because her death forced Edward Kennedy to strive for a higher standard.

NOTES

Introduction

1. "Statement from the Kennedy Family," *Boston Globe*, August 26, 2009.
2. Canellos, *Last Lion*. *Last Lion*, written by a team of reporters at the *Boston Globe*, is the most objective account of Ted Kennedy's political career.
3. Several biographers argue that Ted Kennedy struggled with alcohol throughout his political career and that he was a philanderer, a trait that he learned from his father, Joseph P. Kennedy Sr. See Canellos, *Last Lion*, 261–64; Kessler, *The Sins of the Father*, 2, 71–72, 317–18, 371–72; Hersh, *The Dark Side of Camelot*, 237, 242; Leamer, *The Kennedy Men*, 333–34, 387–88, 409, 462, 584, 665; Klein, *Ted Kennedy*, 24–27, 65–66, 78–80, 134–35, 159–66; Clymer, *Edward M. Kennedy*, 92–93, 98, 108, 133, 141, 149, 151, 186–87, 290–91, 374, 434, 474–78; and Nasaw, *The Patriarch*, 47–48, 76–77, 146–47, 163–64, 379–80, 610–11.
4. Ted Kennedy and his first wife, Joan, divorced after his failed 1980 presidential bid. See Clymer, *Edward M. Kennedy*, 315. Mary Jo Kopechne was killed in the automobile that Kennedy was driving on July 18, 1969. See Richard Powers and Alan Lupo, "Ted Kennedy Escapes, Woman Dies as Car Plunges into Vineyard Pond," *Boston Globe*, July 20, 1969. The first high-profile legal case in which Kennedy was involved was in 1970 to determine if there was criminal negligence in Kopechne's death. See Edgartown District Court, *Inquest into the Death of Mary Jo Kopechne*. The second case was the rape trial of his nephew, William Kennedy Smith, in 1991. See "Kennedy, on TV, Discusses Rape Case, Drinking," *USA Today*, June 6, 1991.
5. In a May 2008 interview, Senator John McCain of Arizona called Ted Kennedy the "last lion of the Senate" because he was at that time the "single most effective member to get results." See Canellos, *Last Lion*, ix. The moniker stuck, and there were two books published under that

title, Canellos's *Last Lion* (2009) and Littlefield and Nexon, *Lion of the Senate* (2015).

6. Potoski and Nelson, *Our Mary Jo*, 40, 57, 66.
7. Potoski and Nelson, *Our Mary Jo*, 79–82, 97, 114.
8. Edward M. Kennedy quoted in Zeigler, *Inquest!*, 35–36.
9. John Farrar quoted in "Diver Said He Could've Saved Kopechne If Called Sooner," *New York Times*, July 22, 1969.
10. For those writers who accused Mary Jo Kopechne of having a sexual affair with Senator Edward M. Kennedy, see "The Mysteries of Chappaquiddick," *Time*, August 1, 1969; "A Scandal That Will Not Die," *Newsweek*, August 11, 1969; Jack Anderson, "Washington Merry-Go-Round," *Washington Post*, September 26, 1969; Charles Seib, "Enough of Chappaquiddick," *Washington Post*, November 16, 1979; Bob Weidrich, "Kennedy Short on Character," *Chicago Tribune*, November 18, 1979; McGinnis, *The Last Brother*, 557–58; Porter and Prince, *Jacqueline Kennedy Onassis*, 580–83; and Carr, *Kennedy Babylon*, 185. For those writers who accused Kopechne of having a sexual affair with Senator Robert F. Kennedy, see Heyman, *Bobby and Jackie*, 152–54; and Jerry Oppenheimer, "The Real Story of How Mary Jo Kopechne Was a Victim of the Kennedys TWICE," *Daily Mail*, April 6, 2018, www.dailymail.co.uk/news/article-5582233/How-Mary-Jo-Kopechne-victim-Kennedys-TWICE.html.
11. Janes B. Reston, "Kennedy's Career Feared Imperiled," *New York Times*, July 24, 1969; Rowland Evans and Robert Novak, "Appraising Kennedy Tragedy," *Newark Evening News*, July 24, 1969; "A Scandal That Will Not Die," *Newsweek*, August 11, 1969, 18–22; "Miserable, Tragic Accident May End the Kennedy Era," *Washington Post*, August 1, 1969; "Living with Whispers," *Time*, August 22, 1969, 13–14; "Kennedy's Time of Trial," *Newsweek*, September 8, 1969, 19–23; Tedrow and Tedrow, *Death at Chappaquiddick*, 35–39; Martin Schram, "Chappaquiddick: Millstone of Uncertain Weight," *Washington Post*, November 13, 1979; "Chappaquiddick Pulls Kennedy Down in Poll," *Washington Post*, January 7, 1980; Kappel, *Chappaquiddick Revealed*, 9; McGinniss, *Last Brother*, 603; *Investigative Reports: Chappaquiddick*; and Heyman, *Bobby and Jackie*, 152–54.
12. Judge James A. Boyle quoted in Damore, *Senatorial Privilege*, 193.
13. Paul F. Healy, "The Girl in Ted Kennedy's Car," *Ladies' Home Journal*, October 1969, 66, 147–50; Gwen Kopechne quoted in Suzanne James, "The Truth about Mary Jo," *McCall's Magazine*, September 1970, 65–66,

130–32; and Jane Farrell, "Memories of Mary Jo," *Ladies' Home Journal*, July 25, 1989, 108–13.

14. For those interested in books that deal exclusively with Chappaquiddick, see Hastings, *The Ted Kennedy Episode*; Olsen, *The Bridge at Chappaquiddick*; Rust, *Teddy Bare*; Cutler, *You, the Jury*; Reybold, *The Inspector's Opinion*; Tedrow and Tedrow, *Death at Chappaquiddick*; Sherill, *The Last Kennedy*; Willis, *Chappaquiddick Decision*; Damore, *Senatorial Privilege*; Kappel, *Chappaquiddick Revealed*; Lange and DeWitt, *Chappaquiddick*; Leland and Shaffer, *Left to Die*; Nelson, *Chappaquiddick Tragedy*; and Pinney and Jones, *Chappaquiddick Speaks*.

    Unlike these nonfictional accounts, novelist Joyce Carol Oates gives readers the victim's side of the story in her 1992 fictional account of the Chappaquiddick tragedy, *Black Water*. Although Oates insisted that the novella was "not about Chappaquiddick per se," she did admit that she felt a "horrified fascination and sympathy" for Mary Jo Kopechne (Oates quoted in Richard Bausch, "Her Thoughts while Drowning," *New York Times Book Review*, May 10, 1992).

    The novella is based on the experience of a twenty-six-year-old woman, Kelly Kelleher, a writer for a Boston-based magazine. Kelleher is also interested in politics. A graduate of Brown University, her senior honors thesis was about a powerful New England senator whom she meets at a Fourth of July party. The senator, who is older, married, and drunk, invites her back to his hotel room. After leaving the party, he takes the "old" Ferry Road instead of the "new" one. Driving recklessly, the car crashes through a guardrail into a marsh, landing passenger side down.

    The senator uses Kelly's body to jettison himself upward, out of the driver's side door. Kelly, badly injured and delirious, tries to free herself. During her last moments alive, as she struggles to keep her head in an air bubble, readers are given glimpses of her childhood and adolescence and flashbacks that reveal the senator's seduction. Composer John Duffy turned the novella into an opera, which premiered at the American Music Theater Festival in April 1997 ("Black Water: An American Opera," Celestial Timepiece: A Joyce Carol Oates Home Page, accessed April 12, 2009).

1. Humble Origins

1. For the early history of the Wyoming Valley, see Miner, *History of Wyoming*; Spear, *Wyoming Valley History Revisited*; Stefon, "The Wyoming Valley"; Hanlon and Zbiek, *The Wyoming Valley*; Moyer, *Wild Yankees*.

2. Northeast Pennsylvania's anthracite region is located across eight counties: Lackawanna, Luzerne, Carbon, Columbia, Northumberland, Schuylkill, Lebanon, and Dauphin.
3. Miller and Sharpless, *Kingdom of Coal*, 3–5, 52–68. In 1880 these four coalfields produced 27,974,532 tons of coal with a total workforce of 73,373 men. Three decades later, annual production had nearly tripled to 83,683,994 tons, and the total workforce had swelled to 168,175 men. By 1917, the peak year of production, the four anthracite fields turned out 100,445,299 tons of coal with a total workforce of 156,148 men.
4. The anthracite region's northern coalfield produced nearly thirty-five million tons of coal annually between 1910 and 1917. See Commonwealth of Pennsylvania, *Report of the Department of the Mine*, 18.
5. Greene, *The Slavic Community on Strike*, 2–3; and Barendse, *Social Expectations and Perception*, 226.
6. Miller and Sharpless, *Kingdom of Coal*, 125–21.
7. Population statistics for immigrants in the period 1875–1915 taken from table 4, "Region and Country or Area of Birth of the Foreign-Born Population, with Geographic Detail Shown in Decennial Census Publications of 1850 to 1930," in Gibson and Lennon, "Historical Census Statistics." Population statistics for eight-county anthracite region taken from *Federal Pennsylvania Census Records* for 1870, 1880, 1900, 1910, 1920.
8. Oscar Handlin, in his Pulitzer Prize–winning work, *The Uprooted*, was the first historian to concentrate on Eastern European immigration and assimilation into American life. He emphasized the importance of ethnic consciousness as an important first step in the assimilation process, particularly in urban areas where the members of the same ethnic group would congregate in order to translate their new American culture. A decade later, John Higham offered a more compelling argument by attributing nativism as the primary motivating factor in forcing immigrants to assimilate. Nativist attitudes demanded that immigrants conform to traditional Protestant American values. See Higham, *Strangers in the Land*.

   Barendse, *Social Expectations and Perception*, and Greene, *For God and Country*, both agree with Higham's argument and apply it to the Polish and Lithuanian immigrants of northeastern Pennsylvania. They argue further that for these two ethnic groups, the assimilation process was interrupted by a labor market divided along ethnic lines. This split market resulted in severe social animosities between these newly arrived eastern Europeans and the members of the more established northern European immigrants, most notably the English and the Welsh.

9. Potoski and Nelson, *Our Mary Jo*, 19–21. The original spelling was "Kopeczny" but was changed to "Kopechne" (pronounced *Ko-peck-nee*) in the United States. The ten children of Joseph and Johanna Kopechne were Mary (born 1863), Johanna (1865), Jenny (1867), Anna (1869), Frank (1876), William (1878), Gisela (1882), Louis (1883), Regina (1884), and John (1889).
10. Potoski and Nelson, *Our Mary Jo*, 18. Potoski claims that Joseph Kopechne was of Lithuanian extraction, though the surname is more commonly identified with the Czech Republic. But Kopechne's ancestors might have migrated south from Lithuania in the Baltic region to Hungary. Both countries were united under the same rulers for centuries, dating to 1386, when Jagello, the Grand Duke of Lithuania, married Hedwig, the daughter of the Hungarian and Polish monarch Louis the Great, and was crowned a king of Poland. See Engel, *The Realm of St. Stephen*, 297–98; and Frost, *The Oxford History of Poland-Lithuania, Volume I*, 278.
11. "Passenger List for Steamship, S.S. *Moravia*," Hamburg, Germany Passenger Lists, October 29, 1890–November 17, 1890, Ancestry.com. The ss *Moravia* was built in 1883 by A. and J. Inglis of Glasgow and purchased the same year by the Hamburg-American Line. She was a 3,739 gross ton ship, 361.3 feet long by 40.7 feet high. The steamship could accommodate 100 first-class and 1,200 third-class passengers. Her maiden voyage came on November 18, 1883, from Hamburg to Le Havre and New York. On November 25, 1898, she commenced her last Hamburg–Le Havre–New York voyage, and later the same year she was sold to Sloman of Hamburg, who intended to name her *Parma*, though this was never done. In January 1899 she sailed from Hamburg for New York but on February 12, 1899, was wrecked on Sable Island in the Canadian Maritimes, with no loss of life. See Bonsor, *North Atlantic Seaway*, 393.
12. Potoski and Nelson, *Our Mary Jo*, 19, 21–22. The eight children of Frank and Mary Kopechne were Louise (born 1900), George (1904), Antoinette (1907), Elizabeth (1908), Frances (1910), Joseph (1913), Edward (1916), and Raymond (1918). See 1920 U.S. Federal Census, Forty Fort Ward 2, Luzerne County, Pennsylvania, Roll T625_1592, Page 15A, Enumeration District 45, Ancestry.com.
13. Harold Aurand, "Child Labor and the Welfare of Children in an Anthracite Coal Mining Town," in Aurand, *Coal Towns*, 54; Roberts,

Anthracite Coal Communities, 181; Bartoletti, *Growing Up in Coal Country*, 34–37.

14. Frank and Mary's highest level of education is listed as "Elementary, 6th grade" in the 1940 Federal Census, Forty Fort, Luzerne, Pennsylvania, Roll M-T0627-03551, Page 12B, Enumeration District 40-60, Ancestry.com.
15. Potoski and Nelson, *Our Mary Jo*, 22–23.
16. Potoski and Nelson, *Our Mary Jo*, 24; and 1930 U.S. Federal Census, Kingston, Luzerne County, Pennsylvania, Roll 2069, Page 1A, Enumeration District 0102, Ancestry.com.
17. Potoski and Nelson, *Our Mary Jo*, 25; and 1920 U.S. Federal Census, Edwardsville Ward 7, Luzerne County, Pennsylvania, Roll T625_1591, Page 4B, Enumeration District 39, Ancestry.com.
18. Potoski and Nelson, *Our Mary Jo*, 26.
19. Potoski and Nelson, *Our Mary Jo*, 27.
20. Potoski and Nelson, *Our Mary Jo*, 28.
21. Potoski and Nelson, *Our Mary Jo*, 28; and 1930 U.S. Federal Census, Kingston, Luzerne County, Pennsylvania, Roll 2069, Page 1A, Enumeration District 0102, Ancestry.com.
22. Dublin and Licht, *The Face of Decline*, 59–66.
23. Dublin and Licht, *Face of Decline*, 62–68, 76, 182.
24. Kashatus, *Valley with a Heart*, viii; "WBRE's 'Little Bill' Phillips," *Times Leader* (Wilkes-Barre PA), May 13, 1937.
25. Potoski and Nelson, *Our Mary Jo*, 30.
26. Potoski and Nelson, *Our Mary Jo*, 32.
27. Joe Kopechne quoted in Rosemary K. Updyke, "Civilian Conservation Corps: Swiftwater Man Learned from Hard Times," *Pocono Post*, August 4–10, 1995.
28. Potoski and Nelson, *Our Mary Jo*, 32, 37, 40; and Updyke, "Civilian Conservation Corps," 33. Nesbitt Memorial Hospital is identified at Mary Jo's place of birth in "Death Took Kennedy to Coal Mining Town," *Lebanon (PA) Daily News*, July 23, 1969.
29. Joe Kopechne quoted in Potoski and Nelson, *Our Mary Jo*, 40.
30. Potoski and Nelson, *Our Mary Jo*, 41; Dublin and Licht, *Face of Decline*, 157.
31. Paul F. Healy, "The Girl in Ted Kennedy's Car," *Ladies' Home Journal*, October 1969, 147; and Alan Stenfors, interview with the author, Scituate, Massachusetts, May 10, 2018.
32. Potoski and Nelson, *Our Mary Jo*, 42.
33. Stenfors interview.

34. Healy, "Girl in Ted Kennedy's Car," 147.
35. Emalene Fargnoli Renna, interview with the author, Bainbridge Island, Washington, October 25, 2009; League of Women Voters, *This Is East Orange*, 9, 41.
36. Renna interview.
37. Renna interview.
38. Potoski and Nelson, *Our Mary Jo*, 40.
39. Potoski and Nelson, *Our Mary Jo*, 40, 50, 15–16.
40. Potoski and Nelson, *Our Mary Jo*, 26; Carol Caprik, email to author, November 22, 2009; Renna interview.
41. Renna interview; Caprik email.
42. Renna interview.
43. Renna interview; Potoski and Nelson, *Our Mary Jo*, 43, 50, 53; Renna interview.
44. Renna interview.
45. Donald Prial, "Friends Recall Mary Jo as Warm, Lively Person," *Newark Evening News*, July 21, 1969.
46. Our Lady of the Valley, *1958 Yearbook*, 62.

2. The Call to Serve

1. Renna interview.
2. Chambers, *Celebrating the Past*, 1–3, 9, 38.
3. Chambers, *Celebrating the Past*, 49.
4. Elly Gardner Kluge, interview with the author, Arlington, Virginia, October 11, 2009; Renna interview.
5. Sister Rita Margaret Chambers, interview with the author, Caldwell College, Caldwell, New Jersey, September 16, 2009.
6. Renna and Kluge interviews.
7. Chambers interview.
8. Manchester, *The Glory and the Dream*, 576–77.
9. Nancy Smack, interview with the author, Bishop, California, December 17, 2009.
10. Patricia Ann Murphy, interview with the author, Bloomfield, New Jersey, September 16, 2009.
11. Peter McKeown to Mr. and Mrs. Joseph Kopechne, San Francisco, July 24, 1969, Kopechne Estate.
12. "Mary-Jo Anne Kopechne," Caldwell College, *1962 Yearbook*, 138.
13. Hebblethwaite, *John XXIII*, 425.

14. Chambers interview.
15. Chambers, *Celebrating the Past*, 57, 64.
16. See issues of Caldwell College newspaper, *The Kettle*, and issues of the Montgomery Catholic High School newspaper, *Dixie Echoes*, for the years 1959–62.
17. Renna, Kluge, Smack interviews; Donald Prial, "Friends Recall Mary Jo as Warm, Lively Person," *Newark Evening News*, July 21, 1969.
18. For details on Joseph P. Kennedy's wealth and career, see Whalen, *The Founding Father*; Koskoff, *Joseph P. Kennedy*; Kessler, *The Sins of the Father*; and Nasaw, *The Patriarch*. In 1914 Joe Kennedy, at age twenty-five, was the youngest bank president in America. He first made a large fortune as a stock market and commodity investor and later rolled over his profits by investing in real estate and a wide range of business industries across the United States, including Radio-Keith-Orpheum Studios, Somerset Importers of Scotch, and Chicago's Merchandise Mart. By age forty, Kennedy was a multimillionaire. To prevent inheritance taxes from consuming the bulk of his estate, the Hollywood mogul began funneling his fortune into trust funds for his nine children as early as 1926. Kennedy's wealth has been estimated between $200 and $500 million at the time of his death on November 18, 1969. See Koskoff, *Joseph P. Kennedy*, 325, 331; Kessler, *Sins of the Father*, 423; and Nasaw, *The Patriarch*, xxi.
19. Hersh, *The Dark Side of Camelot*, 63–64; Davis, *The Kennedys*, 94; and Nasaw, *The Patriarch*, 492–96.
20. Leamer, *The Kennedy Men*, 313, 434; Koskoff, *Joseph P. Kennedy*, 425–26; and Nasaw, *The Patriarch*, 716–18.
21. Leamer, *The Kennedy Men*, 349.
22. From a very young age, Joseph P. Kennedy Jr. was allegedly groomed by his father to be the first Roman Catholic president of the United States. On June 24, 1941, before his final year of law school at Harvard, Joe Jr. enlisted in the U.S. Navy Reserve. He piloted land-based Liberator patrol bombers on antisubmarine details during two tours of duty in the winter of 1943–44. Although Kennedy had completed twenty-five combat missions and was eligible to return home, he volunteered for a secret bombing mission off the coast of Normandy, France, in August 1944. Kennedy, age twenty-nine, was killed when the bombs exploded prematurely exploded. See Elgood, *Crisis Hunter*, 13–14; Axelrod, *Lost Destiny*, 32–33; and Renahan, *The Kennedys at War*, 303–5.
23. John F. Kennedy quoted in Steel, *In Love with Night*, 33.

24. Oliphant and Wilkie, *Road to Camelot*, 3–4, 26–32.
25. Joseph P. Kennedy quoted in Oliphant and Wilkie, *Road to Camelot*, 7; Sorensen, *Counselor*, 170.
26. Sorensen, *Kennedy*, 83; Carty, *A Catholic in the White House?*, 129–57; Casey, *The Making of a Catholic President*, 4, 8. Sorensen's report was titled the "Bailey Memorandum" to distance Kennedy from the argument. John Bailey, state chairman of the Connecticut Democratic Party, was a fervent Kennedy supporter and had the report distributed to party officials before the 1956 national convention to promote JFK as Adlai Stevenson's running mate. William B. Prendergast, in *The Catholic Voter in American Politics*, argues that since the 1960 presidential election, when nearly 78 percent of Catholic voters supported Kennedy, Catholics gradually defected from the Democratic Party and by the end of the twentieth century coveted an independent status (186).
27. Oliphant and Wilkie, *Road to Camelot*, 131–35, 150–52.
28. Rorabaugh, *Kennedy and the Promise of the Sixties*, ix–x; Halberstam, *The Fifties*, 180–87; and MacKenzie and Weisbrot, *The Liberal Hour*, 14–37.
29. Oliphant and Wilkie, *Road to Camelot*, 203–4.
30. Clarke, *Ask Not*, 41–42. Kennedy's obsession with tanning was also a way to dispel rumors of poor health, which were actually true. Kennedy suffered from Addison's disease, a severe adrenal insufficiency. To hide the pallid complexion that often accompanies the disease, Kennedy, beginning with his first congressional campaign in 1946, traveled with a sun lamp, which he used frequently to maintain a dark tan.
31. See Hoffmann, *Theodore H. White*, 107–44; and Rick Perlstein, "Kennedy Week: The Myth of Camelot and the Dangers of Sycophantic Consensus Journalism," *The Nation*, November 23, 2013, www.thenation.com/article/Kennedy-week-myth-camelot-and-dangers-syncophantic-consensus-journalism/. JFK also courted Robert Drew, a former *Life* magazine correspondent turned documentary filmmaker, to create a visual recording of his presidential campaign. The result was a fifty-three-minute short titled "Primary," which features close-up footage of the Massachusetts senator as he traveled across the nation seeking votes. See "Primary," *Kennedy Films*.
32. Interview with John Mohrhauser, Asbury Park, New Jersey, April 27, 2010.
33. Mohrhauser interview.
34. Interview with Dick Toole, Berkeley Heights, New Jersey, February 3, 2010.
35. Toole interview.

36. Toole and Mohrhauser interviews.
37. White, *Making of the President*, 259–60.
38. O'Toole, *The Faithful*, 197–98.
39. White, *Making of the President*, 150–79.
40. See "Remarks of Senator John F. Kennedy on Church and State; Delivered to Greater Houston Ministerial Association, Houston, Texas, September 12, 1960," quoted in White, *Making of the President*, 391–93; and Massa, "A Catholic for President?"
41. Interestingly, Arthur M. Schlesinger Jr., a Harvard University history professor whom Kennedy would appoint to his cabinet as his official historian, argued that there wasn't much difference between the platforms and voting records of the young Democratic nominee and Nixon. But Schlesinger did laud Kennedy's abilities and potential for growth while scorning Nixon for having "no ideas, only methods" and for "caring only about winning." See Schlesinger, *Kennedy or Nixon*.
42. Kraus, *The Great Debates*; and Kallina, *Kennedy v. Nixon*.
43. "Final Presidential Vote, 1960," in White, *Making of the President*, 385–87.
44. Clarke, *Ask Not*, 190–201. Clarke offers a detailed paragraph-by-paragraph explication of Kennedy's inaugural address. Although many historians noted that the speech was restricted to foreign policy concerns, specifically the Cold War, Clarke argues that there were several allusions to domestic issues. For example, phrases like "man holds in his mortal hands the power to abolish all forms of human poverty" could have easily referred to the poverty in Appalachia as well as in the Third World. Similarly, when Kennedy spoke about "paying any price . . . to assure the survival and success of liberty," he might have been alluding to the promise he made to black voters about insuring their civil rights. Clarke, *Ask Not*, 209.
45. The most comprehensive book on Kennedy's administration and his New Frontier program is Schlesinger, *A Thousand Days*.
46. Bryant, *The Bystander*, 11–12, 466–68.
47. Levingston, *Kennedy and King*, viii–x; and "Crisis," *Kennedy Films*.
48. Seaborg, *Kennedy, Khrushchev*, 176, 199. Some misguided conspiracy theories maintain that Kennedy's decision to pursue detente with the Soviet Union provoked the CIA into engineering his assassination. See George M. Anderson, "Unmasking the Truth," *America*, May 12, 2011, 36–40; Vincent Canby, "JFK: When Everything Amounts to Nothing," *New York*

Times, December 20, 1991; and "JFK: The CIA, Vietnam and the Plot to Assassinate John F. Kennedy," *Publishers Weekly*, August 31, 1992.

49. Halberstam, *The Best and the Brightest*, 299–300; and Rust, *Kennedy in Vietnam*, 181–82.
50. Gwen Kopechne quoted in Suzanne James, "The Truth about Mary Jo," *McCall's Magazine*, September 1970, 66.
51. See Reverend J. Edwin Stuardi, Superintendent of Schools, to Mary Jo Kopechne, Montgomery AL, June 22, 1962, Kopechne Estate; and "School History," Montgomery Catholic Preparatory School, June 13, 2018, www.montgomerycatholic.org/domain/10.
52. Stuardi to Kopechne; "Northern Lay Apostle Joins Faculty at CHS," *Dixie Echoes*, September 7, 1962.
53. Interview with Lynn Jehle, Montgomery, May 13, 2015.
54. Interview with Maureen Clark, Montgomery, May 29, 2015.
55. Judith Hadden to the author, Kill Devil Hills, North Carolina, May 22, 2018.
56. Hadden to author.
57. Potoski and Nelson, *Our Mary Jo*, 64.
58. Hadden to author.
59. Hadden to author.
60. See Clark and Jehle interviews.
61. Branch, *Parting the Waters*, 143–205, 451–90.
62. Branch, *Parting the Waters*, 708–12.
63. Potoski and Nelson, *Our Mary Jo*, 66.
64. Evans, *Personal Politics*, 61, 82.
65. Gwen Kopechne quoted in Suzanne James, "The Truth about Mary Jo," *McCall's Magazine*, September 1970, 66. See Mohrhauser interview; Hadden to author.

3. True Believer

1. Potoski and Nelson, *Our Mary Jo*, 52.
2. Paul F. Healy, "The Girl in Ted Kennedy's Car," *Ladies' Home Journal*, October 1969, 66.
3. Gwen Kopechne quoted in James, "Truth about Mary Jo," 66.
4. "George Smathers, 93; Former Florida Senator," *Washington Post*, January 21, 2007.
5. Mudd, *The Place to Be*, 95.

6. Alford, *Once Upon a Secret*; Dallek, *An Unfinished Life*, 376, 475–80; Ernest R. May and Philip D. Zelikow, "Camelot Confidential," *Diplomatic History*, Fall 1998, 642–53; Reeves, *President Kennedy*, 287–90, 315–16; Parmet, *JFK*, 305–7.
7. Gwen Kopechne quoted in "Mary Jo Kopechne: A Fan of the Kennedys," *Daily Herald* (Big Spring TX), July 23, 1969.
8. E.C. (anonymous source), interview with author, Palo Alto, January 10, 2010.
9. Baker, *Wheeling and Dealing*, 80.
10. Baker, *Wheeling and Dealing*, 79. In 1967 Baker was sentenced to three years in federal prison for taking bribes and arranging sexual favors in exchange for congressional votes and government contracts. See Baker, *Wheeling and Dealing*, 201.
11. "Investigations: Bobby's Night Life," *Time*, November 8, 1963, http://content.time.com/time/magazine/article/0,9171,896999,00.html.
12. Schreiber, *The Bobby Baker Affair*.
13. Collins, *When Everything Changed*, 33–36; Friedan, *The Feminine Mystique*, 424.
14. Giele, *Two Paths*, 169–70; Kluge interview; Jeannie Main, interview with the author, Washington DC, January 21, 2015; and Renna interview.
15. Kluge, Main, and Renna interviews.
16. Potoski and Nelson, *Our Mary Jo*, 52.
17. Solvi Eggerz, "Mary Jo Was Dedicated to the Kennedys," *Roll Call*, July 25, 1969; Potoski and Nelson, *Our Mary Jo*, 52.
18. Sorensen, *The Kennedy Legacy*, 201–7; Gwen Kopechne quoted in Jane Farrell, "Memories of Mary Jo," *Ladies' Home Journal*, July 25, 1989, 110.
19. Interview with Owen Lopez, Santa Fe, November 18, 2009; interview with Carol Teague Condon, Point Pleasant Beach, New Jersey, January 23, 2015; and Potoski and Nelson, *Our Mary Jo*, 82.
20. Kluge and Renna interviews; Paul F. Healy, "The Girl in Ted Kennedy's Car," *Ladies' Home Journal*, October 1969, 147.
21. Jacqueline Kennedy quoted by Theodore H. White, "For President Kennedy: An Epilogue," *Life*, December 6, 1963, 158–59. See also Jacqueline Bouvier Kennedy to Harold Macmillan, Washington DC, January 30, 1964, quoted in Kennedy, *The Historic Conversations*, 247n29; and Smith, *Grace and Power*, xvii–xix. Documentary film director Robert Drew helped to craft the Camelot legend with several short films on JFK. The final one, "Faces of November," was a poetic tribute to the fallen president. See "Faces of November," *Kennedy Films*.

22. Theodore H. White, "Handwritten Notes on Camelot Documents"; White, "For President Kennedy," Theodore H. White Personal Papers, John F. Kennedy Library and Museum.
23. See Hoffmann, *Theodore H. White*, 162–63; and Rick Perlstein, "Kennedy Week: The Myth of Camelot and the Dangers of Sycophantic Consensus Journalism," *The Nation*, November 23, 2013.
24. Jacqueline Kennedy quoted by White, "For President Kennedy," 158.
25. Schlesinger, *A Thousand Days*, 1030–31.
26. For conspiracy theories involving the JFK assassination, see Lifton, *Best Evidence*; Waldron with Hartmann, *Ultimate Sacrifice*; and Nolan, *CIA Rogues*. For public distrust of U.S. foreign policy during the Vietnam War, see Halberstam, *The Best and the Brightest*; and McNamara, *In Retrospect*. For the decline of the U.S. presidency, see Schlesinger, *The Imperial Presidency*; and McKenna, *All His Bright Light Gone*.
27. Hilty, *Robert Kennedy*, 6–7; and *RFK*.
28. Adlai Stevenson quoted in Hersh, *Bobby and J. Edgar*, 6.
29. Schlesinger, *Robert Kennedy and His Times*, 348; and *RFK*.
30. Mahoney, *Sons and Brothers*, 86–87; and Hilty, *Brother Protector*, 186–87.
31. Joe Kennedy quoted in Koskoff, *Joseph P. Kennedy*, 461; and Joe Kennedy quoted in Kessler, *Sins of the Father*, 306.
32. Neff, *Vendetta*; Goldfarb, *Perfect Villains, Imperfect Heroes*.
33. Hersh, *Bobby and J. Edgar*, 219, 485.
34. Schlesinger, *Robert Kennedy and His Times*, 614–20; Wofford, *Of Kennedys and Kings*, 384–406; and Bryan Bender and Neil Swidey, "Robert F. Kennedy Saw Conspiracy in JFK's Assassination," *Boston Globe*, November 24, 2013.
35. Nicholas Katzenback quoted in Talbot, *Brothers*, 277.
36. Hersh, *Bobby and J. Edgar*, 448; *RFK*.
37. Mahoney, *Sons and Brothers*, 301–2.
38. Goodwin, *Remembering America*, 450.
39. Guthman, *We Band of Brothers*, 247.
40. Bohrer, *Revolution of Robert Kennedy*, 107–8; Shakespeare quotation from *Romeo and Juliet*, act III, scene II, lines 23–27.
41. Philip Quarles, "Robert F. Kennedy Announces His Senate Candidacy, 1964," Annotations: The NEH Preservation Project, November 5, 2012, www.wnyc.org/story/192691-robert-kennedy/; Schlesinger, *Robert Kennedy and His Times*, 666–76.

42. Alden Whitman, "Keating Dies at 74; Envoy, Ex-Senator," *New York Times*, May 6, 1975.
43. Bohrer, *Revolution of Robert Kennedy*, 114–15; Schlesinger, *Robert Kennedy and His Times*, 668–69.
44. James Desmond, "Bobby Claims Victory over Keating," *New York Daily News*, November 4, 1964; Schlesinger, *Robert Kennedy and His Times*, 675.
45. Schlesinger, *Robert Kennedy and His Times*, 676–77.
46. Adam Bernstein, "Frank Mankiewicz, Political and Media Insider, Dies at 90," *Washington Post*, October 23, 2014. Ed Guthman, RFK's press secretary at Justice, returned to his newspaper career in 1965. He was replaced by Wes Barthelmes, a reporter who had been working for Congresswoman Edith Green. Barthelmes, overwhelmed by the demands on him, resigned after one year, and he was replaced by Mankiewicz. See Schlesinger, *Robert Kennedy and His Times*, 676–77.
47. "Obituary: Wendell Pigman, Legislative Aide," *New York Times*, March 20, 1973; interview with Judith Cromwell, Saint Louis, January 25, 2015; Jeannie Main interview.
48. Esther Newberg, recorded interview with Rosemary Keough, May 22, 1969, 2, Robert F. Kennedy Oral History Project, John F. Kennedy Library and Museum, https://archive1.jfklibrary.org/RFKOH/Newberg,%20Esther%20R/RFKOH-ERN-01/RFKOH-ERN-01-TR.pdf.
49. Cromwell interview; Bohrer, *Revolution of Robert Kennedy*, 158.
50. Schlesinger, *Robert Kennedy and His Times*, 677.
51. Paul F. Healy, "The Girl in Ted Kennedy's Car," *Ladies' Home Journal*, October 1969, 66.
52. Memorandum, Joe Dolan to RFK, March 11, 1965, Joseph F. Dolan Personal Papers, Box 1: "Memoranda, December 5, 1964–April 15, 1965," John F. Kennedy Library and Museum.
53. Wendell Pigman quoted in Healy, "Girl in Ted Kennedy's Car," 148; Cromwell and Main interviews.
54. Angela Novello to Mr. and Mrs. Joseph Kopechne, Washington DC, August 31, 1969, Kopechne Estate.
55. Interview with Donald McFadden, Wilkes-Barre, May 10, 2010.
56. Nicholas Katzenbach quoted in Schlesinger, *Robert Kennedy and His Times*, 241.
57. Ronald Steel in his book *In Love with Night*, 149.
58. Cromwell interview.
59. Frank Mankiewicz quoted in Healy, "Girl in Ted Kennedy's Car," 148.

60. Potoski and Nelson, *Our Mary Jo*, 95.
61. Interview with Melody Miller, Washington DC, March 15, 2015.
62. Novello to Mr. and Mrs. Joseph Kopechne.
63. Ethel Kennedy to Mr. and Mrs. Joseph Kopechne, McLean VA, July 22, 1969, Kopechne Estate.
64. Ethel Kennedy to Mr. and Mrs. Joseph Kopechne.
65. Hersh, *Edward Kennedy*, 346.
66. Frank Mankiewicz quoted in Suzanne James, "The Truth about Mary Jo," *McCall's Magazine*, September 1970, 132; Senator George Smathers quoted in Heyman, *Bobby and Jackie*, 152–53. Wes Barthelmes, who preceded Mankiewicz as RFK's press secretary, expressed similar sentiments about Kopechne. See Barthelmes quoted in Solvi Eggerz, "Mary Jo Was Dedicated to the Kennedys," *Roll Call*, July 25, 1969.
67. Frank Mankiewicz quoted in Potoski, *Our Mary Jo*, 81; Cromwell interview.
68. Potoski and Nelson, *Our Mary Jo*, 97; Healy, "Girl in Ted Kennedy's Car," 148.
69. Lopez interview; Potoski and Nelson, *Our Mary Jo*, 89; Cromwell and Main interviews; Oppenheimer, *RFK Jr.*, 89.
70. Lopez interview; Lopez quoted in James, "Truth about Mary Jo," 130.
71. James, "Truth about Mary Jo," 130.
72. Schlesinger, *Robert Kennedy and His Times*, 786–89.
73. Steel, *In Love with Night*, 125–27.
74. RFK, "Speech on Child Poverty and Hunger," University of Notre Dame, South Bend, April 4, 1968, in Guthman and Allen, *RFK*, 361–63.
75. Coles quoted in Thomas, *Robert Kennedy*, 340, 20–21.
76. Coles quoted in Thomas, *Robert Kennedy*, 339–40; Cromwell interview.
77. Halberstam, *The Best and the Brightest*, 272–76.
78. Wofford, *Of Kennedys and Kings*, 421–22.
79. Schlesinger, *Robert Kennedy and His Times*, 732, 739–40, 770–71; Kennedy, *American Values*, 325–26.
80. RFK quoted in Schlesinger, *Robert Kennedy and His Times*, 773.
81. Kluge interview.

4. Boiler Room Girl

1. Ted Kennedy quoted in Schlesinger, *Robert Kennedy and His Times*, 680.
2. Schlesinger, *Robert Kennedy and His Times*, 681; and *RFK*.
3. Ted Kennedy quoted in Schlesinger, *Robert Kennedy and His Times*, 680–81.

4. Schlesinger, *Robert Kennedy and His Times*, 681. During his time on the McCarthy Army hearings and the Rackets probe in the 1950s, RFK made the acquaintances of such senators as George McGovern (South Dakota), Frank Church (Idaho), Birch Bayh (Indiana), and Claiborne Pell (Rhode Island).
5. Tye, *Bobby Kennedy*, 389–90.
6. Jeff Greenfield, "When Bobby Decided to Run," *Politico*, March 17, 2018, www.politico.com/magazine/story/2018/03/17/bobby-kennedy-election-1968-217648.
7. Greenfield, "When Bobby Decided to Run."
8. White, *Making of the President*, 101–3; Clarke, *The Last Campaign*, 20–22; *RFK*.
9. RFK quoted in Gutman and Allen, *RFK: Words for Our Times*, 322–24.
10. Steel, *In Love With Night*, 170–71.
11. Hersh, *Edward Kennedy*, 347.
12. Solvi Eggerz, "Mary Jo Was Dedicated to the Kennedys," *Roll Call*, July 25, 1969.
13. Interview with K. Dun Gifford, Cambridge, Massachusetts, January 5, 2010.
14. Newberg interview with Keough; Gifford interview; and Damore, *Senatorial Privilege*, 118–19. The concept of a Boiler Room as an intelligence-gathering operation was devised by Larry O'Brien and Dave Hackett during JFK's 1960 presidential campaign.
15. "Who's Who at the Kennedy Inquest," *Time*, September 5, 1969, www.time.com/time/magazine/article/0,9171,901341–4,00.html.
16. Gifford interview.
17. Mary Jo Kopechne quoted in Damore, *Senatorial Privilege*, 119–20; Jimmy Smith quoted in *Boston Globe*, August 24, 1969.
18. Barbara Coleman, recorded interview by Ann Campbell, January 9, 1970, 36, Robert F. Kennedy Oral History Project, John F. Kennedy Library and Museum.
19. Paul F. Healy, "The Girl in Ted Kennedy's Car," *Ladies' Home Journal*, October 1969, 148; Gwen Kopechne quoted in Suzanne James, "The Truth about Mary Jo," *McCall's Magazine*, September 1970, 66.
20. Maureen Dowd, "What's a Modern Girl to Do?," *New York Times*, October 30, 2005; Baumgardner and Richards, *Manifesta*, 325–42; and Giele, *Two Paths*, 1–4. The ideology and philosophy of feminism has changed since the women's rights movement began in the mid-nineteenth century. The initial wave of feminism centered around women's suffrage

beginning with the 1848 Seneca Falls Convention in upstate New York. In the late 1960s, a second wave of feminism emerged among two distinctive groups: equal rights feminists, mostly older white women who fought for equality in the workplace and home by seeking antidiscrimination laws in the job market and greater educational opportunities; and radical feminists, mostly young white women who demanded greater equality in a male-dominated society by deconstructing gender roles and recognizing lesbians. A third wave of feminism was initiated by minority women in the mid-1990s to address the failures of the second wave. Some historians argue that a fourth wave of feminism exists today and that it uses the internet and social media to spread awareness of feminist concerns. An example is the #MeToo campaign, which employs hashtag activism.

21. Giele, *Two Paths*, 165; and Evans, *Personal Politics*, 9–11.
22. Collins, *When Everything Changed*, 5–8.
23. Main interview.
24. Interview with Adam Walinsky, Colorado Springs, June 18, 2018.
25. Gifford interview.
26. Hersh, *Edward Kennedy*, 346.
27. Gifford interview.
28. Barbara Coleman, interview with Ann Campbell, Washington DC, January 9, 1970, 56, Robert F. Kennedy Oral History Project, John F. Kennedy Library and Museum.
29. Hersh, *Edward Kennedy*, 347.
30. Heyman, *Bobby and Jackie*, 152–53.
31. Heyman, *RFK*, 516.
32. Jerry Oppenheimer, "The Real Story of How Mary Jo Kopechne Was a Victim of the Kennedys TWICE," *Daily Mail*, April 6, 2018.
33. Margalit Fox, "C. David Heymann, Biographer of the Rich and Famous, Dies at 67," *New York Times*, May 10, 2012.
34. See Review of *The Other Mrs. Kennedy: Ethel Skakel Kennedy: An American Drama of Power, Privilege, and Politics*, by Jerry Oppenheimer, *Publishers Weekly*, accessed August 2, 2018, www.publishersweekly.com/9780312110406; Jonathan I. Lyons, Review of *RFK, Jr.: Robert F. Kennedy, Jr., and the Dark Side of the Dream*, by Jerry Oppenheimer, *Publishers Weekly*, accessed August 2, 2018, www.publishersweekly.com/9781250032959.
35. Wendell Pigman quoted in Solvi Eggerz, "Mary Jo Was Dedicated to the Kennedys," *Roll Call*, July 25, 1969.

36. Main interview; Paul F. Healy, "The Girl in Ted Kennedy's Car," *Ladies' Home Journal*, October 1969, 148.
37. News of King's death on April 4, 1968, prompted riots and fires in cities across America. Kennedy, who was campaigning in Indiana, was urged to cancel a rally in inner-city Indianapolis that night. But RFK refused, insisting that he would speak to the crowd despite the very real threat of violence. His extemporaneous talk was arguably the most moving of all the speeches he gave during the 1968 presidential campaign. See *A Ripple of Hope*.
38. Edelman, *Searching for America's Heart*, 94.
39. Cromwell, Gifford, Main, and Walinsky interviews.
40. Nolan, *CIA Rogues*, 181. Sirhan was convicted of murder and is serving a life sentence at the Richard J. Donovan Correctional Facility in San Diego County, California. See "Robert Kennedy Assassin, Sirhan Sirhan, Denied Parole: Official," *Newsweek*, February 11, 2016, www.newsweek.com/robert-kennedy-assassin-sirhan-sirhan-denied-parole-official-425598.
41. Klagsbrun and Whitney, *Assassination*, 81–84. There is a growing body of literature contending that a conspiracy to kill RFK involved the Central Intelligence Agency and the Los Angeles Police Department. For conspiracy theories on RFK's assassination, see Melanson, *The Robert F. Kennedy Assassination*; Turner and Christian, *The Assassination of Robert F. Kennedy*; Kaiser, *RFK Must Die!*; Faura, *The Polka Dot File*; O'Sullivan, *Who Killed Bobby?*; Tate and Johnson, *The Assassination of Robert F. Kennedy*.
42. Frank Mankiewicz quoted in *Ted Kennedy, Part 2*.
43. Dun Gifford quoted in *Ted Kennedy, Part 2*.
44. Klagsbrun and Whitney, *Assassination*, 193–96.
45. Klagsbrun and Whitney, *Assassination*, 197–207.
46. Canellos, *Last Lion*, 136–38.
47. Ted Kennedy quoted in Hersh, *Education of Edward Kennedy*, 351.
48. Clymer, *Edward M. Kennedy*, 141–42.
49. Joe Gargan quoted in Damore, *Senatorial Privilege*, 68.
50. Cromwell interview.
51. Damore, *Senatorial Privilege*, 67–68.
52. Damore, *Senatorial Privilege*, 154; Nance Lyons, interview by Janet Heininger, May 9, 2008, Edward M. Kennedy Oral History Project,

Miller Center, University of Virginia, millercenter.org/poh/transcripts /ohp_2008_0309_lyons.pdf.

53. Gifford interview; Gifford quoted in *Ted Kennedy, Part 2*.
54. Canellos, *Last Lion*, 148.
55. Cromwell interview.
56. See “Who’s Who at the Kennedy Inquest,” *Time*, September 5, 1969; Melody Miller, interview by Janet Heininger, Edward M. Kennedy Oral History Project, Miller Center, University of Virginia.
57. Tye, *Bobby Kennedy*, 394.
58. Gwen and Joseph Kopechne quoted in Jane Farrell, “Memories of Mary Jo,” *Ladies’ Home Journal*, July 25, 1989, 110.
59. Mary Jo Kopechne quoted by Sister Margaret Anne in Robert L. Ward, “Nun Recalls Mary Jo: An Active, Popular Girl,” *Boston Globe*, July 20, 1969.
60. Paul F. Healy, “The Girl in Ted Kennedy’s Car,” *Ladies’ Home Journal*, October 1969, 150; Potoski and Nelson, *Our Mary Jo*, 110.
61. Gifford and Main interviews; Potoski and Nelson, *Our Mary Jo*, 149. Matt Reese was an insurance salesman when he was asked to join John Kennedy’s presidential campaign in West Virginia in 1959. Working out of the Kanawha Hotel in Charleston, he organized all fifty-five counties and recruited thousands of campaign volunteers. JFK’s success in the battleground state propelled Reese into national prominence. In 1961 he joined the Democratic National Committee as deputy chairman. Three years later, he campaigned for Lyndon Johnson’s reelection bid. In 1966 Reese established his own campaign consulting business in Washington DC, working with such notable Democratic candidates as Tip O’Neill, John Glenn, and Jay Rockefeller. During his career, Reese worked on more than 450 campaigns. He sold his consulting business in 1986 and taught at Harvard University and later at George Washington University. He died on December 1, 1998, at his home in McLean, Virginia. He was seventy-one years old.
62. Interview with Michael Bonafede, Denver, December 16, 2015; Healy, “Girl in Ted Kennedy’s Car,” 150; Bonafede interview. McNichol lost the election. See Fred Brown, “Ex-Governor McNichol Dies at 83,” *Denver Post*, November 26, 1997.
63. Mary Jo quoted by Sister Regina in Donald Prial, “Friends Recall Mary Jo as Warm, Lively Person,” *Newark Evening News*, July 21, 1969.

64. Gwen Kopechne quoted in Suzanne James, "The Truth about Mary Jo," *McCall's Magazine*, September 1970, 131.
65. Reynold Reimer quoted in Healy, "Girl in Ted Kennedy's Car," 148, 150.
66. Biographer Joe McGinniss contends that just before the Chappaquiddick reunion, Mary Jo had "ended a long intense relationship with a marine officer stationed at Quantico and was in a rather unsettled emotional condition." See McGinniss, *The Last Brother*, 557–58. But the allegation does not square with the accounts of her parents and friends, who insisted that she was happy and content with her personal and professional lives. See Joseph and Gwen Kopechne quoted in James, "Truth about Mary Jo," 131; Kluge, Cromwell, and Main interviews.
67. Matt Reese quoted in Healy, "Girl in Ted Kennedy's Car," 150.
68. Joe Kopechne quoted in James, "Truth about Mary Jo," 131.
69. Gwen Kopechne quoted in James, "Truth about Mary Jo," 131; Healy, "Girl in Ted Kennedy's Car," 150.
70. James, "Truth about Mary Jo," 131; Potoski and Nelson, *Our Mary Jo*, 115.
71. Kurson, *Rocket Men*, 5, 312–14.
72. Mary Jo Kopechne quoted in April Reese to Mr. and Mrs. Joseph Kopechne, Washington DC, July 20, 1969, Kopechne Estate.
73. Reese to Mr. and Mrs. Joseph Kopechne.
74. Reese to Mr. and Mrs. Joseph Kopechne.
75. Gwen Kopechne quoted in James, "Truth about Mary Jo," 131.

5. Chappaquiddick

1. Pinney and Jones, *Chappaquiddick Speaks*, 1. For details on geography of Martha's Vineyard and Chappaquiddick, an Indian name meaning "separate island," see the accounts of longtime residents: Nelson, *Chappaquiddick Tragedy*, 18; and Leland and Shaffer, *Left to Die*, ix–xii.
2. E. Kennedy, *True Compass*, 287–88.
3. EMK testimony quoted in Edgartown District Court, *Inquest into the Death of Mary Jo Kopechne*, 2.
4. Vivian Cadden, "What Happened at Chappaquiddick," *McCall's Magazine*, August 1974, 80.
5. Jack Crimmins testimony quoted in Edgartown District Court, *Inquest into the Death of Mary Jo Kopechne*, 49; and David, *Good Ted, Bad Ted*, 136.
6. Cadden, "What Happened at Chappaquiddick," 81.
7. Cadden, "What Happened at Chappaquiddick," 81.

8. Pinney and Jones, *Chappaquiddick Speaks*, iii.
9. "Who's Who at the Kennedy Inquest," *Time*, September 5, 1969.
10. Gifford interview.
11. Tip O'Neill quoted in McGinniss, *The Last Brother*, 529.
12. Manchester, *The Glory and the Dream*, 1183.
13. Koskoff, *Joseph P. Kennedy*, 474.
14. Canellos, *Last Lion*, 146–47.
15. E. Kennedy, *True Compass*, 282, 281.
16. McGinniss, *Last Brother*, 533.
17. EMK, Jack Crimmins, and Joseph Gargan testimonies in Edgartown District Court, *Inquest into the Death of Mary Jo Kopechne*, 3, 49, 32; McGinniss, *Last Brother*, 534.
18. EMK and Raymond LaRosa testimonies in Edgartown District Court, *Inquest into the Death of Mary Jo Kopechne*, 3, 14.
19. Cadden, "What Happened at Chappaquiddick," 120.
20. Gargan testimony in Edgartown District Court, *Inquest into the Death of Mary Jo Kopechne*, 33.
21. Tretter quoted in Hersh, *Education of Edward Kennedy*, 392.
22. Canellos, *Last Lion*, 151.
23. Foster Silva quoted in Leland and Shaffer, *Left to Die*, 4.
24. EMK and Crimmins testimonies in Edgartown District Court, *Inquest into the Death of Mary Jo Kopechne*, 4, 51.
25. EMK, "Statement of Accident Submitted to Chief Arena," inquest exhibit 2 in Damore, *Senatorial Privilege*, 438.
26. Leland and Shaffer, *Left to Die*, 4–5, ix–x; Nelson, *Chappaquiddick Tragedy*, 24; EMK testimony in Edgartown District Court, *Inquest into the Death of Mary Jo Kopechne*, 5; Damore, *Senatorial Privilege*, 20.
27. EMK, "Statement of Accident." See also Pinney and Jones, *Chappaquiddick Speaks*, 304; Leland and Shaffer, *Left to Die*, 4; Canellos, *Last Lion*, 152.
28. EMK testimony in Edgartown District Court, *Inquest into the Death of Mary Jo Kopechne*, 8.
29. EMK, Gargan, and Markham testimonies in Edgartown District Court, *Inquest into the Death of Mary Jo Kopechne*, 9–10, 35, 44–45, 36.
30. EMK testimony in Edgartown District Court, *Inquest into the Death of Mary Jo Kopechne*, 12.
31. EMK and Russell Peachy testimonies in Edgartown District Court, *Inquest into the Death of Mary Jo Kopechne*, 10, 65.

32. Ross Richards testimony in Edgartown District Court, *Inquest into the Death of Mary Jo Kopechne*, 38.
33. EMK testimony in Edgartown District Court, *Inquest into the Death of Mary Jo Kopechne*, 10–11.
34. Steve Ewing quoted in *Investigative Reports: Chappaquiddick*, 15:37–15:44.
35. EMK testimony in Edgartown District Court, *Inquest into the Death of Mary Jo Kopechne*, 46; Gargan quoted in Damore, *Senatorial Privilege*, 91.
36. Damore, *Senatorial Privilege*, 91.
37. Nance Lyons and Joe Gargan quoted in Damore, *Senatorial Privilege*, 91–92. In a 2008 interview, Nance Lyons emphatically denied that she made the suggestion to have someone else drive the car instead of Kennedy. Instead, she insisted that Gargan made the suggestion and that "it was the [Boiler Room] women who derailed that 'brilliant' idea." She added, "We refused to go along—not that I think the Senator was aware of that proposal." See Nance Lyons, interview with Janet Heininger, May 9, 2008, Edward M. Kennedy Oral History Project, Miller Center, University of Virginia, millercenter.org/poh/transcripts/ohp_2008_0309_lyons.pdf.
38. Jim Arena quoted in Canellos, *Last Lion*, 157–58; Damore, *Senatorial Privilege*, 7.
39. Damore, *Senatorial Privilege*, 7–8; John Farrar testimony in Edgartown District Court, *Inquest into the Death of Mary Jo Kopechne*, 78; and David, *Good Ted, Bad Ted*, 140.
40. Farrar testimony in Edgartown District Court, *Inquest into the Death of Mary Jo Kopechne*, 79.
41. Arena quoted in Damore, *Senatorial Privilege*, 9.
42. "Lack of Autopsy Unusual," *Evening News* (Newark), July 25, 1969.
43. Farrar and Dominick Arena testimonies in Edgartown District Court, *Inquest into the death of Mary Jo Kopechne*, 85; Damore, *Senatorial Privilege*, 9–10.
44. Gwen Kopechne quoted in Suzanne James, "The Truth about Mary Jo," *McCall's Magazine*, September 1970, 130; Joe Kopechne quoted in McGinniss, *Last Brother*, 556.
45. EMK and Arena quoted in Damore, *Senatorial Privilege*, 18–19; EMK, "Statement of Accident."
46. Damore, *Senatorial Privilege*, 24–25.
47. Interview with Liz Trotta, New York, July 28, 2018.

48. James R. Dickenson, "Richard Drayne, Press Aide in Kennedy Campaigns, Dies," *Washington Post*, June 20, 1987.
49. Trotta interview.
50. Canellos, *Last Lion*, 161; McGinniss, *Last Brother*, 553.
51. Dun Gifford quoted in *Investigative Report: Chappaquiddick*, 35:09–35:21.
52. Joe Kopechne quoted in Damore, *Senatorial Privilege*, 139.
53. Michael Graham quoted in *Scandalous: Chappaquiddick*, ep. 1: "The Bridge," 45:01–46:08.
54. See Richard Powers and Alan Lupo, "Ted Kennedy Escapes, Woman Dies as Car Plunges into Vineyard Pond," *Boston Globe*, July 20, 1969. The three stories that appeared on the front page were Richard Powers and Alan Lupo, "Senator Wanders in Daze for Hours"; Timothy Leland, "'There's a Car in the Water'"; and Ken O. Botwright, "Mother in Shock: Ted First to Call Victim's Father." See Victor K. McElheney, "All Is Go for Moon Landing," *Boston Globe*, July 20, 1969.
55. Canellos, *Last Lion*, 164; Arena quoted in Richard Harwood, "Kennedy Cleared of Any Negligence," *Washington Post*, July 22, 1969.
56. McGinniss, *Last Brother*, 560; Leamer, *The Kennedy Women*, 647.
57. Theodore Sorensen, interview by James S. Young, December 7, 2006, Edward M. Kennedy Oral History Project, Miller Center, University of Virginia, millercenter.org/poh/transcripts/ohp_2006_1207_sorensen.pdf.
58. McGinniss, *Last Brother*, 560, 552; Leamer, *The Kennedy Women*, 647.
59. Esther Newberg was quoted in the *Chicago Tribune*, July 25, 1969; *New York Times*, July 23, 1969; and the *Worcester (MA) Gazette*, July 23, 1969.
60. McGinniss, *Last Brother*, 581; Sorensen interview.
61. See McNamara, *Eunice*, 235; and Taraborelli, *After Camelot*, 101. Hanify quoted in McGinniss, *Last Brother*, 581.
62. Ethel Kennedy quoted in *Boston Globe*, July 21, 1969. Nancy Cummings of *Newsweek* was taken aback by Ethel Kennedy's statement. She viewed it as "patronizing as hell." According to Cummings, "'typing' was the operative word to signify Mary Jo had been devoted in her service to the Kennedys. All that was required to account for her death apparently was a posthumous pat on the head. No amount of public relations was going to get around the fact that Mary Jo Kopechne had died in Ted Kennedy's car and he had taken ten hours to tell the police about it." See Cummings quoted in Damore, *Senatorial Privilege*, 115.

63. Liz Trotta quoted in *Scandalous: Chappaquiddick*, ep. 1: "The Bridge," 46:51.
64. Helen Kielty quoted in Libby Brennan, "Funeral Aide Recalls Scene Here in 1969," *Sunday Independent* (Wilkes-Barre PA), July 16, 1989.
65. Damore, *Senatorial Privilege*, 141–42.
66. Joe Kopechne quoted in McGinniss, *Last Brother*, 571.
67. "Kennedy Attends Funeral of Girl Killed in Auto Wreck," *New Mexican* (Santa Fe), July 22, 1969.
68. Joe Kopechne quoted in Don Prial, "Sen. Kennedy, Wife Attend Girl's Rites," *Evening News* (Newark), July 22, 1969; and Damore, *Senatorial Privilege*, 139.
69. Joe Kopechne quoted in Oppenheimer, *RFK Jr.*, 34.
70. For details of the funeral mass and the gravesite service, see Prial, "Sen. Kennedy, Wife Attend Girl's Rites"; "Kennedy Offers Prayers at Funeral for Crash Victim," *Capitol Times* (Madison WI), July 22, 1969; "Death Took Kennedy to Coal Mining Town," *Lebanon (PA) Daily News*, July 23, 1969; Linda Miller, "Chappaquiddick: Twenty Years Later, Local Residents Recall Kopechne Funeral, Kennedy," *Times Leader* (Wilkes-Barre PA), July 18, 1989; Joe Cooper, "Maintaining Dignity Was Primary Concern," *Sunday Independent* (Wilkes-Barre PA), July 16, 1989; and Brennan, "Funeral Aide Recalls Scene."
71. EMK and Liz Trotta quoted in "Kennedy Attends Kopechne Funeral," *Boston Herald Traveler*, June 23, 1969.
72. Trotta interview.
73. EMK testimony quoted in Edgartown District Court, *Commonwealth v. Edward M. Kennedy*, transcript published in *New York Times*, July 26, 1969.
74. Judge James A. Boyle and Arena quoted in Edgartown District Court, *Commonwealth v. Edward M. Kennedy*.
75. Boyle quoted in *Commonwealth v. Edward M. Kennedy*.
76. Sorensen interview. According to Sorensen, the statement Kennedy read on national television was a "consensus view" prepared by all the lawyers who formed the senator's crisis management during the days immediately after the Chappaquiddick accident. While Sorensen admitted Kennedy "participated some in what had to be said," Burke Marshall and Steve Smith had the "most input on that speech."
77. McGinniss, *Last Brother*, 589.

78. EMK, "Televised Speech on Chappaquiddick," WHDH-TV Boston, quoted in Damore, *Senatorial Privilege*, 204–5; "Ted Kennedy Car Accident in Chappaquiddick," *Newsweek*, August 3, 1969, www.newsweek.com/ted-kennedy-car-accident-chappaquiddick-207070.
79. For public opinion poll and quotes from Gwen Kopechne, Tom McIntyre, and Edmund Muskie, see Canellos, *Last Lion*, 172.
80. Steve Kurkjian quoted in *Ted Kennedy, Part 3*, 7:34–7:47.
81. Trotta interview.
82. Dun Gifford quoted in *Investigative Report: Chappaquiddick*, 18:37–19:04.
83. Leland and Shaffer, *Left to Die*, 35–38.
84. Interview with Joseph Flanagan, Forty Fort, May 17, 2010.
85. Judge Bernard Brominski quoted in Luzerne Court of Common Pleas, "Decision: Kopechne, Petition for Exhumation and Autopsy" (No. 1114 of 1969), 13, Luzerne County Court House, Wilkes-Barre.
86. Leland and Shaffer, *Left to Die*, xiii–xiv.
87. See Edgartown District Court, *Inquest into the Death of Mary Jo Kopechne*; and Leland and Shaffer, *Left to Die*, 39.
88. Boyle quoted in Edgartown District Court, *Inquest into the Death of Mary Jo Kopechne*, 123–26.
89. "End of the Affair," *Time*, April 20, 1970; and Leland and Shaffer, *Left to Die*, 99–107.
90. Interview with Leslie Leland, Vineyard Haven, Massachusetts, January 8, 2010. For a more detailed account of Leland's frustrations with the grand jury session, see Leland and Shaffer, *Left to Die*, 109–14.

6. Unanswered Questions

1. For conspiracy theories on Chappaquiddick, see Hastings, *The Ted Kennedy Episode*; Olsen, *The Bridge at Chappaquiddick*; Rust, *Teddy Bare*; Cutler, *You, the Jury*; Reybold, *The Inspector's Opinion*; Tedrow and Tedrow, *Death at Chappaquiddick*; Sherill, *The Last Kennedy*; Willis, *Chappaquiddick Decision*; Damore, *Senatorial Privilege*; Kappel, *Chappaquiddick Revealed*; Lange and DeWitt, *Chappaquiddick*; Leland and Shaffer, *Left to Die*; Nelson, *Chappaquiddick Tragedy*; and Pinney and Jones, *Chappaquiddick Speaks*.
2. For the legal definition of a conspiracy, see *Black's Online Law Dictionary*, 2nd ed., accessed February 2, 2019, https://thelawdictionary.org/letter/c/page/160/. A conspiracy occurs when two or more peo-

ple collude to abuse power or to break the law. A conspiracy can be civil, criminal, or political. In all cases, a conspiracy is a crime separate from the criminal act for which it was developed. Conspiracies and conspiracy theories are an inextricable part of U.S. history. They offer Americans an explanation for a seemingly inexplicable event or crisis situation and, often, a scapegoat for behavior that does not conform to our nation's democratic values. The obsession began with the Salem witchcraft episode in the late seventeenth century and became more common in the eighteenth and nineteenth centuries with the dramatic increase of foreign immigration to the United States. Most of these conspiracy theories were based on a collective paranoia that alien forces were plotting to take over American government and society. See Hofstadter, *The Paranoid Style*. In the twentieth century, Americans came to believe that the federal government and its various agencies were the conspirators because so many high-level political conspiracies reflect these distinguishing features and they've been uncovered by the press, especially since the 1950s. Unlike the imagined conspiracies of the previous centuries, which were promoted by social groups with limited influence, the government enjoys the unchecked authority to conspire against its own citizens. For better and worse, the existence of such proven conspiracies as McCarthyism and Watergate have helped feed the belief in conspiracy theories as well as the American people's distrust of their own government. Olmsted, *Real Enemies*.

3. For mainstream press accounts suggesting that Mary Jo Kopechne had a sexual affair with Senator Edward M. Kennedy, see "The Mysteries of Chappaquiddick," *Time*, August 1, 1969; "A Scandal That Will Not Die," *Newsweek*, August 11, 1969; Jack Anderson, "Washington Merry-Go-Round," *Washington Post*, September 26, 1969.
4. Gwen Kopechne quoted in Jane Farrell, "Memories of Mary Jo," *Ladies' Home Journal*, July 25, 1989, 112.
5. For writers and authors who reinforced the initial press accounts of an affair between Kopechne and Kennedy, see Charles Seib, "Enough of Chappaquiddick," *Washington Post*, November 16, 1979; Bob Weidrich, "Kennedy Short on Character," *Chicago Tribune*, November 18, 1979; McGinnis, *The Last Brother*, 557–58; Porter and Prince, *Jacqueline Kennedy Onassis*, 580–83; and Carr, *Kennedy Babylon*, 185.
6. Bernie Flynn quoted in *Investigative Reports: Chappaquiddick*, 1:18:27–1:18:32.

7. Rosemary Keough quoted in *Investigative Reports: Chappaquiddick*, 8:55–9:26.
8. K. Dun Gifford quoted in *Ted Kennedy, Part 3*, 6:43–6:47.
9. Joan Kennedy quoted in Chellis, *Living with the Kennedys*, 43–45.
10. Maxine Cheshire, "The Mysterious Helga Wagner," *Washington Post*, March 13, 1980; Hersh, *Edward Kennedy*, 365–66; and Leamer, *The Kennedy Women*, 648.
11. Leamer, *Sons of Camelot*, 124–25.
12. Hersh, *Edward Kennedy*, 359.
13. Miller interview.
14. EMK, "Statement of Accident."
15. EMK quoted in Hersh, *Edward Kennedy*, 358–59.
16. EMK testimony quoted in Edgartown District Court, *Inquest into the Death of Mary Jo Kopechne*, 10.
17. EMK testimony in Edgartown District Court, *Inquest into the Death of Mary Jo Kopechne*, 4.
18. Gwen Kopechne quoted in Jane Farrell, "Memories of Mary Jo," *Ladies' Home Journal*, July 25, 1989, 112; and in Suzanne James, "The Truth about Mary Jo," *McCall's Magazine*, September 1970, 132.
19. Vladislas Farago, in a manuscript titled *Worse than a Crime*, was the first writer to identify Keough as the other woman in Kennedy's car. Originally on Avon's 1980 book list, the work was scratched by the publisher after EMK lost the Democratic nomination to Jimmy Carter in 1980 and was ousted from the national spotlight. See Lange and DeWitt, *Chappaquiddick*, 77–78, 269–70. In 2016 Donald F. Nelson resurrected the theory in his book *Chappaquiddick Tragedy*.
20. Farrar and Look testimonies in Edgartown District Court, *Inquest into the Death of Mary Jo Kopechne*, 79, 72–74.
21. Rosemary Keough quoted in Damore, *Senatorial Privilege*, 399; and in *Boston Globe*, October 30, 1974; Nelson, *Chappaquiddick Tragedy*, 175.
22. Rosemary Keough quoted in *Investigative Reports: Chappaquiddick*, 1:28:45–1:29:21 and 8:55–9:26.
23. Lange and DeWitt, *Chappaquiddick*, 77–78.
24. EMK quoted in Spotlight, "Chappaquiddick: The Conflicts Are Still Unresolved Five Years Later," *Boston Globe*, October 29, 1974.
25. EMK and Gargan testimonies in Edgartown District Court, *Inquest into the Death of Mary Jo Kopechne*, 3, 32, 33; Canellos, *Last Lion*, 151.
26. Foster Silva quoted in Leland and Shaffer, *Left to Die*, 4.

27. Jack Crimmins testimony quoted in Edgartown District Court, *Inquest into the Death of Mary Jo Kopechne*, 49.
28. David, *Good Ted, Bad Ted*, 136. David assumes that the two bottles of rum that were consumed were fifths of liquor.
29. David, *Good Ted, Bad Ted*, 134–35.
30. John J. McHugh testimony quoted in Edgartown District Court, *Inquest into the Death of Mary Jo Kopechne*, 39–40; David, *Good Ted, Bad Ted*, 134–35; McGinniss, *Last Brother*, 583. It is important to note that in 1969, most states considered a person legally intoxicated when their blood-alcohol level reached 0.10 percent, which was 0.05 percent lower than the 0.15 blood-alcohol reading in Massachusetts.
31. Olsen, *The Bridge at Chappaquiddick*, 267–68.
32. David Guay quoted in *Investigative Reports: Chappaquiddick*, 1:24:57–1:25:09.
33. Robert DuBois quoted in *Investigative Reports: Chappaquiddick*, 1:25:17–1:27:08.
34. Lange and DeWitt, *Chappaquiddick*, 69–77.
35. Donald R. Mills, the associate medical examiner for Dukes County who examined Kopechne's corpse, believed that Kopechne "died of drowning." See Mills quoted in Zeigler, *Inquest!*, 108–10.
36. Michael Putzel and Richard Pyle, "Air Lack Caused Kopechne Death, Local Diver Says," Associated Press, March 9, 1976. Several authors make the same argument that Kopechne drowned almost immediately, including Lange and DeWitt, *Chappaquiddick*, 88–89; Kappel, *Chappaquiddick Revealed*, 72; Spitz and Fisher, *Medicolegal Investigation of Death*, chapter 15; and Olsen, *The Bridge at Chappaquiddick*, 144–45.
37. John Farrar first mentioned his theory that Kopechne suffocated in a July 22, 1969, *New York Times* article. He repeated the theory at the January 1970 inquest hearing. See Farrar testimony in Edgartown District Court, *Inquest into the Death of Mary Jo Kopechne*, 78. The suffocation theory was also argued by Damore in *Senatorial Privilege* and by Tedrow and Tedrow in *Death at Chappaquiddick*.
38. John Farrar quoted in "Mary Jo's Rescue Possible," *Ocala (FL) Star-Banner*, September 1, 1969; and in *Investigative Reports: Chappaquiddick*, 43:36–44:27 and 46:36–46:42.
39. EMK testimony in Edgartown District Court, *Inquest into the Death of Mary Jo Kopechne*, 8.

40. Sylvia Malm quoted in *Investigative Reports: Chappaquiddick*, 57:49–58:09.
41. *Investigative Reports: Chappaquiddick*, 58:18–58:30.
42. Gargan testimony in Edgartown District Court, *Inquest into the death of Mary Jo Kopechne.*
43. EMK and Markham testimonies in Edgartown District Court, *Inquest into the Death of Mary Jo Kopechne*, 9–12, 45–46.
44. Look testimony in Edgartown District Court, *Inquest into the Death of Mary Jo Kopechne*, 72–73.
45. EMK, "Televised Speech on Chappaquiddick," WHDH-TV Boston, quoted in Damore, *Senatorial Privilege*, 204–5.
46. Bernie Flynn quoted in *Investigative Reports: Chappaquiddick*, 1:15:22–1:15:38.
47. Damore, *Senatorial Privilege*, 25.
48. McGinniss, *Last Brother*, 558.
49. Rosemary Keough quoted in *Investigative Reports: Chappaquiddick*, 24:33–24:47; Damore, *Senatorial Privilege*, 25.
50. Farrar and Frieh quoted in *Investigative Reports: Chappaquiddick*, 15:26–15:49.
51. Mills quoted by Farrar in *Investigative Reports: Chappaquiddick*, 13:22–13:26.
52. Dr. Robert Nevin quoted in *Investigative Reports: Chappaquiddick*, 14:04–14:21.
53. Dr. Donald Mills quoted in "Lack of Autopsy Unusual," *Evening News* (Newark), July 25, 1969.
54. *Investigative Reports: Chappaquiddick*, 13:36–13:41.
55. See Luzerne Court of Common Pleas, "Decision," 1–4.
56. Gwen Kopechne quoted in "Lack of Autopsy Unusual."
57. Gwen Kopechne quoted in "Autopsy Request Dropped," *Evening News* (Newark), July 26, 1969.
58. Flanagan interview.
59. Gwen Kopechne quoted in Suzanne James, "The Truth about Mary Jo," *McCall's Magazine*, September 1970, 131–32.
60. Judge Bernard C. Brominski quoted in Luzerne Court of Common Pleas, "Decision," 13; and in *Investigative Reports: Chappaquiddick*, 38:39–39:05.

61. Judge Bernard C. Brominski quoted in Linda Miller, "Chappaquiddick: Twenty Years Later, Local Residents Recall Kopechne Funeral, Kennedy," *Times Leader* (Wilkes-Barre PA), July 18, 1989.
62. Gwen Kopechne quoted in *Investigative Reports: Chappaquiddick.*
63. McFadden interview.
64. Leland interview.
65. Gifford quoted in *Investigative Reports: Chappaquiddick*, 1:13:34–1:13:55 and 37:55–38:33.
66. See Massachusetts General Laws, chapter 265, section 13, accessed September 12, 2018, www.federalcharges.com/massachusetts-manslaughter-laws/.
67. Walter Steele quoted in *Investigative Reports: Chappaquiddick*, 27:29–28:12.
68. EMK testimony and Judge James A. Boyle and Arena quoted in Edgartown District Court, *Commonwealth v. Edward M. Kennedy.*
69. Boyle's sentence in Edgartown District Court, *Commonwealth v. Edward M. Kennedy.*
70. Leland and Shaffer, *Left to Die*, 35–37.
71. Edmund Dinis quoted in Leland and Shaffer, *Left to Die*, 37.
72. Leland interview; and Leland and Shaffer, *Left to Die*, 37–39.
73. Leland and Shaffer, *Left to Die*, 31–33; Leland interview.
74. Nelson, *Kennedy's Second Passenger*, 155–56.
75. Leland interview; Leland and Shaffer, *Left to Die*, 91, 99, 95–98.
76. For rights and responsibilities of a grand jury, see Massachusetts General Laws, accessed September 15, 2018, www.federalcharges.com/massachusetts-grandjury-laws/. For Judge Paquet's refusal to allow jurors to subpoena witnesses who had already testified at the January 5–10, 1970, inquest hearing, see Leland and Shaffer, *Left to Die*, 102.
77. Leland and Shaffer, *Left to Die*, 102–3.
78. Leland and Shaffer, *Left to Die*, 106.
79. Leland interview.

7. Broken Hearts

1. Gwen Kopechne quoted in Jane Farrell, "Memories of Mary Jo," *Ladies' Home Journal*, July 25, 1989, 112.
2. Potoski and Nelson, *Our Mary Jo*, 41, 43, 127.
3. The *National Enquirer* led all other tabloids in making the unfounded accusations against Mary Jo Kopechne with "Ted Kennedy's Dark Secret—Mary Jo Kopechne Was Pregnant."

4. Jack Anderson quoted in McGinniss, *Last Brother*, 603.
5. Rowland Evans and Robert Novak, "Appraising Kennedy Tragedy," *Newark Evening News*, July 24, 1969.
6. James Reston, "Senator Kennedy's Impossible Question," *New York Times*, July 27, 1969. Some writers maintain that Reston was so smitten with the Kennedy family that he went to great lengths to portray Ted as the victim of Chappaquiddick instead of Mary Jo and her parents. See Stack, *Scotty*; and Jack Shafer, "For the Love of Teddy: James Reston's Inexplicable Kennedy Crush," *Slate*, August 26, 2009.
7. Among the *New York Times* editorials that were most sympathetic to Kennedy were Reston, "Kennedy's Career Feared Imperiled," July 24, 1969; "The Latest Kennedy Tragedy," July 24, 1969; "A Diligent Senator," July 26, 1969; and "A Tragic Accident Imperils a Great Career," July 27, 1969.
8. Gwen Kopechne quoted by Suzanne James, "The Truth about Mary Jo," *McCall's Magazine*, September 1970, 66.
9. The Kopechnes received more than two dozen letters, mostly in 1969 and 1970 before and after the exhumation hearing. Writers accused Mary Jo of having an affair with Ted Kennedy and being pregnant by him. After the Kopechnes went to court to prevent the exhumation of their daughter's body, letter writers accused them of being bribed by the Kennedy family. See Letters, "Exhumation Hearing," Kopechne Estate.
10. "A Boston Native" to Mr. and Mrs. Joseph Kopechne, Cohasset MA, November 14, 1970, Kopechne Estate.
11. Anonymous to Mr. and Mrs. Joseph Kopechne, New Bedford MA, October 19, 1969, Kopechne Estate.
12. Mrs. O. Kabrisky to Mr. and Mrs. Joseph Kopechne, Boston, August 14, 1969, Kopechne Estate.
13. Anonymous to the Kopechnes, Evansville IN, October 11, 1969, Kopechne Estate.
14. Anonymous to Mrs. Kopechne, Sturbridge MA, October 20, 1969, Kopechne Estate.
15. "A Mother" to Mrs. Kopechne, Boston, October 28, 1969, Kopechne Estate.
16. Gwen Kopechne quoted by James, "Truth About Mary Jo," 130, 66.
17. Joe Kopechne quoted by James, "Truth About Mary Jo," 130.
18. Gwen Kopechne quoted by James, "Truth about Mary Jo," 66, 131–32.
19. Potoski and Nelson, *Our Mary Jo*, 8. Most of the sympathy letters were received in 1969 and 1970, but every anniversary of Mary Jo's death

brought more until, with the passage of time, they dwindled. The Kopechnes kept all of the letters in a stack of boxes in the basement of their Swiftwater, Pennsylvania, home. When the couple moved to an assisted living facility, Georgetta Potoski, their niece and executor, took them and in 2014 wrote a family memoir based on her recollections of Mary Jo and the letters of those who knew and loved her.

20. Joseph Kopechne quoted in Jane Farrell, "Memories of Mary Jo," *Ladies' Home Journal*, July 25, 1989, 112.
21. Michael Putzel and Richard Pyle, "Air Lack Caused Kopechne Death, Local Diver Says," Associated Press, March 9, 1976.
22. Flanagan interview. See also Joseph Flanagan quoted in "Kennedy Pays $140,000 Settlement, but 'Blanks' in the Story," *Boston Globe*, November 5, 1974.
23. "Scholarship for Miss Kopechne," *Progress* (Caldwell NY), August 14, 1969. See also "Kopechne Scholarship Fund Planned," *Washington Star*, August 12, 1969; and "Kopechne Fund Set at College," *Pittsburgh Post-Gazette*, August 12, 1969.
24. Chambers interview.
25. Potoski and Nelson, *Our Mary Jo*, 127.
26. Sylvia Wright, "Kennedy Returns to Work," *Life*, August 1969, 38.
27. Clymer, *Edward M. Kennedy*, 171–77.
28. John Dean quoted in Bryan Bender, "Nixon Sought Dirt on Mary Jo Kopechne FBI Files Show," *Boston Globe*, June 14, 2010.
29. Hersh, *Bobby and J. Edgar*, 510.
30. Peter Ulasewicz quoted in *1969*, ep. 3: "The Girl in the Car," May 7, 2019, 40:54 mins., https://abc.go.com/shows/1969/episode-guide/season-01/03-the-girl-in-the-car.
31. Liz McNeil quoted in "The Girl in the Car," 25:14–25:20.
32. Memorandum, "Overlooked Damaging Aspect of Chappaquiddick Tragedy," Jack Caulfield to John D. Erlichman, White House, Washington DC, September 10, 1969, FBI Document File No. 139-4089-2232, vault.fbi.gov.
33. Gentry, *J. Edgar Hoover*, 642.
34. A Massachusetts informant speculated that Albert S. Patterson was an alias for E. Howard Hunt of Watergate infamy. According to a recently declassified document, the informant told FBI agents that Hunt "had falsified documents in an effort to defame John F. Kennedy and Robert F. Kennedy" and was also intent on destroying Ted Kennedy's career.

See U.S. Department of Justice, "FBI Memorandum: Albert S. Patterson," May 14, 1973, FBI Doc. No. BS 66-4051, accessed June 10, 2018, vault.fbi.gov.

35. See Albert S. Patterson to Honorable John C. Stennis, New York, August 20, 1971; Albert S. Patterson to Benjamin R. Fern, New York, September 3, 1971; and Albert S. Patterson to Honorable John C. Stennis, New York, July 29, 1972, FBI Doc. No. 139-4089-2224, vault.fbi.gov.

36. Albert S. Patterson, "All Honorable Men (and Women)—or Perjury at Edgartown," 1972, FBI Doc. No. 139-4089-2224, vault.fbi.gov. Patterson also stated that the other Boiler Room Girls lied about Mary Jo Kopechne being a "longtime and dear friend" when the average length of their acquaintance was just twenty-seven months.

37. See Dilys A. Reynolds, Town Clerk, to FBI Director J. Edgar Hoover, Sturbridge MA, July 23, 1970, FBI Doc. No. 11-55152-155; U.S. Justice Department, "Threats against Senator Edward M. Kennedy"; FBI Chicago to Director, September 2, 1969, FBI Doc. No. 94-55752-69, vault.fbi.gov; and David Lightman, "Ted Kennedy Got Constant Death Threats, FBI Files Show," *Seattle Times*, June 14, 2010.

38. Nasaw, *The Patriarch*, 766.

39. Kessler, *Sins of the Father*, 419–20; McGinniss, *Last Brother*, 549–50.

40. Rita Dallas quoted in Kessler, *Sins of the Father*, 419–20.

41. Kessler, *Sins of the Father*, 787; and Koskoff, *Joseph P. Kennedy*, 477.

42. Burton Hersh quoted in *Scandalous: Chappaquiddick*, ep. 3: "His Turn," 10:41.

43. Joan Kennedy quoted in Leamer, *Kennedy Women*, 651, 48; Clymer, *Edward M. Kennedy*, 205–8.

44. See "Kennedy's Wife Faces Drunken Driving Count," *New York Times*, October 10, 1974; and Canellos, *Last Lion*, chapter 3.

45. Clymer, *Edward M. Kennedy*, 259, 325, 354.

46. Canellos, *Last Lion*, chapter 3.

47. R. J. Apple Jr., "Despite His Lead in the Gallup Poll, Kennedy Insists He Won't Run for President in '72," *New York Times*, May 23, 1971.

48. *Scandalous: Chappaquiddick*, ep. 3: "His Turn," 11:48–13:13.

49. Clymer, *Edward M. Kennedy*, 187–90.

50. Moritz, *Current Biography Yearbook, 1978*, 227.

51. Clymer, *Edward M. Kennedy*, 198–99, 212–15, 217–19; and Moritz, *Current Biography Yearbook*, 228.

52. *Scandalous: Chappaquiddick*, ep. 3: "His Turn," 16:16–16:51.

53. Spotlight, "Chappaquiddick: The Conflicts Are Still Unresolved Five Years Later," *Boston Globe*, October 29, 1974; *Scandalous: Chappaquiddick*, ep. 3: "His Turn," 18:08–22:21.
54. EMK quoted in R. J. Apple Jr., "Kennedy Rules Out '76 Presidential Race," *New York Times*, September 24, 1974.
55. "Chappaquiddick Women Still Tight-Lipped," *Boston Globe*, November 5, 1974.
56. Nance Lyons interview by Heininger.
57. Nance Lyons interview by Heininger.
58. Jane Farrell, "Memories of Mary Jo," *Ladies' Home Journal*, July 25, 1989, 153; Leland and Shaffer, *Left To Die*, 26–27.
59. E. Kennedy, *True Compass*, 288–89.
60. Farrell, "Memories of Mary Jo," 112, 153; Dawn Shurmaitis, "Memories Sustain Grieving Parents," *Times Leader*, July 10, 1994.
61. Potoski and Nelson, *Our Mary Jo*, 127.
62. Gwen Kopechne and Joe Kopechne quoted in Farrell, "Memories of Mary Jo," 153.
63. David Espo, interview by James S. Young, March 25, 2010, Edward M. Kennedy Oral History Project, Miller Center, University of Virginia, millercenter.org/poh/transcripts/ohp_2010_0325_espo.pdf; and Mark L. Hoffman, "Here He Comes! . . . Ted!," *Times Leader*, April 17, 1980.
64. Espo interview.
65. Hoffman, "Here He Comes!"
66. Clymer, *Edward M. Kennedy*, 284–85, 294–99.
67. EMK quoted in Mudd, *The Place to Be*, 355–56; and Brian Lamb, "Interview of Roger Mudd, Former CBS Correspondent and Author, Part II," C-SPAN.
68. EMK quoted in *Scandalous: Chappaquiddick*, ep. 3: "His Turn," 31:05–31:30.
69. See *Chicago Tribune*, March 18, 1980; *Chicago Sun-Times*, March 18, 1980; and *Boston Globe*, March 18, 1980.
70. Clymer, *Edward M. Kennedy*, 309, 312–19. For the most complete treatment of Ted Kennedy's relationship with President Jimmy Carter and the 1980 presidential election, see Ward, *Camelot's End*.
71. Clymer, *Edward M. Kennedy*, 341–42, 385.
72. Amand Ruggeri, "Kennedy's Legacy of Legislative Success," *U.S. News and World Report*, September 1, 2009, www.usnews.com/news/articles/2009/09/01/kennedys-legacy-of-legislative-success; Giselle Edwards,

"The Top 10 Ted Kennedy Legislations," *Ranker*, November 1, 2018, www.ranker.com/list/top-10-ted-kennedy-legislations/litgoddess; and "Ted Kennedy's Diverse Legislative Career," *Newsweek*, August 25, 2009, www.newsweek.com/ted-kennedys-diverse-legislative-career-78961. For EMK's legislative achievements during the period 1994 to 2008, see Littlefield and Nexon, *Lion of the Senate*. Kennedy authored more than 2,500 bills during his senatorial career. Of those bills, several hundred were signed into law. See Michelle Cottle, "The Last Brother: Edward M. Kennedy, 1932–2009: The Legislator," *Newsweek Special Commemorative Edition*, August 2009, 56.

73. EMK quoted in George Esper, "Mrs. Kopechne: A Million Memories," *Sunday Independent* (Wilkes-Barre PA), July 16, 1989.
74. Joe and Gwen Kopechne quoted in Farrell, "Memories of Mary Jo," 112, 153.
75. Kappel, *Chappaquiddick Revealed*, 126.
76. Gwen Kopechne quoted in "Kopechnes Want New Probe of Mary Jo's Death," *Citizens Voice* (Wilkes-Barre PA), November 4, 1989.
77. "Kopechnes Want New Probe."
78. Gwen Kopechne quoted in Farrell, "Memories of Mary Jo," 153; Esper, "Mrs. Kopechne."
79. Joe and Gwen Kopechne quoted in Farrell, "Memories of Mary Jo," 153; Esper, "Mrs. Kopechne."
80. Brian Jarvis, "Family at Peace," *Citizens Voice* (Wilkes-Barre PA), January 12, 2008; Potoski and Nelson, *Our Mary Jo*, 127.
81. "Statement from the Kennedy Family," *Boston Globe*, August 26, 2009.
82. E. Kennedy, *True Compass*, 288–92.

8. Mary Jo's Legacy

1. Sally Quinn, "Mary Jo," *Washington Post*, July 26, 1969.
2. See Chambers, Cromwell, Dougherty, Kluge, Lopez, Lutolf, Mohrhauser, Renna, and Toole interviews.
3. Joseph P. Kennedy Sr. quoted in Hersh, *Bobby and J. Edgar*, ix.
4. For concise summaries of the Kennedy brothers' political achievements, see Mears and Buell, *The Kennedy Brothers*; and Sullivan, *The Kennedys*.
5. Watts, *JFK and the Masculine Mystique*, 5–7. Watts argues that JFK benefited from a crisis of manhood in post–World War II America, a time when men became "ensnared by bureaucracy, softened by suburban comfort and emasculated by a generation of newly-aggressive women."

Kennedy, with his youth and vigor, created a powerful "masculine mystique" that was at the center of his administration's Cold War policies.

6. For the most comprehensive books on these subjects, see Wyden, *Bay of Pigs*; R. Kennedy, *Thirteen Days*; Dobbs, *One Minute to Midnight*; Seaborg, *Kennedy, Khrushchev*; Rust, *Kennedy in Vietnam*; and Halberstam, *The Best and the Brightest.*
7. Brinkley, *American Moonshot.*
8. Rice, *The Bold Experiment.*
9. Levingston, *Kennedy and King*; and Bryant, *The Bystander.*
10. In October 2017 the Trump administration, through the John F. Kennedy Assassination Records Collection Act of 1992, authorized the release of another 2,900 document files pertaining to the assassination of JFK. Among the trove were documents pertaining to JFK's extramarital affairs and his relationships with organized crime figures. Bruce Fessier's online article "Presidents' Playground: JFK's Desert Ties included Mob Entanglements, Affairs and Political Repercussions," *Desert Sun*, October 24, 2017, gives a detailed account of the president's sordid past. See also Exner, *Mafia Moll*; Lertzman and Birns, *Dr. Feelgood*; "Historic Presidential Affairs That Never Made It to the Tabloids," History.com, May 7, 2018.
11. Miroff, *Pragmatic Illusions*, 89–100; Ashley May, "JFK Files: How the CIA Planned to Murder Castro Using Mafia and Poison Pills," *USA Today*, October 28, 2017; Thomas Maier, "Inside the CIA's Plot to Kill Fidel Castro—With Mafia Help," *Politico*, February 24, 2018, www.politico.com/magazine/story/2018/02/24/fidel-castro-cia-mafia-plot-216977.
12. See Waldron, *Ultimate Sacrifice*; Russo and Molton, "Did Castro OK the Kennedy Assassination?"; and Nolan, *CIA Rogues.*
13. Steel, *In Love with Night*, 17; and Bohrer, *Revolution of Robert Kennedy*, introduction.
14. Margolick and Brinkley, *The Promise and the Dream*; and Bender, *One Night in America.*
15. Shesol, *Mutual Contempt.*
16. Nolan, *CIA Rogues*, 171–278.
17. Rorabaugh, *Kennedy and the Promise of the 1960s*; and Kennedy, *Robert F. Kennedy.*
18. Hastings, *Ted Kennedy Episode*; Olsen, *Bridge at Chappaquiddick*; and Rust, *Teddy Bare.*

19. Cutler, *You, the Jury*; Reybold, *Inspector's Opinion*; Tedrow and Tedrow, *Death at Chappaquiddick*; Sherill, *Last Kennedy*; and Willis, *Chappaquiddick Decision*.
20. Damore, *Senatorial Privilege*. Damore was given a $150,000 advance for his manuscript by Random House in 1982. Five years later, the publishing house rejected the manuscript, calling it "libelous," and demanded the return of the advance. Damore insisted that his research was sound and that Random House was bowing to the Kennedy family. He took his case to court and eventually reached a settlement with the publisher. In 1988 Regnery Gateway, a small, conservative house, brought the book out, and it immediately became a big seller. Damore fell on hard times afterward. Divorced and broke, he died by suicide in early October 1995. See Robert McG. Thomas Jr., "Leo J. Damore, 66, Author of a Book on Chappaquiddick," *New York Times*, October 4, 1995.
21. Kappel, *Chappaquiddick Revealed*; and Lange and DeWitt, *Chappaquiddick*; Leland and Shaffer, *Left to Die*; Nelson, *Chappaquiddick Tragedy*; Pinney and Jones, *Chappaquiddick Speaks*.
22. Paper, *John F. Kennedy*; Miroff, *Pragmatic Illusions*; Parmet, *Jack*; Parmet, *JFK*; Reeves, *A Question of Character*; Chomsky, *Rethinking Camelot*; Exner, *Mafia Moll*; Lertzman and Birns, *Dr. Feelgood*; Nolan, *CIA Rogues*; Alford, *Once Upon a Secret*.
23. Kessler, *The Sins of the Father*; Hersh, *The Dark Side of Camelot*; Klein, *The Kennedy Curse*; Evans, *Nemesis*; Heyman, *Bobby and Jackie*; Sloan, *The Politics of Deception*; and Carr, *Kennedy Babylon*.
24. Counter-revisionist accounts include Bernstein, *Promises Kept*; Thomas, *Robert Kennedy*; Dallek, *An Unfinished Life*; Canellos, *Last Lion*; Brinkley, *John F. Kennedy, 1961–1963*; Andersen, *These Few Precious Days*; Tye, *Bobby Kennedy*; and Bohrer, *Revolution of Robert F. Kennedy*.
25. See *Chappaquiddick*. Sec also Maria Puente, "Chappa-what? Everything You Should Know about Ted Kennedy and the 'Chappaquiddick' Movie," *USA Today*, April 4, 2018. One reviewer wrote that the film was both "ambiguous and damning" in its portrayal of Ted Kennedy. According to Jake Coyle of the Associated Press, there are elements in the movie that "make Teddy a sympathetic figure," but Allen and Logan "cast an equally critical eye on him as he launches into full damage-control mode." See Coyle, "Review: 'Chappaquiddick' Is a Profile in Cowardice," Associated Press, April 5, 2018.

26. Dan Zak, "What Really Happened at Chappaquiddick? The Truth We'll Never Know," *Washington Post*, April 4, 2018.
27. Zak, "What Really Happened." See also Bill O'Boyle, "Book Will Tell Who Mary Jo Kopechne Really Was," *Times Leader* (Wilkes-Barre PA), July 18, 2014.
28. Georgetta Potoski quoted in Liz McNeil, "Kennedy Family Scandal: What Really Happened at Chappaquiddick?," *People*, April 9, 2018, 65.
29. E. Kennedy, *True Compass*, 292.

BIBLIOGRAPHY

Archives

Edward M. Kennedy Institute for the Senate, Boston / Miller Center, University of Virginia

Edgartown District Court, *Inquest into the Death of Mary Jo Kopechne*

Edward M. Kennedy Oral History Project

John F. Kennedy Library and Museum, Boston

Joseph F. Dolan, Personal Papers

Robert F. Kennedy Oral History Project

Theodore H. White, Personal Papers

Kopechne Estate, Plymouth PA

Anonymous letters, 1969–72

Caldwell College, *1962 Yearbook*, Bloomfield NJ

Family photographs, 1944–2002

Letters of condolence, 1969–72

Our Lady of the Valley Catholic High School, *1958 Yearbook*, Orange NJ

Personal letters to Mary Jo Kopechne, 1962–69

U.S. Justice Department, Washington DC

Federal Bureau of Investigation, "Chappaquiddick Files"

Published Sources

Alford, Mimi. *Once Upon a Secret: My Affair with President John F. Kennedy and Its Aftermath*. New York: Random House, 2012.

Andersen, Christopher. *These Few Precious Days: The Final Year of Jack with Jackie*. New York: Gallery Books, 2013.

Aurand, Harold, ed. *Coal Towns: A Contemporary Perspective, 1899–1923*. Lexington MA: Ginn Custom Publishing, 1980.

Axelrod, Alan. *Lost Destiny: Joe Kennedy, Jr., and the Doomed WWII Mission to Save London*. New York: St. Martin's Press, 2015.

Baker, Bobby. *Wheeling and Dealing: Confessions of a Capitol Hill Operator.* New York: W. W. Norton, 1978.

Barendse, Michael. *Social Expectations and Perception: The Case of the Slavic Anthracite Workers.* University Park: Penn State University Press, 1981.

Bartoletti, Susan. *Growing Up in Coal Country.* Boston: Houghton Mifflin, 1996.

Baumgardner, Jennifer, and Amy Richards. *Manifesta: Young Women, Feminism and the Future.* New York: Macmillan, 2000.

Bender, Steven W. *One Night in America: Robert Kennedy, Cesar Chavez and the Dream of Dignity.* New York: Routledge, 2007.

Bernstein, Irving. *Promises Kept: John F. Kennedy's New Frontier.* New York: Oxford University Press, 1991.

Bohrer, John R. *The Revolution of Robert Kennedy: From Power to Protest after JFK.* New York: Bloomsbury Press, 2017.

Bonsor, N. P. *North Atlantic Seaway.* Vol. 1. Wheat Ridge CO: Brookside Publications, 1975.

Branch, Taylor. *Parting the Waters: America in the King Years, 1954–63.* New York: Simon and Schuster, 1989.

Brinkley, Alan. *John F. Kennedy, 1961–1963.* New York: Times Books, 2012.

Brinkley, Douglas. *American Moonshot: John F. Kennedy and the Great Space Race.* New York: Harper, 2019.

Bryant, Nick. *The Bystander: John F. Kennedy and the Struggle for Black Equality.* New York: Basic Books, 2006.

Canellos, Peter S., ed., and the Team from the *Boston Globe. Last Lion: The Fall and Rise of Ted Kennedy.* New York: Simon and Schuster, 2009.

Carr, Howie. *Kennedy Babylon: A Century of Scandal and Depravity.* Wellesley MA: Frandel, 2017.

Carty, Thomas J. *A Catholic in the White House? Religion, Politics, and John F. Kennedy's Presidential Campaign.* New York: Palgrave Macmillan, 2004.

Casey, Shaun. *The Making of a Catholic President: Kennedy vs. Nixon 1960.* New York: Oxford University Press, 2009.

Chambers, Sister Rita Margaret. *Celebrating the Past, Shaping the Future: A Short History of Caldwell College, 1939–1989.* Caldwell NJ: Caldwell College, 1989.

Chappaquiddick. Directed by John Curran. Written by Taylor Allen and Andrew Logan. Produced by Entertainment Studios Motion Pictures, 2018.

Chellis, Marcia. *Living with the Kennedys: The Joan Kennedy Story.* New York: Simon and Schuster, 1985.

Chomsky, Noam. *Rethinking Camelot: JFK, the Vietnam War and U.S. Political Culture*. Cambridge MA: South End Press, 1993.

Clarke, Thurston. *Ask Not: The Inauguration of John F. Kennedy and the Speech That Changed America*. New York: Henry Holt, 2004.

———. *The Last Campaign: Robert F. Kennedy and 82 Days That Inspired America*. New York: Henry Holt, 2008.

Clymer, Adam. *Edward M. Kennedy: A Biography*. New York: Harper Perennial, 2009.

Collins, Gail. *When Everything Changed: The Amazing Journey of American Women from 1960 to the Present*. Boston: Little, Brown, 2010.

Commonwealth of Pennsylvania. *Report of the Department of the Mine, Part I—Anthracite*. Harrisburg: Commonwealth of Pennsylvania, 1924.

Cutler, Robert B. *You, the Jury*. Self-published, 1973.

Dallek, Robert. *An Unfinished Life: John F. Kennedy, 1917–1963*. Boston: Little, Brown, 2003.

Damore, Leo. *Senatorial Privilege: The Chappaquiddick Cover-Up*. Washington DC: Regnery Gateway, 1988.

Davis, John H. *The Kennedys: Dynasty and Disaster*. New York: S.P.I., 1993.

Dobbs, Michael. *One Minute to Midnight: Kennedy, Khrushchev and Castro on the Brink of Nuclear War*. New York: Alfred A. Knopf, 2008.

Dublin, Thomas, and Walter Licht. *The Face of Decline: The Pennsylvania Anthracite Region in the Twentieth Century*. Ithaca: Cornell University Press, 2005.

Edelman, Peter. *Searching for America's Heart: RFK and the Renewal of Hope*. Boston: Houghton Mifflin, 2001.

Edgartown District Court. *Inquest into the Death of Mary Jo Kopechne*. New York: EVR Productions, 1970.

Elgood, Paul. *Crisis Hunter: The Last Flight of Joseph P. Kennedy, Jr.* Brighton, UK: Columbia Point, 2014.

Engel, Pal. *The Realm of St. Stephen: A History of Medieval Hungary, 895–1526*. London: Bloomsbury, I. B. Tauris Publishers, 2001.

Evans, Peter. *Nemesis: The True Story of Aristotle Onassis, Jackie O, and the Love Triangle That Brought Down the Kennedys*. New York: William Morrow, 2005.

Evans, Sara. *Personal Politics: The Roots of Women's Liberation in the Civil Rights Movement and the New Left*. New York: Knopf, 1980.

Exner, Judith Campbell. *Mafia Moll: The Judith Exner Story; The Life of the Mistress of John F. Kennedy*. Ishi Press, 2008.

Faura, Fernando. *The Polka Dot File on the Robert Kennedy Killing: The Paris Peace Talks Connection*. Walterville OR: Trine Day, 2016.

Friedan, Betty. *The Feminine Mystique*. New York: W. W. Norton, 1963; paperback ed., 2013.

Frost, Robert. *The Oxford History of Poland-Lithuania, Volume I: The Making of the Polish-Lithuanian Union, 1385–1569*. New York: Oxford University Press, 2015.

Gentry, Curt. *J. Edgar Hoover: The Man and the Secrets*. New York: W. W. Norton, 1991.

Gibson, J. Campbell, and Emily Lennon. "Historical Census Statistics on the Foreign-born Population of the United States: 1850–1990." Washington DC: Population Division, U.S. Bureau of the Census, 1999.

Giele, Janet Z. *Two Paths to Women's Equality: Temperance, Suffrage and the Origins of Modern Feminism*. New York: Twayne, 1995.

Goldfarb, Ronald. *Perfect Villains, Imperfect Heroes: Robert Kennedy's War against Organized Crime*. New York: Random House, 1996.

Goodwin, Richard. *Remembering America*. New York: Harper and Row, 1988.

Greene, Victor. *For God and Country: The Rise of Polish and Lithuanian Consciousness in America, 1860–1910*. Madison: Historical Society of Wisconsin, 1975.

———. *The Slavic Community on Strike: Immigrant Labor in Pennsylvania Anthracite*. South Bend IN: Notre Dame University, 1968.

Guthman, Edwin O. *We Band of Brothers*. New York: Harper and Row, 1971.

Guthman, Edwin O., and C. Richard Allen, eds. *RFK: His Words for Our Times*. New York: William Morrow, 2018.

Halberstam, David. *The Best and the Brightest*. New York: Ballantine Books, 1992.

———. *The Fifties*. New York: Ballantine Books, 1993.

Handlin, Oscar. *The Uprooted: The Epic Story of the Great Migrations That Made the American People*. New York: Grosset and Dunlap, 1951.

Hanlon, Edward F., and Paul J. Zbiek. *The Wyoming Valley: An American Portrait*. Sun Valley CA: American Historical Press, 2003.

Hastings, Don. *The Ted Kennedy Episode*. Dallas: Reliable Press, 1969.

Hebblethwaite, Peter. *John XXIII: Pope of the Council*. New York: Harper Collins, 1994.

Hersh, Burton. *Bobby and J. Edgar: The Historic Face-off Between the Kennedys and J. Edgar Hoover That Transformed America*. New York: Basic Books, 2008.

———. *The Education of Edward Kennedy: A Family Biography*. New York: William Morrow, 1972.

———. *Edward Kennedy: An Intimate Biography*. Berkeley CA: Counterpoint, 2010.

Hersh, Seymour. *The Dark Side of Camelot*. Boston: Little, Brown, 1997.

Heyman, C. David. *Bobby and Jackie: A Love Story*. New York: Atria Books, 2009.

———. *RFK: A Candid Biography of Robert F. Kennedy*. New York: Dutton, 1998.

Higham, John. *Strangers in the Land: Patterns of American Nativism, 1860–1925*. New York: Atheneum, 1967.

Hilty, James W. *Robert Kennedy: Brother Protector*. Philadelphia: Temple University Press, 1997.

Hoffmann, Joyce. *Theodore H. White and Journalism as Illusion*. Columbia: University of Missouri Press, 1995.

Hofstadter, Richard. *The Paranoid Style in American Politics and Other Essays*. Cambridge MA: Harvard University Press, 1996.

Investigative Reports: Chappaquiddick. Cat. AAE-74211. Produced by Otmoor Productions and A&E Television Networks, 1994.

Kaiser, Robert Blair. *RFK Must Die! Chasing the Mystery of the Robert Kennedy Assassination*. New York: Overlook Press, 2008.

Kallina, Edmund F., Jr. *Kennedy v. Nixon: The Presidential Election of 1960*. Gainesville: University Press of Florida, 2011.

Kappel, Kenneth. *Chappaquiddick Revealed: What Really Happened*. New York: Shapolsky Publishing, Inc., 1989.

Kashatus, William C. *Valley with a Heart: Northeastern Pennsylvania's Wyoming Valley*. Wilkes-Barre PA: Luzerne County Historical Society, 2013.

Kennedy, Edward M. *True Compass: A Memoir*. New York: Hachette Books, 2009.

Kennedy, Jacqueline. *The Historic Conversations on Life with John F. Kennedy*. Edited by Michael Beschloss. New York: Hyperion, 2011.

Kennedy, Kerry. *Robert F. Kennedy: Ripples of Hope*. New York: Center Street, 2018.

Kennedy, Robert F., Jr. *American Values: Lessons I Learned from My Family*. New York: Harper Collins, 2018.

———. *Thirteen Days: A Memoir of the Cuban Missile Crisis*. New York: W. W. Norton, 1969.

The Kennedy Films. Produced by Robert Drew and Associates, 1960–1964, Criterion Collection.

Kessler, Ronald. *The Sins of the Father: Joseph P. Kennedy and the Dynasty He Founded*. New York: Warner Books, 1996.

Klagsbrun, Francine, and David C. Whitney. *Assassination: Robert F. Kennedy, 1925–1968*. New York: Cowles Education Corporation, 1968.

Klein, Edward. *The Kennedy Curse: Why Tragedy Has Haunted America's First Family for 150 Years*. New York: St. Martin's Griffin, 2004.

———. *Ted Kennedy: The Dream That Never Died*. New York: Crown, 2009.

Koskoff, David E. *Joseph P. Kennedy: A Life and Times*. Engelwood Cliffs NJ: Prentice Hall, 1974.

Kraus, Sidney. *The Great Debates: Kennedy v. Nixon, 1960*. Bloomington: Indiana University Press, 2001.

Kurson, Robert. *Rocket Men: The Daring Odyssey of Apollo 8 and the Astronauts Who Made Man's First Journey to the Moon*. New York: Random House, 2018.

Lange, James, and Katherine DeWitt. *Chappaquiddick: The Real Story*. New York: St. Martin's Press, 1992.

League of Women Voters. *This Is East Orange: A Handbook and Map*. East Orange NJ: League of Women Voters, 1965. www.eohistory.info/EOTimeLine/ThisIsEastOrange.pdf.

Leamer, Laurence. *The Kennedy Men*. New York: St. Martin's Press, 2001.

———. *The Kennedy Women: The Saga of an American Family*. New York: Fawcett Books, 1994.

———. *Sons of Camelot: The Fate of an American Dynasty*. New York: William Morrow, 2004.

Leland, Leslie, and J. B. Shaffer. *Left to Die: Chappaquiddick Grand Jury Foreman Reveals Explosive, Never-Told-Before Information*. New York: Strategic Book Publishing, 2009.

Lertzman, Richard A., and William J. Birns. *Dr. Feelgood: The Shocking Story of the Doctor Who May Have Changed History by Treating and Drugging JFK, Marilyn, Elvis and Other Prominent Figures*. New York: Skyhorse Publishing 2013.

Lester, David. *Good Ted, Bad Ted: The Two Faces of Edward M. Kennedy*. New York: Carol Publishing Group, 1993.

Levingston, Steven. *Kennedy and King: The President, the Pastor, and the Battle over Civil Rights*. New York: Hachette, 2017.

Lifton, David S. *Best Evidence: Disguise ad Deception in the Assassination of John F. Kennedy*. New York: Dell Publishing Company, 1980.

Littlefield, Nick, and David Nexon. *Lion of the Senate: When Ted Kennedy Rallied the Democrats in a GOP Congress*. New York: Simon and Schuster, 2015.

MacKenzie, G. Calvin, and Robert Weisbrot. *The Liberal Hour: Washington and the Politics of Change in the 1960s*. New York: Penguin, 2001.

Mahoney, Richard D. *Sons and Brothers: The Days of Jack and Bobby Kennedy*. New York: Arcade Publishing, 1999.

Manchester, William. *The Glory and the Dream: A Narrative History of America, 1932–1972*. Boston: Little, Brown, 1973; paperback ed., 1975.

Margolick, David, and Douglas Brinkley. *The Promise and the Dream: The Untold Story of Martin Luther King, Jr. And Robert F. Kennedy*. New York: Rosetta Books, 2018.

"Mary Jo Kopechne." Academic panel discussion, Northeastern Pennsylvania History Conference, October 12, 2018. Produced by Pennsylvania Cable Network and in association with Luzerne County Community College.

Massa, Mark S. "A Catholic for President? John F. Kennedy and the 'Secular' Theology of the Houston Speech, 1960." *Journal of Church and State* 39 (1997): 297–317.

McGinnis, Joe. *The Last Brother: The Rise and Fall of Teddy Kennedy*. New York: Simon and Schuster, 1993.

McKenna, Peter. *All His Bright Light Gone: The Death of John F. Kennedy and the Decline of America*. New York: New Frontier, 2016.

McNamara, Eileen. *Eunice: The Kennedy Who Changed the World*. New York: Simon and Schuster, 2018.

McNamara, Robert S. *In Retrospect: The Tragedy and Lessons of Vietnam*. New York: Times Books, 1995.

Mears, Walter R., and Hal Buell. *The Kennedy Brothers*. New York: Tess Press, 2009.

Melanson, Philip H. *The Robert F. Kennedy Assassination: New Revelations on the Conspiracy and Cover-Up, 1968–1991*. Shapolsky Publishers, 1991.

Miller, Donald L., and Richard F. Sharpless. *The Kingdom of Coal: Work Enterprise and Ethnic Communities in the Mine Fields*. Philadelphia: University of Pennsylvania, 1985.

Miner, Charles. *History of Wyoming*. Philadelphia, 1845.

Miroff, Bruce. *Pragmatic Illusions: The Presidential Politics of John F. Kennedy*. New York: Longman, 1976.

Moritz, Charles, ed. *Current Biography Yearbook*. Hackensack NJ: H. W. Wilson, 1978.

Moyer, Paul B. *Wild Yankees: The Struggle for Independence along Pennsylvania's Revolutionary Frontier*. Ithaca NY: Cornell University, 2007.

Mudd, Roger. *The Place to Be: Washington, CBS, and the Glory Days of Television News*. New York: Public Affairs, 2008.

Nasaw, David. *The Patriarch: The Remarkable Life and Turbulent Times of Joseph P. Kennedy*. New York: Penguin, 2012.

Neff, James. *Vendetta: Bobby Kennedy Versus Jimmy Hoffa*. New York: Back Bay Books, 2015.

Nelson, Donald. *Chappaquiddick Tragedy: Kennedy's Second Passenger Revealed*. Gretna LA: Pelican, 2016.

Nolan, Patrick. *CIA Rogues and the Killing of the Kennedys: How and Why U.S. Agents Conspired to Assassinate JFK and RFK*. New York: Skyhorse Press, 2013.

Oates, Joyce Carol. *Black Water*. New York: Dutton, 1992.

Oliphant, Thomas, and Curtis Wilkie. *The Road to Camelot: Inside JFK's Five-Year Campaign*. New York: Simon Schuster, 2017.

Olmsted, Kathryn S. *Real Enemies: Conspiracy Theories and American Democracy, World War I to 9/11*. New York: Oxford University Press, 2008.

Olsen, Jack. *The Bridge at Chappaquiddick*. Boston: Little, Brown, 1970.

Oppenheimer, Jerry. *RFK Jr.: Robert F. Kennedy, Jr. and the Dark Side of the Dream*. New York: St. Martin's Press, 2015.

O'Sullivan, Shane. *Who Killed Bobby? The Unsolved Murder of Robert F. Kennedy*. New York: Skyhorse, 2018.

O'Toole, J. M. *The Faithful: A History of Catholics in America*. Cambridge MA: Harvard University Press, 2008.

Paper, Lewis J. *John F. Kennedy: The Promise and the Performance*. New York: DaCapo, 1975.

Parmet, Herbert S. *Jack: The Struggles of John F. Kennedy*. New York: Dial Press, 1980.

———. *JFK: The Presidency of John F. Kennedy*. New York: Penguin, 1989.

Pinney, Bill, with Carol Jones. *Chappaquiddick Speaks*. Coconut Grove FL: Stormy Weather Press, 2017.

Porter Darwin, and Danforth Prince. *Jacqueline Kennedy Onassis: A Life beyond Her Wildest Dreams*. Staten Island: Blood Moon Productions, 2014.

Potoski, Georgetta, and William Nelson. *Our Mary Jo*. Plymouth PA: privately published, 2014.

Prendergast, William B. *The Catholic Voter in American Politics: The Passing of the Democratic Monolith*. Washington DC: Georgetown University Press, 1999.

Reeves, Richard. *President Kennedy: Profile of Power*. New York: Simon and Schuster, 1993.

Reeves, Thomas C. *A Question of Character: A Life of John F. Kennedy*. New York: Free Press, 1991.

Renahan, Edward J., Jr. *The Kennedys at War, 1937–1945*. New York: Random House, 2002.

Reybold, Malcolm. *The Inspector's Opinion*. New York: Saturday Review Press, 1975.

RFK. Produced by David Grubin for PBS's American Experience Series and in association with the British Broadcasting Corporation, 2004.

Rice, Gerard T. *The Bold Experiment: JFK's Peace Corps*. South Bend IN: University of Notre Dame Press, 1985.

Richards, Amy. *Manifesta: Young Women, Feminism and the Future*. New York: Macmillan, 2000.

A Ripple of Hope. Directed by Donald Boggs, Covenant Productions, Anderson University for PBS, 2009.

Roberts, Peter. *Anthracite Coal Communities*. New York: Macmillan, 1904.

Rorabaugh, W. J. *Kennedy and the Promise of the Sixties*. London: Cambridge University Press, 2002.

Russo, Gus, and Stephen Molton. "Did Castro OK the Kennedy Assassination?" *American Heritage* 58, no. 6 (Winter 2009). www.americanheritage.com/content/did-castro-ok-kennedy-assassination.

Rust, William J. *Kennedy in Vietnam: American Vietnam Policy, 1960–1963*. New York: Charles Scribner, 1985.

Rust, Zad. *Teddy Bare: The Last of the Kennedy Clan*. Boston: Western Islands, 1971.

Scandalous: Chappaquiddick. Narrated by Bruce McGill. Produced by FOX News Network, 2018.

Schlesinger, Arthur M., Jr. *The Imperial Presidency*. Boston: Houghton Mifflin, 1973.

———. *Kennedy or Nixon: Does It Make Any Difference?* New York: Macmillan, 1960.

———. *Robert Kennedy and His Times*. Boston: Houghton Mifflin, 1978.

———. *A Thousand Days: John F. Kennedy in the White House*. Boston: Houghton Mifflin, 1965.

Schreiber, George R. *The Bobby Baker Affair: How to Make Millions in Washington*. Chicago: Henry Regnery, 1964.

Seaborg, Glenn T. *Kennedy, Khrushchev and the Test Ban*. Berkeley: University of California Press, 1981.

Sherill, Robert. *The Last Kennedy*. New York: Dial Press, 1976.

Shesol, Jeff. *Mutual Contempt: Lyndon Johnson, Robert Kennedy and the Feud That Defined a Decade*. New York: W. W. Norton, 1998.

Sloan, Patrick J. *The Politics of Deception: JFK's Secret Decisions on Vietnam, Civil Rights and Cuba*. New York: Thomas Dunne, 2015.

Smith, Salley B. *Grace and Power: The Private World of the Kennedy White House*. New York: Random House, 2004.

Sorensen, Theodore C. *Counselor: A Life at the Edge of History*. New York: Harper Collins, 2009.

———. *Kennedy*. New York: Harper and Row, 1965.

———. *The Kennedy Legacy: A Peaceful Revolution for the Seventies*. New York: New American Library, 1970.

Spear, Sheldon. *Wyoming Valley History Revisited*. Shavertown PA: JeMags, 1994.

Spitz, Werner U., and Russell S. Fisher. *Medicolegal Investigation of Death*. Springfield IL: Charles C. Thomas, 1980.

Stack, John F. *Scotty: James B. Reston and the Rise and Fall of American Journalism*. Lincoln: University of Nebraska Press, 2006.

Steel, Ronald. *In Love with Night: The American Romance with Robert Kennedy*. New York: Simon and Schuster, 2000.

Stefon, Frederick J. "The Wyoming Valley." In *Beyond Philadelphia: The American Revolution in the Pennsylvania Hinterlands*, edited by John B. Frantz and William Pencak, 133–52. University Park: Penn State Press, 1998.

Sullivan, Robert, ed. *The Kennedys: End of a Dynasty*. New York: Time-Life Books, 2009.

Talbot, David. *Brothers: The Hidden History of the Kennedy Years*. New York: Free Press, 2007.

Taraborelli, J. Randy. *After Camelot*. New York: Grand Central Publishing, 2012.

Tate, Tim, and Brad Johnson. *The Assassination of Robert F. Kennedy: Crime, Conspiracy and Cover-Up—A New Investigation*. London: Thistle, 2018.

Ted Kennedy, Part 2: With Bobby, After Bobby. Produced by Ann Silvio, *Boston Globe*, based on reporting by Neil Swidey, August 26, 2009.

Ted Kennedy, Part 3: Questions After Chappaquiddick. Produced by Ann Silvio, *Boston Globe*, based on reporting by Neil Swidey, Jenna Russell, Sam Allis, Joseph P. Kahn, and Susan Milligan, August 26, 2009.

Tedrow, Thomas, and Richard Tedrow. *Death at Chappaquiddick*. Gretna LA: Pelican Publishing, 1976.

Thomas, Evan. *Robert Kennedy: His Life*. New York: Simon and Schuster, 2000.

Turner, William, and John Christian. *The Assassination of Robert F. Kennedy*. New York: Basic Books, 2006.

Tye, Larry. *Bobby Kennedy: The Making of a Liberal Icon*. New York: Random House, 2016.

Waldron, Lamar, with Thom Hartmann. *Ultimate Sacrifice: John and Robert Kennedy, the Plan for a Coup in Cuba, and the Murder of JFK*. New York: Carroll and Graf, 2005.

Ward, Jon. *Camelot's End: Kennedy vs. Carter and the Fight that Broke the Democratic Party*. New York: Hachette, 2019.

Watts, Steven. *JFK and the Masculine Mystique: Sex and Power on the New Frontier*. New York: St. Martin's Press, 2016.

Whalen, Richard. *The Founding Father: The Story of Joseph P. Kennedy*. Washington DC: Regnery Gateway, 1964.

White, Theodore H. *The Making of the President, 1968*. New York: Harper, 2010.

Willis, Larryann C. *Chappaquiddick Decision*. Portland: Better Books, 1980.

Wofford, Harris. *Of Kennedys and Kings: Making Sense of the Sixties*. Pittsburgh: University of Pittsburgh Press, 1992.

Wyden, Peter. *Bay of Pigs: The Untold Story*. New York: Simon and Schuster, 1979.

Zeigler, Henry A., ed. *Inquest! Excerpts from the Official Testimonies at the Inquest into the Death of Mary Jo Kopechne*. New York: Tower Publications, 1970.

INDEX